PRAISE FOR

SOMEONE WOULD HAVE TALKED
BY LARRY HANCOCK

*This important book shows additional light on the dark
faces that subverted the political life of this republic.*

-Gerald McKnight, Author of"Breach of Trust: How the
Warren Commision Failed the Nation and Why"

*Once Again Hancock opens doors that the CIA and FBI would prefer stay
closed. By probing newly released documents and bringing forth witnesses to the
fore, Hancock's tireless research conclusively proves there is stil plenty we don't
know about the perpatration and cover-up of the Kennedy assassination. For
the "last word" on the tragedy of November 22, 1963, read Hancock's book!*

- Dick Russell, Author of"The Man Who Knew Too
Much" and"On the Trail of the JFK Assassins"

*Larry Hancock has put countless hours into the study of the files made available
under the JFK Records Act, and it was worth the effort. His wide-ranging
document-based research, coupled with Larry's practical skeptisism, and an
eye for detail makes this book an invaluable guide to making sense of Dallas.*

- Rex Bradford, Mary Ferrell Foundation

*The thousands of primary source materias he uses paint a disturbing
and compelling picture of the assassination of President John F.
Kennedy. Making these documents available on his website, Hancock
invites the reader to look at the documents and use them to repeat his
work and challenge his conclusions. Such intellectual courage is rare.
This is a significant contribution to our nation's historigraphy.*

-Dr. Thomas L. Pearcy, Former Joint Historian, US Department of State

2010 update available from www.jfklancer.com and larry-hancock.com, Kindle from amazon.com

NEXUS

First Edition ISBN: 978-0-9774657-8-1

    United States - Foreign Relations - Cuba

    World Politics - 1950 - 1980

    Cold War

    Kennedy, John F., 1927-1963

The goal of JFK Lancer Productions & Publications, Inc. is to make research materials concerning President John F. Kennedy easily available to everyone. Our prime concern is the accuracy of history and the true story of the turbulent 1960's. We are results oriented and actively support the continued investigation of the JFK assassination and related events.

For more information:

www.jfklancer.com

www.larry-hancock.com

NEXUS

LARRY HANCOCK

The CIA and Political Assassination

JFK Lancer Productions & Publications, Inc.

PREFACE

In the three editions of *Someone Would Have Talked*, I presented sources and circumstantial evidence suggesting that certain CIA officers instigated a joint action against President Kennedy — using individuals, networks, and assets, which had previously been used in a series of efforts to eliminate Fidel Castro and senior members of his regime. Anecdotal evidence, including remarks by certain senior CIA officers, suggests that action evolved through the activities of individuals within the CIA's Department of Plans (Operations).

What *Someone Would Have Talked* — some 480 pages in its most recent (2010 paperback) edition — does not do is to provide a full picture of the culture and conditions which could allow such an act to be instigated by CIA personnel and then not be exposed by an Agency investigation. In essence, that work deals with "what happened" rather than "how could something like that happen?" In other words, how can you take a position that CIA officers were involved and yet maintain that it was not an act of the Agency as a whole?

The only way to respond to that question is to engage in a historical study of how political assassination evolved within the Central Intelligence Agency. How did it start, how was it conducted (how will you recognize it when you see it), who gave the orders, and perhaps most importantly, who were the people actually involved in such actions as political assassination and even on a grander scale, "executive action" of senior political leaders during the 1950's and 1960's.

While many of those questions were quite mysterious for a considerable time, much detailed research is now available (including that of various Congressional investigations of the 1970's), as well as a host of actual documents on the subject of Agency political assassination (many of the documents are quite dry and still "crypted" with code words and agency name crypts, which have only recently become known). Equally important, only in the last decade have biographies and oral histories on some of the key Agency personnel allowed much deeper insights into internal social networks, as well as the sorts of dialogs that really made things happen inside the shadow world of covert operations — the things that never showed up in memos, were obfuscated with agreed upon "agency speak" and often were never sanctioned with as a designated project (which meant waiving normal agency internal security procedures and virtually all oversight), in other words, the way such things were done under "extreme deniability."

To properly address such a subject, it is necessary to present background on the Agency as well as the personalities of certain of its inner circle covert personnel. It's also necessary and to trace the development of a "culture" that viewed murder as simply another tactic — justified by a variety of national security concerns. In this study, we will examine a culture that considered any perceived weakness in the face of Communist expansion as being equivalent to treason; a culture in which an obsession with national security could and did override all other moral and legal constraints. It's not a particularly pretty story, and it will be necessary to "wade" into it in some depth, but I feel that the reader will learn a good deal about the Agency, and about American cold war history. A great deal of it will be new; it certainly was to me, even after a decade of working on the subject.

CONTENTS

ACKNOWLEDGMENTS

To those readers who kept pressing me to take the final step, to dive in and deal with the realities of the Central Intelligence Agency and its real world connections to political assassination – thanks, I think. To those who prefer the movie and action novel versions of such things to the actual historical record, sorry about that.

And in regard to the true historical record, my thanks go to Mary Ferrell, Anna Marie Kuhns Walko, Debra Conway, Malcolm Blunt, and Rex Bradford for decades of work in digging the actual documents out of the National Archives, of sorting them, organizing them and then taking the extra effort to make them available for serious historical research. They were the front-line citizen warriors, devoting their time and personal resources in an effort largely bypassed or ignored by professional historians.

There were investigative reporters who did deal with the Agency, especially in more recent years, and they have provided critical information and insights. For their work and their books, I owe a great deal to Professor John Newman, to Bayard Stockton, Tom Mangold, Michael Holzman, and Jefferson Morley – their data was critical to this work, and any faults in using or interpreting it are my own.

Others, who have yet to publish, include John Sanders, whose ground breaking research on John Roselli will hopefully appear in print one day but has already provided a substantial improvement in our knowledge of Roselli's true allegiances and activities.

Then there is Bill Simpich, the absolute master of the flood of new CIA and FBI operational documents released over the last decade. I can recall wondering what we might learn about the true activities of the CIA's Miami field station if someone took the time to obsessively review and correlate the thousands of pages of new releases. Bill took that a step further, addressing not only the operations and counter intelligence activities of the Miami Station but also of Mexico City and James Angleton's counter intelligence staff members, who formed a separate network throughout the Agency. Bill is the absolute master of who did what to whom within the Agency in the early 60's and holds my utmost respect for his work – and thanks for sharing it with me.

Then there were the handful of researchers who served as a support group, running down documents, sources and names – and serving as friendly critics during the development of this work – my thanks to Zach Robinson, Greg Parker, Stuart Wexler, and Professor John Williams.

Finally, in memory of an individual who holds my utmost respect (I only wish I had known her in person), a very special recognition is due. This work is dedicated to the courage and memory of Lisa Howard, and what might have been…

Larry Hancock, 2011

INTRODUCTION

Editors remind their reporters, "Don't forget to tell a good story."

With *NEXUS*, Larry Hancock not only offers a bird's eye view into JFK assassination story – he also gets the facts right. Many researchers unearth remarkable vignettes. Others conduct groundbreaking interviews. But the most important thing is to put it all into a story that people will understand, and remember. Larry's story is impossible to forget.

He has spent many years doing the research, a number of his sources can be found in his ever-expanding (as of 2010 in its third edition) book, *Someone Would Have Talked*. In this new work, *NEXUS*, he offers his analysis not only of the JFK case, but also of the culture of the Central Intelligence Agency itself.

Without analysis, good research is barren. The figures in *NEXUS* have room to breath and develop. While Larry readily admits when he doesn't have all the answers, he uses primary research to pave the way towards what we do know and what we must understand. His analysis shows what is possible when citizens have access to actual documents; he could not have written *NEXUS* without reviewing internal memoranda, routing slips, cover documents, cut-out requests, after-action reports, and a host of day-to-day operational Agency documents. And he pulls them all together in a story unlike any previously written about the CIA or the Kennedy assassination.

That story exists only because, over time, the American people have risen up and demanded the release of information, which have revealed the truth of the nation's covert operations during the height of the cold war. It is time to pass on the lessons learned from the release of the JFK records, and to bring about a fundamental change in the way in which American citizens obtain information from their government – especially at a time when we still continue to struggle with seemingly endless (and needless) foreign wars and regime change.

In *NEXUS*, Larry starts by relating the CIA's central role in the Guatemala coup of 1954, naming the people who brought about "regime change" in that elected government – Tracy Barnes, Henry Hecksher, Howard Hunt, Rip Robertson, David Phillips, and David Morales. He traces their careers until all are reunited in 1960, in a project to engineer a similar regime change in Cuba. *NEXUS* digs into how they worked together, who mentored and directed them, and how they eventually came to view their Commander in Chief.

The story heats up when they all come to deal with the Agency's dramatic failure in the landing of Brigade 2506 at the Bay of Pigs. *NEXUS* relates how that failure appears to have largely been the fault of one man – but not the man who ended up shouldering the responsibility in the history books and garnering the hatred of the CIA officers involved, but a man seemingly seduced by the possibility of covert political assassination. In addition to detailing the role of the "magic button" in the abortive Cuban invasion, NEXUS also explores the actual role of "Operation 40," the cadre trained and prepared to become the "backbone of the new regime" following the anticipated victory. Stories have long circled about that group, portraying them as torturers and terrorists. Instead, we find that the personnel had been very specially selected and trained by the CIA, specifically by counter-intelligence and covert operations officer David Morales. As Larry shows, there was a great deal of continuity in these sorts of Agency projects; it turns out that there is no surprise in finding that one of the covert warriors of Guatemala would become the father of the anti-Castro Cuban Intelligence Service.

Following his exploration of the Bay of Pigs failure, NEXUS continues with the story of how Bill Harvey, David Morales, and former Havana casino figure John Roselli were teamed up to finish off Fidel once and for all. Readers are treated to the intricacies of programs and operations such as "Mongoose," "ZR/RIFLE," "TILT" and "AM/WORLD," as well as the effects of the Cuban missile crisis and the designation of Robert Kennedy as the de facto head of the secret war against Castro.

And then, the "bolt out of the blue," the fury of the officers conducting the secret war when they learn that the President has begun fast track, personal negotiations for an accommodation with Fidel Castro – at the same time, they are still running missions into Cuba, risking lives and taking casualties.

From the general subjects of the CIA, regime change, and political assassination, Larry proceeds to the story of the three men who actually provide a realistic view into the murder of President Kennedy, men whose own remarks suggest their knowledge of a joint action against JFK. NEXUS critically examines these three men and other "shadow warriors" against Fidel Castro — warriors such as Rip Robertson, Roy Hargraves, and Felipe Vidal, what they did and what they said during the summer and autumn of 1963. Once you have read it you will have a true appreciation of the truly chaotic nature of the relationship between CIA officers, "employees", "assets", "surrogates" and "fellow travelers."

The release of the CIA's operational archives produced by the JFK Records Act has given researchers the equivalent of a Hubble telescope, capable of looking into the inner worlds of the CIA and FBI during the early cold war era. We now have access to the very "sources and methods" that the Agency vowed to protect at any cost. And we live in a time in which the power and authority of the mainstream media are shifting to the more robust and transparent models of information access via the Internet. In NEXUS, Larry points us to an unparalleled opportunity not only to resolve the historical truths of the JFK assassination but also to fully understand the nature and risk of the national security apparatus created in the earliest days of the cold war, as long ago as 1947.

Bill Simpich

Author of the forthcoming book, Double Image, a look at how CIA counter intelligence molded the JFK case

1   A CREATURE OF ITS TIME

In 1947, during the earliest years of the "Cold War," the CIA was conceptualized as a function that would serve to consolidate and analyze intelligence. Its charter specifically directed it to correlate and evaluate intelligence, advise the National Security Council on intelligence coordination, and make recommendations for such coordination. A fourth element in its charter spoke to performing services of common concern to other intelligence organizations.

It was widely recognized that covert activities would be a fundamental element of the CIA's role. The aggressive security practices it would face in combating the nation's primary perceived threat (expansion by the Communist nations) left little "open source" information available. There was no question that foreign intelligence collection would have to use clandestine operations to obtain vital information.[1] Doolittle Report

But beyond covert intelligence collection, a final item in the CIA's charter designated that it would also perform "other duties related to intelligence" as the National Security Council might direct from time to time. That fifth and final element has been cited as authorization for what developed as one of the Agency's major activities – covert action operations involving both political and paramilitary operations.[2]

Almost immediately, perhaps due to the fact that a great many of its first officers had served in the Office of Strategic Services during WWII and were very much action oriented, covert operations grew to be a major function of the Agency. Initially designated as "Operations," the covert action arm was eventually (with the intention to obfuscate) renamed as "Plans." The Directorate of Operations/ Plans engaged in clandestine collection of information, psychological warfare, and covert operations, ranging from political action within foreign countries to special affairs (paramilitary) activities.[3]

In the 1960's, the clandestine Directorate included Foreign Intelligence, Signals/Communications/Technical Intelligence (designated as Staff D), Counter Intelligence (initially referred to as Staff C) and Covert Actions. Covert actions (also referred to as "special operation" or "special activities") included covert intelligence collection, psychological/propaganda work, political action personnel, and paramilitary staff. The Counter Intelligence function operated in very close association with the Agencies' Office of Security. The Directorate of Operations/Plans was headed by a Deputy Director (DDP/DDO) and

Assistant Deputy Director (ADDP/ADDO), and each of its functions was staffed at CIA headquarters and also within the global geographic divisions of the agency.

Operations personnel also served under cover (generally either State Department or Military) within U.S. embassies or covertly, attached to foreign CIA stations. In some instances, such as in Mexico City, some CIA personnel would be under diplomatic cover associated with the U.S. Embassy and separate, totally covert field operations personnel would also be in place.

Independent "cover" companies were also used to shield personnel and activities, both overseas and domestically. Those companies would generally be real businesses with actual business staff and operations, effectively providing a cover for operational CIA personnel and projects. The owners or senior management of those businesses essentially allowed normal business activities to provide cover for activities ranging from simply providing a legitimate employment reference for individuals to much more complex projects ranging from aerial surveillance (during the cold war, certain airlines had planes with specially constructed camera compartments operating on routes into and over targeted countries) to highly complex technical activities (Howard Hughes' companies are now well known for such activities). During the secret war against Cuba, islands in the Caribbean where oil and mineral exploration were taking place were covertly used for CIA operations, with the approval of the private companies involved, and Freeport Sulphur ore carriers were reported to have been used to carry cargo other than nickel.

Beyond "cover" companies, the Agency also used/uses "front" companies, which are real operating companies doing real business, with the Agency as a primary customer. Front companies were common in the areas of logistics, especially air and marine transport. Examples include Air America, Southern Air Transport, and Sea Supply. For its own field activities, the Agency often used "dummy" companies as covers – these companies were nothing more than "shells" used to conceal CIA operations (Zenith Technical Services was the shell for the CIA's huge field station in Miami, internally known as JMWAVE).

The CIA officers, who will be discussed in the context of the Kennedy assassination "nexus," worked within the Directorate of Operations as well as with Staff D. Because of the technical nature of its activities, Staff D personnel were to be found both at headquarters and associated with field offices; headquarters personnel would also be sent globally for specific missions and, as we will see, there were some efforts to recruit Staff D assets overseas. The same seems to have been true for Counter Intelligence, which even maintained its own communications system independent of the other Directorates and functions. Compartmentalization was seen as simply a basic part of CIA organization (and life); it was a fundamental and essential security measure. However, to some extent, such pervasive compartmentalization also presented a real risk.

And as we will see, the individuals who comprised the "nexus" addressed in this study were exceptionally senior, well experienced and well connected — quite competent to use compartmentalization to "game the system."

UNDECLARED WAR:

Almost from its inception, the Agency was forced to deal with the fact that many of its covert operations were illegal. Studies conducted prior to its formation had been based on the premise that it was necessary for the United States to aggressively confront the Communists. To counter the "vicious covert activities of the USSR" the CIA would be expected use any and all tactics. Both law and morality would have to be sacrificed to the needs of self-defense. The working assumption was that the United States was still engaged in a war, albeit an undeclared one.

This may be difficult to fully appreciate for readers not familiar with the years of the 1950's and 1960's. Indeed, many would be surprised to realize that senior officers of the United States Army Air Force had begun preparing plans for preemptive atomic attacks on the Soviet Union even before the official surrender of Japan – with the Soviets felt to be years away from having atomic bombs of their own. A document titled *A Strategic Chart of Certain Russian and Manchurian Urban Areas* had been sent to General Leslie Groves, the head of the U.S. atomic bomb project, on August 30, 1945. The document included a selection of 15 key Soviet cities and estimated how many atomic weapons would be needed to destroy each.[4]

In October 1945, the Joint Chiefs' own Joint Intelligence Committee drafted a plan for a first strike on the Soviet Union, using some twenty to thirty atomic bombs. The plan addressed two situations, responding to Soviet aggression or as a preventive strike at the point where the Soviets might themselves be able to attack the U.S. with a certainty of victory. The Joint Chiefs had quickly reached the conclusion that there was simply no way to "defend" against an atomic attack, you either prevented it through strength or you were essentially eliminated if your opponent convinced themselves to strike first. Although the U.S. never endorsed the concept of preventive war, it became an ongoing concern; the National Security Council responded by forming the Net Evaluation Subcommittee. The name of the committee failed to reflect its true task. It was chartered with evaluating the net strategic balance between the United States and the Soviet Union. It would advise the NSC of points at which either country was felt to have an overwhelming advantage. This would be translated into "defensive" and "offensive" recommendations.[5]

This was the strategic situation, the emotional situation that existed at the birth of the Central Intelligence Agency. It and its officers were viewed not simply as intelligence officers, but at least in regard to the covert/clandestine operations arena, as actual combatants. The language contained in National Security Council document #68, drafted in 1948, was "strident," declaring, "the

Soviet Union is animated by a new, fanatic faith, antithetical to our own and seeks to impose its absolute authority over the rest of the world."

The overall national security posture of the Truman administration envisioned the fact that the Cold War might become "hot" at any time, with the maximum danger occurring in 1954, with a fully atomic capable Soviet Union. Later, during the Eisenhower administration a different fear had evolved. There was no longer a specific year of maximum danger but rather, as President Eisenhower himself told a National Security Council meeting in April of 1953, they would have to plan on the "premise of a floating D Day."[6] Readers interested in more detail on the emergence of the "cold war" with Russia should find Norman Graebner's *The National Security: Its Theory and Practice 1945-1960* of interest.[7]

In this context, it is vitally important to appreciate that many CIA officers considered themselves to literally be in an undeclared war and accepted the premise that any act ordered by the President or required in the interest of national security was both legal and morally acceptable. In addition, security considerations were so preeminent, that CIA personnel could not be expected to tell the truth, even under oath.

While a member of the Warren Commission, when asked to confirm that his officers would lie in Court or to Congress, Director Dulles responded as follows:

> MR. DULLES: Yes, but he wouldn't tell.
> THE CHAIRMAN: Wouldn't tell it under oath?
> MR. DULLES: I wouldn't think he would tell it under oath, no.
> THE CHAIRMAN: Why?
> MR. DULLES: He ought not tell it under oath. Maybe not tell it to his own government but wouldn't tell it any other way.
> MR. McCOY: Wouldn't he tell it to his own chief?
> MR. DULLES: He might or might not. If he was a bad one then he wouldn't
> ... I would tell the President of the United States anything, yes, I am under his control. He is my boss. I wouldn't necessarily tell anybody else, unless the President authorized me to do it. We had that come up at times.[8]

Later, another CIA Director, Richard Helms, gave proof to his predecessor's revelation. In 1973, Helms was being considered by the Senate Foreign Relations Committee for appointment as the U.S. Ambassador to Iran. He was quizzed twice about the CIA's activities in Chile in 1970 and the committee had concluded that he had lied to them on both occasions. As expected, this raised considerable questions about conflicts between national security, loyalty and perjury. The Committee pursued legal remedies and Helms' lawyer raised the point that if Helms were to be charged and tried, an adequate defense would require that national secrets be exposed.

His lawyer was adamant that bringing Helms to trial "would involve tremendous costs to the United States and might jeopardize national secrets." Helms, moreover, had "performed outstanding services to the United States Government" during "a most distinguished career." This did not deter committee legal action against Helms and he did come before a Judge; Helms made a personal appeal in regard to his Senate testimony, stating that he was at the mercy of a conflict between his oath to protect and preserve secrets and lying to or otherwise misleading the committee. He claimed that he was simply trying to work through a very difficult situation but he did have to admit to the perjury charge (with the understanding there would be no jail sentence and his pension would be protected). The Judge refused to immediately issue a sentence in accordance with those stipulations, surprising Helms' lawyers. *Four days later the Judge, in court, publicly scolded Helms...*

> "You now stand before this court in disgrace and shame ... There are those employed in the intelligence-security community who feel that they have a license to operate freely outside the dictates of the law. No one, whatever his position, is above the law."

Then in spite of his strong words, the Judge accepted the previous plea bargain, fining Helms $2,000 and giving him a suspended two year sentence. Afterwards, in front of reporters Helms proudly proclaimed, *"I don't feel disgraced at all."* In an aside, one of his lawyers was quoted as adding, "He (Helms) is going to wear this conviction like a badge of honor. He'll wear it like a banner."[9]

A less dramatic but much more far ranging example of the Agency positioning itself above the law can be seen in the highly illegal mail-opening program operated by the CIA during the 1960's. The Church committee, investigating the program (HT/LINQUAL) established and operated by James Angleton, head of Counter Intelligence, determined that senior CIA and FBI officers were well aware of the program's illegality. Agency officers had determined that if it were exposed, it would be necessary to find a scapegoat to take the blame – in fact it had developed "a strategy of complete denial and transferring of blame as approved by the Director of Security in February 1962."[10]

Obviously such attitudes and actions, expressed and confirmed at the highest levels of the CIA, not only made Congressional oversight problematic but ensured that Congressional investigations of the Agency would be challenging, at best, and almost certainly less than comprehensive. Certainly it would be foolish for any Congressional committee or body to assume full CIA cooperation in its efforts.

2   A Culture of Deniability

The CIA evolved a culture of deniability so pervasive that it is difficult to fully appreciate. At one level, deniability meant that even sanctioned operations might not be traced back to any specific order or directive. At another it meant that all the material relating to a field operation was non-traceable to the U.S. much less the Agency. While "sanctioned" projects, regardless of their actual source, were entered into the Agency "crypt" system for tracking and documentation, other projects – such as the Counter Intelligence mail opening project – were given their own designations by the officers running them. One way to make a project internally "deniable," even within the Agency, was simply to not assign it a formal crypt.

Beyond that, projects could have their own "covers." For example William Harvey's executive assassination project was buried under an official crypt assigned to a project (ZRRIFLE) created to recruit burglars to steal foreign government cryptographic information. Truly deniable projects like the executive assassination project were never treated in writing. Officers might also make their own "soft files" to be kept in their desks but not entered into the "system;" we have a certain number of William Harvey's notes on his assassination project only because he took them with him upon leaving the Agency. And of course, all these levels of deniability exposed the Agency to the possibility of officers initiating their own projects – in essence going "rogue." In such an instance, the officer could use "black" money and assets with the implication that the projects were officially sanctioned. Individuals working on such projects would assume they were working on a sanctioned but deniable project.

Deniability was also observed at the level of employees, where matters were especially complicated within the clandestine groups such as Operations/Plans and Staff D. Individuals might well have been hired as temporary contract employees, actually paid by the Agency or they might have been treated as "assets" and paid with cash or in another indirect fashion. Some "assets" were either purely unpaid volunteers or working for "cover" companies and paid on those companies' payrolls, not directly from the Agency. In other instances, individuals might be associated with the Agency simply through some sort of security clearance, allowing them to provide information or to be used operationally; they still would not officially be paid employees falling under the rules of government employment. And of course, even actual clandestine employees would never be officially admitted by the Agency. Upon retirement, personnel would be given generic resumes with non-Agency employment histories. If they were especially clandestine, their Agency service would not show up in either their obituaries or on their tombstones. Such extensive deniability was intended to confound foreign intelligence services; it had a similar effect on Congressional investigations.

Given the obvious nature of clandestine operations and the demands of national security, it became clear very early on that the Agency was going to be forced to deal with instances in which its personnel became involved in violations of criminal statures. As early as 1954, in response to one such instance, the Agency sought and achieved a general "understanding" with the Department of Justice (an agreement kept extremely confidential over decades). This agreement was made in talks between CIA General Counsel Lawrence Houston and Deputy Attorney General William Rogers. Houston stated that there simply was no way in which such cases could be prosecuted without revealing highly classified information. Given the security implications, the Deputy Attorney General responded that it would serve no purpose to refer the case to Justice (since no legal measures could proceed without full disclosure of all information pertinent to the crime).

It would be left to the CIA to evaluate the possibilities of prosecution – informing Justice only if they indicated prosecution was possible without revealing secure information. The Attorney General also took the position that such practices could continue without any formal documentation. On February 23, 1954, Lawrence Houston prepared a memorandum for Allen Dulles, documenting the agreement with the Justice Department. The memorandum makes it clear that in instances of "apparent criminal activities involved with in highly classified and complex covert operations" outside agencies would be "unable to prosecute the case without revealing highly classified matters to public scrutiny." He concluded that in the case of covert operations "there appears to be a balancing of interest in enforcing the law which is in the proper jurisdiction of the Department of Justice and the Director's (CIA) responsibility for protecting intelligence sources and methods." This memorandum and the agreement with Justice with the CIA established a precedent at the highest level of the Agency, which allowed senior CIA officers to place national security ahead of criminal violations of its personnel. This practice was followed over some two decades, with no notification to at least two subsequent Attorney Generals who served during following years.[11]

Readers are referred to an extended discussion of this agreement, including Houston's testimony before a Congressional subcommittee in 1975. In testimony, Houston was forced to admit that the agreement could and did *"in certain cases," have the effect of allowing CIA officers the authority to give immunity to individuals for crimes up to and including murder.* This was done in the face of Federal statutes ordering the reporting of criminal violations. In addition, the practice was carried out through subsequent administrations in which the

Attorney Generals were not notified of the memorandum of understanding. Houston's position was simply that the CIA Director's statutory duty to protect intelligence sources and methods was considered to override normal standards or legal obligations. As one of the Congressmen on the committee noted for the record, this interpretation allowed the Agency to *"put the rule of law under suspension."*[12]

WHATEVER IT TALES:

During the 1970's, following various media revelations, the U.S. Congress convened a committee to investigate reported illegal activities conducted by the CIA; the investigation included the question of whether or not politically targeted murder and assassination had been a practice of the Agency. Despite facing extensive challenges to its work, the committee was able to determine that assassination had indeed been both considered and acted upon as an acceptable action related to national security and the Agencies' various missions. In fact, there is considerable evidence that "elimination" was indeed an accepted tactic, both among Operations senior staff and with certain field officers. One of the earliest documented examples can be seen in one of the CIA's first major missions, the confrontation and elimination of perceived Communist influence in Guatemala.

Shortly after his popular election in 1950, U.S. policymakers began to view Guatemalan President Arbenz, and his government, with considerable concern. By 1952, they were seriously worried that a growing Communist influence over Arbenz might offer a foothold for Soviet influence within Latin America. Perhaps equally important, Arbenz's agrarian reform polices had begun to damage U.S. business interests in the country, especially that of the United Fruit Company (a business with considerable influence and clout within the U.S. government, as well as with high level CIA officers). In general, Agency and intelligence community reports supported the view that the Arbenz regime was coming more and more under Communist influence, a view supported by CIA director Walter Bedell Smith. They began lobbying for a sanctioned support program to assist the anti-Communist elements in the country (the Catholic Church hierarchy, landowners, and business interests, as well as certain university groups and the Army).

Other U.S. government officials, especially within the State Department, were more cautions, offering the view that overreaction would simply indicate U.S. weakness in Latin America ("the spectacle of the elephant shaking with alarm before the mouse"). State proposed a policy of persuasion and cooperative assistance (including defense assistance pacts) with the neighboring states of El Salvador, Nicaragua and Honduras. In the end, State's position was accepted as the public posture but the Truman administration was persuaded by the CIA and eventually approved a covert action program designed to oust Arbenz and his government. The new covert action project was designated by the CIA with the cryptonym, PBFORTUNE.[13]

The PBFORTUNE Guatemala project (and its successor PBSUCCESS) seems to have been heavily influenced by Nicaraguan President Anastasio *Somoza*. In April of 1952, during a visit to Washington, he proposed that if provided with arms and support, he and Guatemalan exile Carlos Castillo Armas could overthrow the Arbenz government. President Truman reportedly asked CIA Director Smith to investigate that option and he dispatched a high level officer to explore the possibility. Available documents identify the officer only as "Jacob R. Seekford"; however, it seems likely that Seekford may have actually been either Tracy Barnes, the officer eventually designated with oversight for the Guatemalan project or one of its senior field officers, Albert Haney, Henry Hecksher or Howard Hunt.[14]

"Seekford" was sent to contact Guatemalan dissidents about armed action against the Arbenz regime. Based on his report, the Chief of Operations proposed to CIA Deputy Director Allen Dulles that the CIA supply Armas with arms and $225,000 in funding. He also proposed that Nicaragua and Honduras be encouraged to provide air support for Armas. The State Department concurred and planning began, only to be terminated after barely a month due to the fact that its security had been blown (a common occurrence in virtually every major Agency Latin American project during the following two decades).[15]

A historical study of the early weeks of the Guatemala project, in its first PBFORTUNE incarnation, revealed that one tactic was discussed frequently and seriously in project planning sessions – proposals for political assassinations. In fact, months before its approval, Director of Operations officers had compiled a "hit list." They worked from an existing Guatemalan Army list of Communists and with information from the CIA Directorate of Intelligence. Their work product was described as a list of "top flight Communists whom the new government would desire to eliminate immediately in event of successful anti-Communist coup." The project officers asked Headquarters to review the eliminations list and also a list of some 16 additional communists/sympathizers who should be locked up after a successful coup. The compilation and review of target lists (sometimes referred to as "black lists", given their high level of secrecy) continued to be a part of the PBSUCCESS project that replaced PBFORTUNE. Some nine months later, Castillo Armas, the Agency client political leader, forwarded Headquarters a "disposal" list which called for the "execution through executive action" of some 58 "category 1" Guatemalans and the imprisonment or exile of another 74 designated as category 2.[16]

At the same time, CIA officer Seekford also reported to headquarters that as of September 1952, General Rafael Trujillo of the Dominican Republican had agreed to aid Castillo Armas in return for the murder of four Santo Dominicans residing in Guatemala. Armas had agreed, but stipulated that the murders were not to be carried out during the military coup due to security reasons. He noted that Armas planed similar eliminations and had already organized and was training special squads for that purpose. The CIA historical report noted that no Headquarters response to the compilation of the lists and Armas elimination squads were located.[17]

After PBFORTUNE was officially terminated, and before its successor, PBSUCCESS, kicked off, the Agency continued to pick up reports of assassination planning on the part of the Guatemalan opposition. In late November 1952, it was reported that in conversation with an Arbenz opposition leader, that individual had confirmed that Castillo Armas had special "K" groups whose mission was to kill all leading political and military leaders, and that the hit list with the location of the homes and offices of all targets had already been drawn up. In December, Seekford related that Castillo Armas planned to make maximum use of the "K" groups. *Another CIA source provided the information that Nicaraguan, Honduran, and Salvadoran soldiers (operating in civilian dress) were designated to infiltrate Guatemala and assassinate unnamed Communist leaders.*[18]

During the period before PBSUCCESS was authorized, the CIA continued its efforts to influence events in Guatemala and a variety of ideas were floated which involved disposal of key figures in the Arbenz government. In 1953, sabotage and propaganda efforts were discussed but beyond that a CIA officer [NAME REDACTED] proposed a plan for first, spreading rumors that the Communists were dissatisfied with Arbenz, then killing him in a fashion that would be "laid to the Commies" and used to create massive Army defections to the Armas forces. A CIA Western Hemisphere memo of 1953 also suggested assassinating key military officers if they refused to convert to the rebel cause and that fall another CIA plan of action included a reference to "neutralizing" key military leaders.

Amazingly, the CIA historical study actually found memoranda and other documents from as early as 1952 and 1953, discussing themes and tactics that would become constants during the following decades i.e. creation of black lists targeting individuals to be killed or imprisoned, the murder of senior military officers in the target regime, acceptance (and very probably support) for deniable assassination squads (composed of both rebels and volunteers provided by third party governments), and sophisticated propaganda/paramilitary options which would include assassination of elected leaders while placing the blame on designated parties (patsy's). We will see a resurgence of all these practices as we move forward in time a decade, to the early 1960's.

Under PBSUCCESS (in 1953 and 1954), the CIA accelerated its support for the Armas effort significantly, from financial and logistic activities to training and propaganda. The effort was lobbied in Washington as being a vital, strategic national security intervention. When Arbenz began arms purchases from Eastern European Soviet clients, Alan Dulles promoted the idea that with the arms, Arbenz could "roll down and seize the Panama Canal." Later CIA officers working in support of the coup managed to bribe a Guatemalan military officer who confirmed that the shipment was simply a boatload of scrap and surplus WWII equipment that the Czechs had managed to successfully dump into Guatemala (for a nice profit). It included cast-off and obsolete antitank guns and artillery (of little value in the jungle) and the entire assembly was mismatched in terms of parts and materials. The determination of the actual content of the shipment occurred after the PBSUCCESS paramilitary CIA officer (William "Rip" Robertson) had (against orders) unsuccessfully attempted to bomb the cargo ship carrying the materials and then tried unsuccessfully to attack the train carrying the shipment.[19]

A more detailed review of PBSUCCESS is necessary to our subject, especially in regard to covert assassination tactics and the management of surrogates used in covert operations. It will also introduce the names of several individuals that this study will follow all the way through to November 1963. The Guatemala project was a seminal environment for many of these individuals to meet, work with each other, and learn to trust each other. For some of the newest members, who were only contract employees at the time, it was also an environment to learn exactly what tactics were accepted and tacitly endorsed by their superiors.

3 | A MODEL FOR SUCCESS

The CIA's own historical study relates that by the fall of 1953, U.S. policymakers were increasingly frustrated as Arbenz seemed to be moving even closer to the Communists, legalizing the Guatemalan Communist Party and suppressing anti-Communist opposition. Perhaps equally as important, he had further infuriated U.S. business interests by expropriating more United Fruit Company holdings as part of his agrarian reform initiatives. These events led the National Security Council to authorize a new covert action project, giving the CIA (Western Hemisphere and the Directorate of Operations/Plans) primary responsibility in the effort. Unlike later similar projects, PBSUCCESS did involve considerable coordination with the State Department. The stated objective was "to remove covertly, and without bloodshed if possible, the menace of the present Communist-controlled government of Guatemala." However, even in its outline, the "roll up" of Communists and collaborators was discussed, a task to follow after a successful coup. At the national policy level, the project was viewed (or at least documented) as being conducted without bloodshed, possibly with the simple imprisonment or deportation of Guatemalan Communists as its final result. In terms of actual operational discussions and field tactical actions, the reality of the operation was dramatically different.

PERSONNEL:

The personnel assigned to the project are still redacted in the available PBSUCCESS documents, however in succeeding years, autobiographies and studies of the Agency have revealed considerable detail. As an example, in David Phillips' autobiography of his CIA career, *The Night Watch*, he described the Guatemala project command structure — beginning at the top Allen Dulles (Deputy Director), Richard Bissell under Dulles, then Frank Wisner (Deputy Director Operations/Plans), then Tracy Barnes (Project Chief) and J.C. King (Director Western Hemisphere). Phillips also wrote about being personally recruited by Tracy Barnes, a "super grade" GS 18 officer in the Directorate of Operations (which Phillips translates as "overseas covert projects e.g. clandestine projects"); Barnes recruited Phillips to head the propaganda activities of the Guatemala project.[20]

It seems clear that Tracy Barnes was assigned as the senior officer in charge of the project and his staff included Albert Haney and Haney's protégé, Henry

Hecksher. Hecksher personally went undercover in Guatemala, recruiting intelligence sources and assets including Army officers. Hecksher also took David Phillips (at that time only a CIA contract employee) into the field in Guatemala. Paramilitary operations and training for the project were conducted by William "Rip" Robertson and David Morales. Howard Hunt was assigned to the project as a political action officer.

Tracy Barnes had been one of the first employees of the newly formed Central Intelligence Agency, later widely viewed and described as one of the "old boys," the core "cadre" of the organization.[21] During WWII, Barnes had served in the OSS and was quite close to and personally endorsed by Allen Dulles; Barnes had assisted with some of Dulles' European OSS projects. Following the war and before joining the CIA, he served in 1950 as a special assistant to the Under Secretary of the Army, and as deputy director of the Psychological Strategy Board during the Korean War, joining the CIA in 1951.

In 1953, Barnes had been appointed Special Assistant for Paramilitary/ Psychological Operations (generally referred to as the "PP" staff, containing both psychological and paramilitary personnel) under Wisner and was assigned to the Guatemala project. There is a general consensus that Barnes' fast track within the agency was heavily influenced both personally by Dulles and by the perceived success of the Guatemala project. But even at the start of the Guatemala project, Barnes was already a super grade officer, reporting to Frank Wisner (former OSS officer) who in turn reported to Richard Bissell. Richard Bissell had served in the OSS during WWII and had extensive social and political connections; he associated with a group of journalists, politicians and government officials that became known as the "Georgetown Set." Bissell had been appointed as administer for the Marshall Plan in Germany and gone on to head the Economic Cooperation Administration. After that, he had worked for the Ford Foundation before Wisner persuaded him to join the CIA. He eventually replaced Wisner as Deputy Director of Operations.

Henry Hecksher had come into the agency from Army Intelligence (Captain) and service in the OSS. He had initially served as acting chief of the Berlin CIA station (under State Department cover) until the arrival of William Harvey. Known for his aggressiveness and anti-Communist passions, in 1953, Hecksher had cabled for permission to issue arms and weapons to the East Berliners during their abortive revolt against the Soviets. After the success of the Guatemala project, Hecksher moved on to the CIA Station in Tokyo, and following that, he became Chief of Station in Laos, where he immediately came into conflict with the U.S. Ambassador. The Ambassador requested his removal but CIA Director Allen Dulles personally denied the request. At one point, when meeting opposition to his actions against the Communists in Laos, Hecksher cabled an apocryphal message to CIA headquarters – asking, "Is headquarters still in friendly hands?"[22]

Rip Robertson and Howard Hunt were both agency employees; Robertson had been in the Marines during WWII, earning two Silver Stars at Saipan, and came into the Agency as a paramilitary officer. His tendency to action and disregard for orders during the Guatemalan project (in particular his attempt to bomb the weapons shipment at sea, against direct orders) put him in the bad graces of certain senior officers (J.C. King), and he left the agency for several years, moving and working in Nicaragua where he had strong ties to the Noriega regime. In contrast, former Army corporal David Morales (with a paratroop training, service in the 82nd Airborne in Germany and experience in Army counter-intelligence) and contract employee David Phillips each distinguished himself with exceptional service in Guatemala and began fast track careers with the Agency.

During his service in Guatemala, Morales was assigned as operations officer on the Psychological/Paramilitary staff; following the success of the project, he became an intelligence officer assigned to Foreign Intelligence and served under State Department covers in several Latin American assignments including service in Cuba. Over the next decade, Morales would rise in rank from being an Army corporal to the equivalent government personnel rank of Lt. Colonel.

David Phillips (aka Paul D. Langevin and Walter B. Bracton), coming into the CIA as a contract employee after being a professional actor and Latin American newspaper operator, was assigned to psychological and propaganda operations in PB/SUCCESS. His efforts proved to be key in the overall operation, saving what had become a stalled military action on Armas part, into virtually the overnight fall of the Arbenz regime. The propaganda effort was so effective that the Guatemalan Army largely defected and indeed there was relatively little bloodshed in the final coup. Phillips was recommended for CIA employment by Tracy Barnes and endorsed by Deputy Director of Operations Wisner (who in his endorsement described Phillips as "exceptionally qualified for covert political and psychological operations").

CIA Director Dulles personally concurred and Phillips was actually allowed to spend considerable time at CIA headquarters before going into covert assignments (CIA security expressed its objection to that but was overridden by senior officers). By the time of his somewhat unusual early retirement, Phillips himself would rise to the rank of GS 18, only one step below the position of Deputy Director or Director of the CIA.[23]

Following the successful coup against Arbenz, Barnes, Hecksher, Hunt, Phillips, Robertson and Morales were all personally introduced to the President and commended for their work in PBSUCCESS. Morales and Phillips would receive highly prestigious CIA awards and in his recommendation for full time employment, the Director of Western Hemisphere, J.C. King, stated that Phillips "developed and sustained a completely notional situation without parallel in psychological warfare....he personally created and directed a psychological weapon which has no equal."

TRAINING:

David Morales was deeply involved in the project's training efforts (as he would later be in the preparations for the initial phase of the Cuba project, which led to the Bay of Pigs disaster). And although the CIA historical study notes that "assassination was not mentioned specifically in the overall plan" it went on to point out that that the project chief "requested a special paper on the liquidation of personnel on 5 January 1954." This paper was to be utilized to brief the training chief for PBSUCCESS before he left to begin training Castillo Armas' forces in Honduras, in January 1954. The next day, another cable requested 20 silencers for .22 caliber rifles – strongly suggesting that Armas' people were indeed going to be prepared for assassinations actions. Documents also show that the chief discussed the training plan with "Seekford" and that Seekford related Armas' request for PBSUCCESS to train to "assassins." The training of the assassination specialists was discussed with Armas again in February of 1954.[24]

Clearly, regardless of any official position being taken in Washington, PBSUCCESS CIA field staff were very much involved with the subject of assassination and actively involved in preparing surrogate personnel to carry out political eliminations. This conclusion is corroborated by the preparation of an actual CIA "Assassination Manual", drafted early in 1952 in support of the Guatemalan project. While titled "A Study of Assassinations" and containing background on the employment and justification of assassinations as well as planning of assassinations, the document provides an in depth study of "techniques," and commentary on devices ranging from bare hands kills though "accidents," the use of drugs, "edged" weapons, various firearms and explosives. In addition, some twenty plus known political assassinations are listed and outlined. All in all, the document has the appearance of a training guide and contains very detailed instructions and advice in regard to the various assassination techniques.[25]

Although the idea of assassination teams ("K" groups) apparently originated with Castillo Armas as early as 1952, the PBSUCCESS project head routinely included two assassination specialists in his training plans. The plans for sabotage teams, in early 1954, also included the creation of a "K" group trained to perform assassinations – focusing on local Communists and Communist properties rather than attacks directly on the Guatemalan army. A chart depicting Armas organization (CALLIGERIS, a cryptonym for Castillo Armas) showed a "K" group and the chart was being distributed in paramilitary training packages in the spring of 1954. A June briefing also mentioned that the sabotage teams would assassinate known Communists once the invasion operations actually began.

PSYCHOLOGICAL WARFARE:

Although not generally discussed in the narratives of PBSUCCESS, and certainly not mentioned in David Phillips' autobiography, it appears that assassination (or the threat of it) was also a significant weapon in the project's propaganda effort. In one instance, "mourning" cards were sent to top Communist leaders – mentioning purges and executions of Communists around the world and hinting at the "forthcoming doom" of the addressees. Death threat letters were also sent to top Guatemalan Communists. These actions, part of the "Nerve War against Individuals" included sending wooden coffins, hangman's nooses and phony bombs to the targeted individuals. Beyond that, the targets were treated to slogans such as "Here Lives a Spy" and "You have only 5 days" on their houses.[26]

The rebel leaders also kept pushing to go beyond threats, pressuring for the "violent disposal" of senior Communist leaders. In one instance, PBSUCCESS headquarters (Lincoln station) pushed back against endorsing immediate murders. Yet the reply included remarks that the idea was not a good one for the present, since it might touch off violent reprisals and noted that *a CIA field officer might wish "to study the suggestion for utility now or in the future."* The CIA historical study notes that the field officers continued to seek Headquarters support for assassinations and for Armas "K" group plans but their inquiry found no documented endorsement from either high-level personnel at either the State Department or the White House.

Still, the study was forced to present the documented evidence that assassination, the preparation of target lists, and special kill squads were a constant in field discussions and in proposals from both Armas and CIA project officers. In March 1954, a PBSUCCESS Headquarters meeting considered the murder of 15-20 of the top Guatemalan leaders by "Trujillo's trained pistoleros." The record indicates that the idea was endorsed by the CIA Director of Operations, with concurrence from the State Department representative. Another attendee stated "such elimination was part of the plan and could be done," objecting only to murders at that particular time. Another unnamed attendee was very much in favor of the assassinations, stating that "knocking off" the leaders might make it possible for the Army to immediately take control.[27]

It is important to note that in virtually none of this planning and discussion was it assumed that CIA employees themselves would be conducting assassinations. Such actions would be done in a totally deniable fashion, by working with the Agency clients, members of the rebel forces (paramilitary trainees) or with individuals provided by other anti-communist sources. Generally speaking, the murders (the "disposal list") would be restricted to those "irrevocably implicated in Communist doctrine and policy," to "out and out proven Communist leaders," or "those few individuals in key government and military positions of tactical importance those removal for psychological, organizational or other reasons is mandatory for the success of military action." The CIA project chief seems to have consistently emphasized to Armas that any assassinations should take place during the actual invasion and coup attacks.[28]

The records reveal that the CIA field officers engaged on constant, ongoing discussion of assassinations, including disposals of specific individuals and a constant dialog about whether they could wait for the military action or would indeed have to be done before hand to ensure success of the coup. On occasion, specific proposals were passed to Headquarters for approval – the historical study found no replies either approving or denying requests. In June 1954, a senior project officer traveled to Washington and submitted a proposal for "specific sabotage and possibly political assassinations" as an alternative to the paramilitary action program. At that time the proposal was rejected "for the immediate future" but a directive was given to generate a more specific plan including individual targets, timing and statement of purpose and advantage for each target. Again, the issue seems simply to have been that of effectiveness and timing, with no fundamental objection the political assassinations. This view is confirmed by the fact that when the chief returned from the Washington meeting, he reported to the PBSUCCESS staff that the consensus in Washington had been that "*Arbenz must go; how does not matter.*"[29]

PARAMILITARY/MILITARY ACTIVITIES:

Despite all the training, the preparation of "K teams," the plans for assassination to soften up the Arbenz regime, in the end, the success of the Guatemalan project appears to have been brought about by a combination of an extremely successful propaganda effort, limited aerial action conducted by mercenary pilots using WWII era aircraft and Arbenz's personal fear of an actual U.S. military intervention to support the exiles. Armas' forces did engage in minor combat, but almost all of it was quite remote from the capital. Arbenz showed no sign of personally becoming involved in military action to repel the attacks. On June 16, 1954, CIA-backed armed Guatemalan exiles entered remote border areas, advancing tentatively. As David Phillips himself described it, the "invasion" consisted of "several trucks crossing the border without opposition... Carlos Armas out front in a battered station wagon."

The rebel forces were divided into four groups, entering at five points to give the image of a massive effort, yet numbering less than 500 men in total. The approach also consciously selected, in order to prevent the effort from being aborted due the destruction of the entire force. Some ten saboteurs were assigned to blow selected bridges and cut telegraph lines. A conscious effort was also made to avoid engagement with the Guatemalan army – the "invasion" was actually more of a psychological device than a serious military effort to match Guatemalan military forces.

Armas' forces moved quite slowly and in its first battle, 122 rebels were crushed by some 33 Guatemalan soldiers. Only 28 of the Armas troops escaped being killed or captured. In another attack, on a heavily defended port city, the local police chief used local dock workers to oppose them and the majority of the rebels were killed or captured, with the few remaining fleeing back to Honduras. Inside three days, two of the four rebel groups had been neutralized.

Amazingly, at that point Arbenz reportedly ordered his military to allow the remaining Armas forces to advance – apparently due to a concern that if they appeared to be totally defeated, the American military would intervene.

Such a fear was not without some cause. In early June, the U.S. Navy had implemented, with both ships and submarines, the practice of stopping and boarding commercial vessels in search of weapons shipments. Operation HARDROCK BAKER was conducted by the Navy, with orders to use force in the effort, even if foreign ships were damaged. During the effort, even British and French ships were challenged, stopped, and inspected. There is no record that any weapons were found during the blockade. Even more aggressively, a force of five amphibious assault ships and an anti-submarine (helicopter equipped) aircraft carrier was deployed off the Guatemalan coast. The landing assault ships were backed with a full Marine Battalion level landing force. Reportedly, rumors were rampant within Guatemala that the Marines would support Armas and Arbenz felt this would encourage his Army commanders to strike a deal with the rebels.

Prior to Armas incursion, CIA sponsored mercenary pilots had already been flying leaflet drops over Guatemala City and other towns and, in conjunction with Armas crossing of the border, WWII fighters and B-26 bombers began strafing runs and bombing of selected targets as part of the propaganda campaign. The news of exile troops "in-country," combined with the aerial attacks seems to have virtually panicked President Arbenz. Earlier, when the PBSUCCESS propaganda campaign had really begun in early May, he had suspended civil liberties, and then ordered an electrical blackout – after Armas' entry, his actions made the Army increasingly worried about continuing to support him.

At that point the CIA officers in PBSUCCESS executed a final psychological stroke, ordering the bombing of the parade ground of the largest military base in the capital city and simultaneously broadcasting that two rebel columns were converging on the capital. Within 24 hours, Arbenz had broadcast a resignation speech, fled to the Mexican embassy with several hundred supporters, and shortly afterwards departed the country. Armas and his troops were flown directly from their remote location to a landing field outside the city, and entered with a victory parade.

It seems clear that the CIA success in Guatemala was largely due to David Phillips' psychological warfare campaign (including the broadcasts of the *Voice of Liberty* radio station operated by Phillips from outside Guatemala), more so than any significant paramilitary victory. The CIA study of assassination in PBSUCCESS blandly stated that despite all the preparations, none of the individuals on the original PBFORTUNE list were killed in the coup, virtually all of them fleeing the country. To a large extent, that appears to have been due to the quick resignation of Arbenz and his immediate departure and most of his supporters, from the country (well before Armas had even moved forces into the capital and took any real control). After the coup and in following years, assassination did become a major factor of Guatemalan life. Armas assumed dictatorial power and even David Phillips was forced to write that under that rule, government security officials organized "death squads" and eliminated any real opposition to the dictatorship. Human Rights group studies suggest that during the next four decades more than 140,000 Guatemalans were either killed or "disappeared."[30]

4 LESSONS FROM GUATEMALA

The CIA's activities in the Guatemalan intervention are valuable background for a variety of reasons. For the Agency, it should have been a dramatic lesson in what tactics did work in what has come to be called "regime change." Even a quick overview of the events suggests that it was not the paramilitary efforts of the project that ousted Arbenz, but rather a combination of the propaganda and intimidation activities, working on an elected President, who was facing very active and internal opposition to his policies, an Army which was at best indecisive and a social agenda – but a leader lacking "tempering" or combat experience. Arbenz had been isolated from his own military, had antagonized it with several of his policies and actions, and in the end definitely proved not to be the type of man who would rush to meet the challenge, leading his own forces.

Yet in 1960, when the CIA cadre from Guatemala was reassembled to oust Fidel Castro in Cuba, they failed to demonstrate that they had personally learned anything of this sort from PBSUCCESS. And, in the end, at the Bay of Pigs, they essentially "rolled the dice" on a largely military solution. That disaster, and the descent into personal denial by many of the CIA personnel involved, was very likely the first step towards the assassination of President Kennedy, the one individual the field officers outspokenly blamed for that failure. We will examine the Cuba project in considerable detail going forward. However, there are other lessons for us to take away from PBSUCCESS.

One of those lessons involves the concept of assassination in support of United States national security. It is also important to note that we would know virtually nothing about the discussions of assassination as an accepted CIA tactic unless the CIA itself had produced the information on PBSUCCESS. It was only during a Congressional investigation (popularly referred to as the Church committee) in the 1970's that records staff within the CIA came across a file folder titled "Eliminations."[31]

The CIA documents group research on that folder and tracking of documents in it revealed all the details we reviewed. As we will see, that was probably the last time such written records were kept (the Agency was very young in 1952, that CIA staff actually prepared memos which discussed or even acknowledged "assassination"). That it continued to be accepted in support of national security actions is a proven fact, it simply became a matter for verbal communication only, and one to be strictly avoided even in group meetings.

Guatemala provides a study in how national security issues translate to actions such as political assassination. At the highest levels there is no indication that the President or the National Security Council was directing the murder of Arbenz, senior members of his regime or even leading Communists in Guatemala. The CIA project plan prepared by the Western Hemisphere Division, combined psychological warfare, economic, diplomatic, and paramilitary actions against Guatemala. PBSUCCESS was to be coordinated with the State Department and its stated objective was "to remove covertly, and without bloodshed if possible, the menace of the present Communist-controlled government of Guatemala." At the highest levels, the Agency, the NSC and the President could rightly deny that they had endorsed any element of political elimination.

Yet in public session, the U.S. Congress had discussed a resolution, proposed by Senator Lyndon Johnson, which was intended to serve as in "an unmistakable warning that we are determined to keep Communism out of the Western Hemisphere." Congressional rhetoric was inflammatory (much on the order of Dulles' proposal that Arbenz might use Czech arms to push to the Panama Canal) with Representative Jack Brooks of Texas endorsing the resolution as: "so basically American and so basically anti-Communist" that support for it was urgent, in light of the fact that "a Communist-dominated government in Guatemala is only 700 miles from Texas – only 960 miles, or a few hours' bomber time, from the refiners, the chemical plants, and the homes of my own Second District in Texas. The Monroe Doctrine–1823–is still a vital, living force. But it needs restatement in light of modern conditions," said Brooks. Fellow Texan Martin Dies agreed: "The Soviet government...has challenged the Monroe Doctrine. To that challenge there can be but one response."[32]

Behind the scenes, Senators were closely in touch with the senior officers of the CIA, encouraging them to take an aggressive stance against the Communists in Guatemala. Senator Wiley of Wisconsin had encouraged Dulles to go public in announcing shipments of Soviet client state weapons to Guatemala as "part of the master plan of world Communism." Senator Smathers of Florida consistently used similar language, warning that "the Politburo of Guatemala" was "taking orders from Moscow" and that the arrival of a cargo ship with armaments "was concrete evidence of Soviet intervention."[33]

In a study titled Congress, the CIA and Guatemala, 1954 – Stabilizing a Red Infection, David Barrett presents the proposition that Congress and the American press was quite aware and quite supportive of American intervention in Guatemala. The CIA certainly was not operating without extended moral support from the American government. And while none of the resolutions addressed tactics, they expressed the "do whatever it takes to stop the Commies" attitude of the earliest days of the cold war.[34]

There is also little doubt that CIA headquarters officers were well aware of the pressure placed on them from Congress as well as the direction given them by the President Eisenhower. And while the President and Congress had recourse to deniability, the CIA staff were the ones on the firing line. As we have seen, in virtually all the PBSUCCESS headquarters meetings there was ample evidence that all options were on the board and nothing was off limits. A document introduced earlier makes that crystal clear:

> "Mr. [NAME REDACTED] then stated that he and Mr. [NAME REDACTED] were there to take stock of the present situation, to determine where we stand now and what are the future prospects. Are things going downhill so fast in Guatemala that PBSUCCESS, as it now stands, may not be enough? Consideration must be given to the much greater pressure which may come from Congress and public opinion on the present administration if the situation in Guatemala does deteriorate. It may be necessary to take more calculated risks than before.... Mr. [NAME REDACTED] then asked Mr. [NAME REDACTED] exactly what was meant by possible additional calculated risks. Messrs. [NAME REDACTED] and [NAME REDACTED] replied: (a) *We might reconsider exploiting the conclusion arrived at by [Dominican Republic leader] Trujillo last year and transmitted to [Venezuelan leader] Perez Jimenez that the best way to bring about the fall of the Arbenz government would be to eliminate 15 to 20 of its leaders with Trujillo's trained pistoleros.... Mr. [NAME REDACTED] replied that he thought the operation could be brought to a conclusion by 15 June; that the program was complex but that we believe the Agency has the capability of doing the job....* Mr. [NAME REDACTED] "...If attributable to the United States, it should not be done. High-level thinking is that an act which can be pinned on the United States will set us back in our relations with Latin American countries by 50 years." [NAME REDACTED] then expressed himself as opposed to the elimination of 15 to 20 Guatemalan leaders as a possible solution to the problem, although stating that such elimination was part of the plan and could be done."[35]

We also reviewed the record of a June 1954 headquarters meeting in which a senior project officer had traveled to Washington, submitting proposal for "specific sabotage and possibly political assassinations" as an alternative to the paramilitary action program. At that time the proposal was rejected "for the immediate future" but a directive was given to generate a more specific plan including individual targets, timing and statement of purpose and advantage for each target. No objection was given to the idea of political assassinations; the issues were simply ones of effectiveness and timing. When the chief returned from the Washington meeting, he reported to the PBSUCCESS staff that his *instructions were simple* – "Arbenz must go; how does not matter."

A CULTURE OF "HOW DOES NOT MATTER:"
Guatemala teaches us a great deal about the cultural development of the CIA itself, especially about the Directorate of Operations, the covert action staff of the Agency. The senior officers responsible for and participating in the

PBSUCCESS project – Dulles, Bissell, and Barnes – would all move into the highest positions within Operations Directorate and the Agency. Their attitudes and conduct would set a culture which remained in effect for the better part of the next two decades, through the Cuba project, the Laos and Vietnam interventions, to a point where CIA covert and paramilitary roles became ever larger, on the order of large scale military operations. It was a culture in which virtually all the most senior officers were extremely anti-Communist, oriented towards "forward leaning" actions, and fundamentally willing to do whatever it took to defeat Soviet expansion. The majority of senior officers were ex-military, ex-OSS or both. Their field officers and staff were also largely ex-military, with WWII service and several were OSS. David Phillips was something of an exception, having been an Air Force bombardier during WWII; Phillips, however, had been shot down, taken prisoner, then became escape group leader for the camp, eventually escaping successfully.

The field personnel of PBSUCCESS would become virtual legends within the CIA and within operations, going on to senior positions. Phillips and Morales would both become super grade officers and receive the coveted CIA medals (presented and recorded only secretly).

Yet in Guatemala, they were all exposed to and routinely considered, supported or facilitated planning for extensive political assassination. Barnes himself routinely attended both field and headquarters meetings with "target lists," "kill teams," and the details of when to kill Arbenz. Arbenz regime leaders and Communist leaders were discussed. The paramilitary staff trained Armas/exile personnel as well as individuals from third nations to be used in assassinations. Even the psychological/propaganda element of the operation published target lists and used the imminent threat of murder and assassination as an integral part of its campaign. It is virtually impossible to conclude that political assassination and murder was not an accepted tactic in the covert war against the Soviets and Communism in general (not performed by Agency employees but by agency surrogates in the form of the exiles which were being supported). Given the actual documents, even the CIA's own internal study was forced to state that the *"plans for assassination pervaded PBFORTUNE and PBSUCCESS, rather than being confined to an early stage of these programs. Even before official approval of PBFORTUNE, CIA officers compiled elimination lists and discussed the concept of assassination with Guatemalan opposition leaders. Until the day that Arbenz resigned in June 1954, the option of assassination was still being considered. Beyond planning, some actual preparations were made. Some assassins were selected, trained, and tentative 'hit lists' were drawn up."*

The best that the report could do was to blunt the impact of that assessment, by asserting that the plans were not implemented – "yet no covert action plan involving assassinations of Guatemalans was ever approved or implemented" – while also stating that no headquarters replies of any sort were located in regard to certain assassination proposals and by pointing out that no evidence had been found that the individuals from the very early PBFORTUNE target list had actually been killed either before or in the final coup.

INSTITUTIONALIZING POLITICAL ASSASSINATION:

Perhaps the best indication that the idea of political assassination and the use of "surrogates" was becoming an ongoing part of CIA Operations "culture" can be found in the fact that two of the senior offices responsible for PBSUCCESS were to become key "approvals" personnel for the more radical operations proposals, including assassinations (referred to as *sensitive or special projects*). Over the last few decades, literature on the CIA has discussed anecdotal reports that Barnes and Bissell became the "deniability" link between such proposals at the most senior Director and Deputy Director levels of the Agency. David Wise describes Barnes' approval of a plan to "incapacitate" an Iraqi colonel, accused of being a Communist sympathizer, with a poison handkerchief. The Church Committee report ("*Alleged Assassination Attempts on Foreign Leaders*") stated that Barnes had approved the poisoning on behalf of Bissell.[36]

Later in March of 1961, Barnes approved the transfer of three rifles to the Dominican Republic for dissidents to use in an assassination attempt against the Dominican president, Rafael Trujillo. One of the guns was found in the possession of the assassins after the shooting. One of Barnes later roles involved the creation of CIA "fronts" and cover companies for various activities. In *Secret History*, Trento describes an incident where Barnes was involved in setting up a cigarette factory in Africa, to be used as an assassinations cover. When Justin O'Donnell, the deputy representing another senior CIA officer in a meeting on the factory, questioned what in the world it would be good for, Barnes became so incensed (over simply being questioned) that O'Donnell was "out on the street" within three weeks of the incident.[37]

In regard to Cuba, it was Bissell who originated the idea of contacting former Havana gambling interests in regard to a *"sensitive project"* (verbal code for assassination) against Fidel Castro.[38]

We will return to the subject of Cuba and Fidel Castro as they pertain to both Barnes and Bissell but in summary, the consensus seems to be that by the late 1950's and early 1960's, Barnes and Bissell were willing to authorize risky actions which were in line with Allen Dulles's own views, yet provided him official deniability. In extended Congressional testimony, Richard Helms indicated that the two men scored political points with Dulles, for doing so while he stood aside, secretly hoping that the two would come to grief over their actions (which they most definitely did in regard to the Cuba project). Helms clearly was upset that Barnes had been promoted to the same level as he; apparently because of Barnes' willingness to sanction the sorts of actions which Dulles and Bissell endorsed – which Helms considered as "cowboy" behavior.[39]

Official deniability became standard practice for political assassinations (even within the Agency), whether they were at the "Executive" level or at the regime/leadership level as seen in the "target lists" from Guatemala. No longer would there be memoranda of discussions or any written records of plans; the use of "surrogates" would become standard practice. Compartmentalization of even verbal discussions became intense, standard practice was to talk around the subject, using suggestive but non-committal wording. As an example, early in the initial Cuba project (August 1960), Richard Bissell initiated an effort to use elements of the "gambling syndicate," formerly active in Havana in a *"sensitive project"* against Fidel Castro. That effort would later become a focus for the Church Committee, although it had to rely almost entirely on oral testimony to reconstruct events. The following, obtained from one interview, clearly illustrates the evolution of such activities, following PBSUCCESS:

> "Approached by Mr. Richard Bissell, DDP, to explore the possibility of mounting a sensitive operation against Fidel Castro. It was thought that certain gambling interests which had formerly been active in Cuba might be willing to assist and might have intelligence assets in Cuba and communications between Miami, Florida and Cuba. Mr. Maheu was approached and asked to establish contact with a member of the gambling syndicate...Mr. Roselli showed interest... indicated that he had some contacts in Miami he might use...met with a courier going back and forth to Cuba...*never became part of the project current at the time for the invasion of Cuba...no memoranda....no written documentation... orally approved by Senior Officials of the Agency.*"[40]

5 FIGHTING FIRE WITH FIRE

Two specific examples give us further appreciation of how difficult it became to track CIA assassination projects – and the nature of the culture that had evolved inside the agency. The culture was based so much on deniability and compartmentalization that extreme acts came to be authorized strictly by word of mouth, with no questions asked and little in the way of specific instructions or direction given.

The first example, a multi-year effort to assassinate Fidel Castro, also introduces the fact that the Agency had devoted considerable effort to the operational use of poisons and drugs, both for assassinations and certain non-lethal activities. That work was done in conjunction with various military projects, largely centered on the Army's biological warfare program housed at the Edgewood Army Chemical Center and at Camp Detrick in Maryland. The CIA's Chemical Division was headed by Dr. Sydney Gottlieb of CIA Technical Services, and it utilized the staff of the Fort Detrick's Special Operations Division (SOD) both for the production of the toxins and work on developing delivery systems. In 1950, the Agency had established an informal agreement with SOD to pursue designated projects. Initial funding (MKNAOMI) was on the order of $500,000 annually and reached a high of $675,000 by the mid-sixties. Confirmation of the MKNAOMI project was revealed in 1977, when Carter administration Defense Secretary Brown requested an internal review of CIA projects which had involved the Department of Defense The Department of Defense's legal counsel conducted the investigation and among other things reported back that MKNAOMI had begun in the early 1950's and was *intended to stockpile severely incapacitating and lethal materials and to develop gadgetry for dissemination of these materials.*

A June 29, 1975 CIA memorandum has also been located which documents the SOD/CIA relationship and *confirms that no written records were kept; management was by verbal instruction and "human continuity."* The memo refers to "swarms of project requests" and cites examples of suicide pills, chemicals to anesthetize occupants to facilitate building entries, "L-pills" and aphrodisiacs for operational use. *The memo notes "some requests for support approved by the CIA had apparently involved assassination."*[41]

It should be noted that statements and memoranda relating to projects such as MKNAOMI often refer to the threat posed by Soviet use of similar toxins; CIA records do show instances of Soviet poison attacks in Europe. These included the apparent use of a mystery agent that created symptoms of multiple sclerosis against some seven Soviet defectors at two CIA safe houses in Berlin.[42]

Several senior CIA officers were privy to the work being done on both lethal chemicals (drugs, poisons and diseases) and non-lethal drugs (including a number of LSD derivatives) for use in interrogation and temporary incapacitation. These officers included Sheffield Edwards (Office of Security), James Angleton (Counter Intelligence), and Richard Bissell (Operations). All three men were members of a group, reportedly (and likely unofficially) referred to as the "Health Alteration Committee." The Church Committee obtained testimony that in 1960 this group endorsed a proposal for a special operation to "incapacitate" an Iraqi Colonel suspected of promoting Soviet interests; the device to be used was a monogrammed, poisoned handkerchief. In the Colonel's case the handkerchief did not reach him prior to a coup, which resulted in his execution. The request for the special action was apparently routed through CIA Counter Intelligence (James Angleton). The Committee had endorsed the action and forwarded its approval to Deputy Director of Operations/Plans (Richard Bissell); the operational approval was signed off for Bissell by Tracy Barnes.

While the "Health Alteration Committee" may have served to screen and approve lethal and incapacitating actions against individuals, as in the instance of the Iraqi Colonel previously discussed. In that instance, a CIA Division head had identified the individual and the potential advantage and requested approval and support). The Agencies' involvement in attempts to murder foreign leaders was apparently much more nebulous (hence deniable). The instances of approved Executive actions recorded by the Church committee reveal no paperwork nor do they suggest that there was a definite process or even a final point of operational approval.

We now know of at a number of efforts to eliminate foreign leaders, which did occur during the 1960's – including attempts supported by Sydney Gottlieb and CIA Technical Services and at least one sophisticated sniper attack plan, supported by the National Photographic Interpretation Center. In all instances the attempts/assassinations were actually carried out by CIA surrogates, not by Agency covert action paramilitary personnel.

LUMUMBA MURDER...

Patrice Lumumba had been elected Prime Minister of the Republic of the Congo, after leading its independence drive from Belgium in 1960. Lumumba was a strong opponent of European colonialism and called for the spread of a pan-Africa movement. In the context of the times, the Eisenhower administration seemed unable to disassociate the rejection of European colonialism and surge in nationalism (whether in Africa, Asia or Latin America) with the spread of Communism and Lumumba seems to have been viewed as simply one more emerging Communist threat. Documents made available to the National

Archives only in the late 1990's, show that President Eisenhower did address the issue of Lumumba at a National Security Council meeting on August 18, 1960. No direct quotations were allowed for the notes of the NSC meetings so the actual dialog of the meeting was not recorded. In a meeting of the Church committee in 1975, the meetings note taker (Robert Johnson) related that Eisenhower had turned to Allen Dulles and said something to the effect that "Lumumba should be eliminated." In later testimony, Johnson was a bit more cautions, saying simply that he could not recall the exact words but that he himself felt they were an order that Lumumba be killed.

Whatever Eisenhower specifically intended, we know that Allen Dulles definitely interpreted the remark as a direction for the CIA to kill Lumumba, because Sydney Gottlieb of CIA Technical Services was dispatched to the Congo with a vial of poison. He was to contact an individual who was to be paid to poison Lumumba. However once again the language being used emphasized "deniability;" on August 26, 1960 Dulles had cabled the CIA station chief in the Congo that "In high quarters here, it is the clear-cut conclusion that if [Lumumba] continues to hold high office, the inevitable result will at best be chaos and at worst pave the way to Communist takeover...His removal must be an urgent and prime objective." The station chief later testified he was amazed when Gottlieb showed up with poison as he had interpreted Dulles cable in terms of political action, not murder.[43]

Circumstances, including a total lack of coordination in regard to individuals sent to the Congo, prevented the poison from being delivered; in the interim Lumumba were captured by political rivals and murdered. The Church Committee concluded that the CIA was not directly involved with the actual murder. The Church Committee's conclusions about exactly who did murder Patrice Lumumba may have been premature, based on more recently available information, but certainly the CIA poison attack itself did not actually happen.

Due to confusion between different case officers, two different CIA "assets" to be involved in the poison delivery were both sent to the Congo and housed in the Regina Hotel in Leopoldville. One man (WIROGUE) had been recruited by the Agency for the specific purpose of "spotting agent candidates," in particular criminals with good connections (including drug smuggling and burglary, to support CIA Staff D covert collections activities). Another man, (ZRRIFLE) was an experienced criminal (active in drug smuggling) who was expected to have contacts to be used in "sensitive operations" ranging from burglary to assassination. Neither man had any contacts or experience in the Congo; objectively the whole poison effort seems to have been about as well organized as a pick-up basketball game. With both men (Europeans) at a hotel, WIROGUE actually tried to recruit ZRRIFLE for the Lumumba poison delivery – because ZRRIFLE had no information on WIROGUE, the offer was refused. WIROGUE gave up on the job, engaged in some local

by ZRRIFLE (Harvey's "Executive Action" program)
the author likely means "QJWIN"
Luxemborg assassin

money making activities and left the Congo on less than good terms with the Agency. ZRRIFLE appears to have simply returned to Europe.[44]

One point, the Lumumba attempt does make perfectly clear, if the senior leadership of the Agency felt it had received a direction to "eliminate" a foreign leader, assassination was a perfectly acceptable tactic. It had the tools to perform deniable assassinations and it had senior officers who were fully prepared to attempt political murders. A second point is that the switch to "deniable" wording had added a totally new element to the situation – "interpretation." Words used loosely (perhaps intentionally) could take on a whole new meaning when translated at different levels within the Agency. And, as in Guatemala (and later in Vietnam with the murder of President Diem), the problem could be considerably magnified when the Agency was working with third parties (exiles, rebels, coup leaders) in "regime change."

TRUJILLO MURDER...

In 1961, Rafael Trujillo, long time head of the Dominican Republic and considered as one of the most brutal Latin American dictators (reportedly responsible for the deaths of more than 50,000 people), was murdered in a machine gun attack in his capital. Trujillo's brutality and his increasing meddling (including a 1960 bomb attack against the President of Venezuela) had turned his long time relationship with the United States into a major embarrassment. Following his assassination, the CIA was widely suspected, due to the association of its personnel with the individuals who had killed Trujillo.

The agency responded by reporting to the Deputy Attorney General that it had "no active part" in the murder. However an internal CIA memorandum shows that that the Agency had indeed had extended involvement with the individuals involved. Such an involvement was confirmed by the fact that one of them was found in possession of a rifle supplied by the CIA and further investigation revealed that Tracy Barnes (apparently again acting for Richard Bissell) had signed off on delivering that weapon and two other rifles to the Dominican Republic via State Department pouch.

We will see that pattern repeated in many similar incidents. Assassinations (more frequently assassination attempts) were not conducted by CIA employees or by any individual directly associated with the Agency. Instead, the acts were carried out by individuals and cliques who had been in contact with, encouraged, and supported by CIA covert officers.

CASTRO MURDER ATTEMPTS...

Unlike the Lumumba plot, there is no solid indication that the various murder attempts against Fidel Castro began at the level of the National Security Council, either under Presidents Eisenhower or Kennedy. It appears instead

see max vongydow's Character in "3 days of the London" film

that the initiatives came from within the CIA Operations Division, tasked with the overthrow of the Castro government. In March 1960 a top-secret policy paper was drafted entitled: "A Program of Covert Action Against the Castro Regime" (code-named JMARC), "to bring about the replacement of the Castro regime with one more...acceptable to the U.S. in such a manner as to avoid any appearance of U.S. intervention." The proposal was largely based in the tactics of PBSUCCESS, viewed as a model for forced regime change and widely viewed as having been extremely successful in Guatemala.

Evan Thomas, in his 1995 book on the CIA, *The Very Best Men: The Early Years of the CIA*, provides two examples illustrating how assassination attempts could begin within operations without any actual sanction, not even a head shake. In one instance, Bissell reportedly "informed" his superior, Allen Dulles, of a plan to kill not only Castro but also other senior regime members including Castro's brother. Bissell simply used alphabetical designations rather than names and Dulles simply listened – he asked no questions and gave no approval, with Bissell later claiming that Dulles fully understood that he was approving the murder of the leaders of the Cuban government. In a second instance, Tracy Barnes, on his own, approved an attempt on Fidel Castro, Raul Castro, and Che Guevera. He was ordered to cancel the attack. He proceeded to do so, but it turned out to be moot, only because the foreign agent involved did not receive Barnes' approval in time to carry out the bombing.[45]

The Church Committee inquiries revealed that Bissell had turned to Sydney Gottlieb and Technical Services for a variety of options, some short of assassination. Gottlieb had offered substances that, if delivered, would make Castro appear incoherent during a major television speech. Another alternative would be saturate Castro's shoes with thallium so that the hair of his beard would fall out, ruining his macho image. Over time Gottlieb also presented lethal assassination options, including the use of a poisoned cigar, a poisoned wetsuit, an exploding conch shell and a poisonous fountain pen.

An actual long-term effort to assassinate Castro began some months after Richard Bissell and Tracy Barnes had been assigned to the JMARC project. This effort was especially significant because it appears that Bissell and Barnes felt that it would take Castro out of the picture and enable a cadre of trained Cuban exiles to successfully enter Cuba and seize power. As we will note later, the CIA's ability to conceal the Castro assassination element of Bissell's and Barnes' planning became a major factor in the disaster at the Bay of Pigs.

As far as recorded testimony goes, the initial Castro murder effort began in the fall of 1960 with Richard Bissell (Operations) and Sheffield Edwards (Office of Security). Their plan was to turn to certain of the Office of Securities' contacts, in particular someone who might have access to the old Havana gambling network and individuals who could line up couriers and assassins within Cuba. Edwards' support chief, Jim O'Connell, initiated the search for such an individual through a Washington private investigative firm – a firm on contract with the Agency for "sensitive matters."

This effort is generally portrayed as the CIA's decision to use the "Mafia" to kill Castro, but a closer study of the details shows that in no way did the Agency reach out to the national crime syndicate to contract an assassination. Their objective was to find criminal contacts that could operate on the ground in a "denied area" and who, because of Castro's acts against the Havana casino owners, could be seen as having an obvious motive. We will examine other instances in which the Agency turned to "underworld" connections for deniable operations. In one Cuba related instance, the Agency had approached Cuban underworld types to break a Technical Services team out of a Cuban prison. As we will see, it was also not unusual for either Staff D or Counter Intelligence to use "underworld" contacts and assets; the Office of Security appears to have routinely assisted with such introductions.

The private investigative firm in question was headed by Robert Maheu. According to Maheu himself, the CIA had been his first client, using him in "cut-out" assignments for jobs in which the Agency could not be officially involved.[46] Maheu had been an FBI special agent from 1940-1947, opening his own firm in 1954. The CIA Office of Security recruited him in 1954, placing him on a $500 a month retainer and granting him a covert security clearance. He performed assignments for the Operations Directorate; whose activities apparently ranged from "procurement of feminine companionship for foreign dignitaries" to wire tapping and bugging operations. In the latter activities, he employed Alan Hughes. Hughes had worked for CIA technical services in support of activities between TSS and the Special Operations Division at Camp Detrick (under Sydney Gottlieb). While working for Maheu, Hughes planted bugs with prostitutes provided to both foreign dignitaries and domestic politicians. He also worked on the electronic security system for Dictator Rafael Trujillo and eventually was involved in a domestic bugging operation which eventually exposed the Roselli/Cuban assassination project to the FBI.[47]

Robert Maheu proposed John Roselli as the right person for the Castro project; Roselli was a well-connected Los Angeles/Las Vegas entertainment and casino figure with a prior history in Cuba. Roselli also had extensive connections with a number of major regional underworld figures. His business card identified him as a "strategist" and he was known to be a deal maker, from organizing film industry investments in Los Angeles, to putting together casino deals in Las Vegas. He had worked in Havana (following scandals which forced Batista to appeal to mob godfather Meyer Lansky for someone to improve the image of the Havana casinos) and had connections to virtually the entire old Havana casino crowd. Maheu and Roselli had become acquainted in the 1950's and CIA Security officer O'Connell had previously met Roselli at Maheu's home in Washington, D.C. Roselli was also well acquainted with a number of influential Washington insiders, including key lobbyists such as Fred Black (a neighbor of both J. Edgar Hoover and Lyndon Johnson).

Roselli met with Maheu and O'Connell at the Hilton Plaza in New York City and agreed to make introductions to people who "knew the Cuban crowd." At a subsequent meeting in Miami, Roselli brought in two other men and introduced them simply as his Cuban contacts, one of whom he described as a courier. The men reportedly rejected the CIA proposal for a rifle attack on Castro, proposing poison since their "people" were not willing to risk being killed in a direct attack. Several weeks later both Maheu and the CIA offices were seriously taken aback when they came to realize that the two men Roselli had involved were actually major Mafia figures from Chicago and Florida (Sam Giancana and Santo Trafficante). With little choice but to proceed, O'Connell requested six poison pills from Technical Services (Gottlieb) and the project moved forward.

In what might be considered "Round One" of the Roselli project (before the exile Brigade landing attempt), Roselli orchestrated at least three poison attempts against Castro, two in March and one in April, immediately prior to the Bay of Pigs Cuban exile landing. At the last moment, the individual designated to coordinate that effort, (Antonio De Varona, a.k.a. Tony Varona), was confined by CIA officer Howard Hunt, along with the rest of the exile leadership. Hunt acted to prevent exile political confrontations at the last moment but his action may well have unwittingly doomed the entire effort by aborting the poison attempt. Ironically, Hunt had himself broached the subject of assassinating Castro with Barnes, but he had been abruptly cut off – being told not to concern himself. Everything was under control.

As knowledge of the CIA/Roselli Castro plots emerged during the Church Committee hearings, various CIA officers affirmed that they had no knowledge of it, suggesting that it was run virtually anonymously at the highest levels and was never a factor in the Cuba project itself or in any way related to it. When questioned, Bissell himself "gave widely varying answers at different times," eventually suggesting to CIA historian Jack Pfeiffer that as he recalled, Sheffield Edwards had brought up the idea. In his own biography, Bissell wrote that he hoped the plot would succeed because *"the end justified the means."* Bissell also noted that if Castro had been killed it could have made the effort to overthrow Castro either "unnecessary or much easier." Given that the poison attempts were under way up to the very last minute, it seems hard to believe that a Castro assassination was not a major factor in Bissell's thoughts on the exile Brigade and its chance for success.[48]

Regardless of Bissell's comments, we now know that the Castro assassination effort was indeed known inside the Agency, beyond Edwards and Bissell. In a 1997 interview with Don Bohning, Jake Esterline, operations head of the Cuba project, described that in the fall of 1960 he received a mysterious request for a large amount of money. The amount could have been $50,00 or even $150,000, but it was far beyond routine approval amounts and it came from J.C. King (King was CIA Western Hemisphere Division head but not actively involved in the Cuba project). Esterline sent the request back to King. It came back with a note saying it had to be approved and quickly because the money was needed (it would come out of the Cuba project budget). Esterline called King and said he wasn't signing without understanding what it was for and King said he would get back to him.

Apparently King got clearance from Bissell and was back the next day briefing Esterline on the outlines of an assassination project, using the "Mafia;" following the briefing, Esterline eventually signed off on requests for some $200,000 for the highly secret project. Esterline eventually came to feel that if the assassination effort had not been expected to succeed, many of the issues with the final Brigade invasion plan might have been addressed – "If Bissell and others hadn't felt they had the 'magic button' I don't think we would have had all the hair splitting over air support." Esterline had also ordered him not to discuss the assassination project with Bissell (Esterline's boss) because he thought that it would be "a hell of a mess." Later Esterline would come to realize the whole project was Bissell's idea and that, among a number of other things (to be discussed later), that realization would lead him to conclude that he was "pretty damn sure that Bissell was not being straight with us on a number of things." Unfortunately, that realization would be many years down the road from 1961.[49]

Although the Roselli linked poison attempts are the most frequently discussed (and the only ones apparently studied in any depth by the Church Committee), new documents suggest that there were several more attempts to kill Castro, some extensively planned and some seemingly much more spontaneous. One particular attack on Raúl Castro appears to have been an autonomous effort, conducted during an operational mission led by Rip Robertson, a JMWAVE operations officer. While engaged in a paramilitary attack on the Santiago de Cuba harbor, Robertson's crew also conducted a machine gun attack on Raúl's home. Other efforts, much more extensively planned, were supported by JMARC field staff at the Miami station and were to be carried out by exile paramilitary trainees inserted into Cuba.

During the period of the Church Committee hearings, the CIA conducted an extensive internal inquiry, in an effort to locate any references to assassination activities, which might have been conducted during its earlier decades. In 2005, researcher Malcolm Blunt located CIA reports prepared during this inquiry and circulated internally within the Agency. A key memo was prepared by Edward Cates of the Imagery Exploitation Group at the National Photographic Interpretation Center. Three of Cates' employees had formerly worked at the CIA JMWAVE field station in Miami and had heard references to assassination plans targeting the two Castro brothers. Eight individuals had heard of multiple operations targeting Fidel Castro and one of which had aimed at his brother Raúl.[50]

The "operational" attacks on Fidel Castro show evidence of having been intensely

(handwritten margin note: CIA IG Report + other testimony.)

planned and orchestrated, but who knew about them above the level of the Cuban project special operations personnel is entirely unknown. The NPIC supported plan was to conduct a sniper attack on Castro while he was traveling to and staying at the Varadero Beach Estate, east of Havana. Castro was known to frequent the estate and the plan had extensive photo interpretation support, including preparation of photographic views and diagrams of the estate. It appears that there were three different attempts to insert Cuban exile shooters for a long-range rifle attack. This plan was definitely related to the CIA Operations group and the name Carl Jenkins (alias James E. Beckhoff), surfaced in association with it. Jenkins was a paramilitary trainer for the Cuba project, specializing in maritime infiltration and exfiltration. It should also be noted that Jenkins went on to become associated with the JMARC successor project (AMWORLD, centered round exile leader Manual Artime), serving as the case officer for Artime's second in command, Rafael Quintero. In September 1963, Jenkins drafted a memo summarizing military actions proposed for the AM/WORLD project. In the section on "Commandos," there was discussion of the use of abductions and assignations targeting Cuban intelligence officers, agents and informants as well as foreign Communists, with the objective of raising the morale of rebels within Cuba. Much later, in the 1990's, Quintero and Jenkins' names would be surfaced in relation to the Kennedy assassination.[51]

Yet another attack plan called for Castro to be assassinated while on or in the area of a yacht that he maintained near the Bay of Pigs. The only reference to that plan, which could be located, referred to a project named "Pathfinder," and the only document which could be located in regard to "Pathfinder" made reference to Frank Sturgis and gave the date of January 20, 1961. Sturgis was a significant figure in the secret war against Cuba, first joining Castro and becoming a major weapons procurer for the rebel forces, achieving a military command level within Castro's regime and later turning on Castro when he began to display communist inclinations. Before his escape from Cuba, Sturgis had approached the CIA with an offer to organize the murder of Castro, using troops under Sturgis' command. Officially, that offer was rejected at that time. Sturgis later became a key informant on exile activities, providing information to the Miami station.

Several sources, including Sturgis himself, suggest he served to brief and prepare a very special group of exiles, in preparation for the overthrow of Castro. Sturgis referred to this group as "Operation 40" – the existence of such a special group has been verified by very well informed sources including Sam Halpern, the *Times* news correspondent in Havana and later Miami. Arthur Schlesinger reported Halpern's information on Operation 40, noting Halpern's "very strong contacts among the exiles." Halpern stated that the CIA has trained a special force, originally of only 40 men with the ostensible purpose of administering liberated areas in Cuba. However, they had also been trained in interrogation, torture, and general terrorism. It was believed they would execute designated Castro regime members and Communists. The more liberal and leftist exile leaders also feared that they might be targeted following a successful coup. Halpern also reported that the groups leader was Captain Luis Sanjenis, who served as chief of intelligence for the group and that the CIA had brought in a Latin American named Felix to conduct the special training for the group.[52]

If Halpern's information is accepted, it is quite significant as it would suggest that the same sort of "blacklist" political elimination plans first seen in our review of the Guatemala project were also a highly covert part of Cuba project. And, as it turns out, almost all the elements described by Halpern can now be independently verified. Documents reveal that David Morales, acting as the Counter Intelligence officer for JMARC, had selected and arranged for extensive and special training for 39 Cuban exiles, designated as AMOTs. A small number of those individuals were infiltrated into Cuba in advance and the rest went in along with the invasion force. The head of the AMOTs was Jose Joachim "Sam" Sanjenis, and documents show that Sanjenis was the individual who recruited Frank Sturgis for CIA activities following Sturgis' escape from Cuba. The AMOTs received special training because they were intended to form the backbone of the new regime in Cuba, also serving as the new Cuban intelligence service. Perhaps most importantly, a JMARC document which reviews Morales' Counter Intelligence program notes that special training was provided by a Chilean ex-police officer and that during the "Action Phase" of the operation the groups primary objective would be to "identify and contain rabid Castro-ites, Cuban Communists, members of the Cuban security services;" they would also develop "black lists" pertinent the that objective.[53]

As final confirmation of both the existence of Operation 40 and its congruence with the Cuban personnel trained and prepared by David Morales, Grayston Lynch (one of the two CIA officers accompanying the Cuban Brigade during the landing at the Bay of Pigs) wrote in 1998 that the ship Lake Charles had transported the men of "Operation 40" to the Cuba landing area. The men had trained in Florida, apart from the regular Brigade members, and were to act as a military government after the overthrow of Castro's regime. Their task would be to administer first the beachhead and following that all of the "liberated" areas in Cuba as the anti-Castro forces advanced.[54]

To some extent, Lynch also confirmed the fears of the liberal/leftist segments of the exile movement. He commented that Manolo Ray and his followers were virtually the same as Castro and noted that when some of Ray's personnel joined the exile 2506 Brigade in training, they were imprisoned. The plan was to transport them to the beachhead in Cuba for legal trial as mutineers. He does not speculate on their punishment, but it seems likely they would never have left the beachhead alive. Instead, he recounts that when the invasion failed they were acclaimed as heroes by the exile radical left and released. It should be noted that when the AMOTs returned to Florida, they were organized into a highly effective counter intelligence group directed at both suspected Castro agents and at the exile community in general. The majority of Cuban counter-intelligence from 1962 until the early 1970's was collected by the group, which came under the supervision of CIA officer Tony Sforza. Reportedly Sanjenis continued as the Cuban leader and maintained extensive files on the Cuban community; as time progressed, the group came to be locally mistrusted, apparently due to blackmail and other activities on the part of some of its members and former members.[55]

The Congressional investigation of the CIA's assassination activities in Cuba led to the Agency conducting its own internal inquiry into files and messages on the subject. Internal memos reveal that, in 1975, five assassinations related messages were discovered. One in particular typifies the sort of deniability the Agency struggled to maintain in respect to its surrogates. In that incident, an Agency associated exile (AMBRONC/S) who would be infiltrated into Cuba three times by the CIA, was taken out twice and captured and executed during his final penetration) sent messages back from Cuba discussing plans to kill Castro and simultaneously sabotage the Havana electrical power system.

Message 1, from March 27, 1961, requested an Agency opinion on the sabotage and plan for attacking Castro at the Havana Sports Palace. No Agency reply was located and in a second cable on March 29, AMBRONC specifically discussed attacking the Havana electrical system after the assassination of Castro — both to occur on April 9. That message did draw a response – which endorsed a "major effort on the date selected". It also suggested others who should be contacted to initiate a general uprising on that date. A final message from the Agent discusses his assembly of some 50 men for the attacks and a plea for U.S. military support, since by itself the effort would fail.

No further related documents were located. The case officer responsible for the agent was interviewed about the Cuba and Castro assassination efforts. The investigation generated a list of other Agency operatives who had been referred to support the attacks. Both the case officer and the Agency inquiry noted that the exile operative had never publicly admitted to working for the CIA, even up to the time of his execution.

These assassination-related messages were apparently not shared with the Congressional committee and appear only in internal CIA commentary on the Committees final report.

This provides us with yet another instance of the pattern in which CIA agents/ surrogates proposed and attempted assassinations but in which the Agency obtained deniability by not actually approving such proposals in official memos or cables (and certainly not using the word assassination themselves) and left itself the out that any such actions were taken at the "initiative" of those individuals without any specific orders having been given.

6 THE END JUSTIFIES THE MEANS – BUT WHO MAKES THE CALL?

In 1954, during PBSUCCESS, political assassination had been proposed by the rebel leaders and seriously considered by the CIA field and headquarters project officers. By the time several of those same officers (Bissell, Barnes, Morales, and Robertson) were assigned to the Castro project (JMARC), targeted assassinations seem to have become an accepted tactic, at least within certain segments of the Agency. A variety of lethal toxins and delivery devices had been developed under the direction of CIA Technical Services. That work was known not only to senior officers in Operations but also in the Office of Security and Counter Intelligence. In 1960, the Agency had been involved in assassination plots against Raphael Trujillo and Patrice Lumumba. And in 1960, while assigned to Staff D, William Harvey was tasked by Richard Helms, Deputy Director of Operations, with setting up a network to effect deniable foreign operations, including political assassinations. Harvey's own notes and documents reflect certain skepticism about the project but show that he took it professionally and as a serious task. His notes of his meeting with Helms referred to the "Magic Button" and "the last resort beyond the last resort."

Former CIA Director Helms gave testimony on Harvey and the ZRRIFLE project, indicating that it was simply a foreign recruiting effort and that the assassination aspect of the project was never implemented, and ordered discontinued when brought to his attention. Given statements (and documents) from ZRRIFLE project officer William Harvey, Helms' statement would have to be considered an outright lie. There is no doubt that William Harvey was directed to implement ZRRIFLE in regard to the assassination of Fidel Castro and Harvey was reporting directly to Helms at the time (paperwork shows that Helms authorized the continuation of ZR RIFLE and payments to the project through 1963). It is also true that (without naming but certainly implying Richard Helms among others) Harvey himself made a number of disdainful comments in regards to the Church Committee testimony of a number of senior CIA officers. As his biographer, Bayard Stockton describes them, Harvey's comments "reflect disappointment, even disgust, with the charades that took place at the Church (Committee) hearings, as sometimes worthy intelligence officers, heretofore men of honor, writhed in their suits, feigned loss of memory, sought to protect reputations or hustled to be seen as protecting secrets vital to the national interest."[56]

At the time Helms was talking to Harvey about a "Magic Button," Harvey was in charge of CIA Staff D. Staff D (Signals intelligence) was one of the most secure CIA departments (along with Counter Intelligence). Harvey had himself earlier run Counter Intelligence before being assigned as Chief of Station in the Agency's most important foreign base – Berlin. He was succeeded in Counter Intelligence by James Angleton. Staff D (sometimes referred to somewhat superficially as either "signals or communications intelligence") was responsible for clandestine collections using covert technical and personnel assets. This involved not only placing wire taps and electronic "bugs" (developed by the audio section of Technical Services/David Christ) but the actual theft of foreign countries' code books and related materials. Personnel used by Staff D included burglary specialists, many with significant criminal backgrounds. Recruitment of such underworld "assets" appears to have been facilitated through information provided by the CIA Office of Security (Sheffield Edwards). Reportedly, James Angleton had access to Staff D assets as well as his own connections; one of his FBI counterparts related that Angleton had access to a New York mob lawyer and, that on occasion, the FBI itself performed domestic "black bag" jobs for Angleton.[57]

In short, given that a good number of Staff D operations were overseas and employed a variety of criminal talent, it seems to have presented an ideal cover for the "Magic Button" – which in 1962 came into action under Harvey in the form of a revival of the Roselli/Castro assassination project (Phase 2). Staff D itself has been described as a "tight, fearless group." Its members included top-of-the line locksmiths, photo experts and building tradesmen…very, very good…no one will ever know the number of embassies all over the world that they entered and relieved of crypto materials." In 1967, the CIA's Inspector General noted that they were recruited "to break into safes and kidnap couriers" while Evan Thomas, author of *The Very Best Men* described them as "a rough bunch with strong ties (if not full-fledged membership) in the underworld. He quoted Sam Halpern as saying "We had to keep the FBI informed when one of them traveled."[58]

Clearly – regardless of senior officers' protests to the Church committee, in the early 1960's – "executive action" was accepted as a necessary tool of the Cold War. A tool not to be used indiscriminately but only on specific projects relating to the highest levels of national security, projects at the forefront of the secret war with the Communists. Sydney Gottlieb, charged with developing and stockpiling lethal poisons and toxins, was directly involved with such executive action, having been involved with the initial attempt to kill Patrice Lumumba, as well as in numerous efforts to assassinate Fidel Castro. In his 1977 testimony to the Church Committee, Gottlieb was truthful enough to state that his actions were in the interest of national security and that "*the country was involved in a real covert war in the sense that the Cold War had spilled over into intelligence activities.*"

As we continue this study, it is critical to keep in mind that the men being discussed all would be considered as intensely patriotic and intensely (perhaps obsessively) anti-Communist. Virtually all of them had served and/or fought during World War II and to them the Cold War was an actual war. They were the country's proactive defense and the weight of denying a Communist victory was on their backs. And as events developed, during the early years of the 1960's it appeared that they might be losing that battle. Rather than "rolling back" Communist expansion, they themselves were in danger of being rolled over, both in Asia and 90 miles off the Florida coast.

BUT HE SAID – OR DID HE?

Of course the ultimate danger in an environment in which murders ranging from "executive action" to the elimination of "black listed" political cadre during regime change involved not only accountability but communication. Apparently senior officers at the level of Dulles, Helms, Angleton, and Bissell routinely discussed a great many subjects in such abstract terms, so much so that certain decisions became subject to personal interpretations. And on occasion, "deniability" proved not only to be an operational tactic but quite useful during Congressional inquiries. The Church committee report concluded:

> "...the system of executive command and control was so ambiguous that it is difficult to be certain at what levels assassination activity was known and authorized. This situation creates the disturbing prospect that Government officials might have undertaken assassination plots without having it uncontrovertibly clear that there was an explicit authorization from Presidents."[59]

7 THE DANGER OF DENIAL

Much has been and will be written about the disastrous landing of Brigade 2506 at the Bay of Pigs in Cuba. Following its dramatic failure, President Kennedy immediately ordered General Maxwell Taylor to head a government committee investigating the failure and the CIA itself initiated an internal, Inspector General led investigation of the Cuba project.[60]

The Inspector General's report proved to be a particularly serious indictment of the project, with a negative assessment of both its organizational structure and the overall management of the effort. In fact the internal CIA report so angered certain senior officers that the Director allowed one of the senior Cuba project officers to right a rebuttal.[61]

Unfortunately neither of those inquiries had access to certain information that has since emerged during the following decades, in particular information and insights provided from the projects' two senior military officers – Jake Esterline and Colonel Jack Hawkins. There information only became known in 2006, with the publication of Don Bohning's book, *The Castro Obsession*.

It will be necessary to review certain aspects of the first Cuba project in order to better understand the thoughts of the CIA officers involved in it, to map it against the project many of them had jointly worked on earlier in Guatemala and most importantly, to paint a full picture of the intense emotional impact it had on all of them. An event so personally overwhelming, it represented the first step towards the ultimate decision to undertake a domestic "executive action" against President Kennedy.

Following the successful ouster of Batista, Fidel Castro's regime had come to be viewed as another primary (and much worse) example of an emerging Soviet client state, a Soviet client only some 90 miles off American shores. By 1959 the Eisenhower administration ordered an effort to oust Castro and his increasingly Russian influenced regime. In March of 1960, a top secret paper was drafted, with the title "A Program of Covert Action against the Castro Regime" with the goal of replacing Castro with a government "more acceptable to the U.S. and in such a manner to avoid any appearance of U.S. intervention."

In order to do that a select group of CIA officers were brought into a project at CIA Headquarters, led by Richard Bissell and Tracy Barnes. While based in Washington, the project began to develop a huge domestic field office in

Miami, Florida (JMWAVE). The operational teams (and their initial tactics) were to a large extent a duplication of Guatemala and PBSUCCESS. Bissell was designated as overall project chief and Barnes his project manager. Henry Hecksher also joined the Cuba project but his role is quite unclear; he was reported at training camps including the Brigade camp in Guatemala. It is also likely that following the Bay of Pigs, he was assigned to covert intelligence activities in Mexico City.[62]

The project was to have a significant propaganda/psychological operations element (headed by David Phillips), a political action effort with Cuban exiles and groups (worked by Frank Bender, an alias for Gerry Droller, and Howard Hunt, both Guatemala alumni), a paramilitary effort to place armed groups inside Cuba (Jake Esterline) and an important Counter Intelligence/ Training effort for special action exile groups (David Morales). As the effort mushroomed, a much more formal military element would be added (Jake Esterline, Colonel Jack Hawkins, Rip Robertson, and Grayston Lynch).

Both Phillips and Morales had recently been in Cuba, Morales operating under a State Department cover and attached to the U.S. Embassy. Phillips was working as a CIA contract employee, totally undercover, with an alias at a public relations business. Both men had been forced to leave Cuba – Morales when his cover was blown by the discovery of his name on a Batista secret police credentials list and Phillips when his activities with anti-Castro activists became known to Cuban intelligence. In his biography, Phillips described being recruited into the new Cuba project; his immediate question was "what's the plan" – the reply was "the Guatemala scenario."[63]

It is extremely important to realize the extent to which the initial Cuba project (Phase 1) looked very much like PBSUCCESS, with a heavy utilization of propaganda, outreach to anti-Castro rebels and an appeal to conservative elements of Cuban society (especially the extremely anti-Communist business families and religious leadership). Over time (and under two administrations), that approach "morphed" into essentially a "go for broke," single, large scale military action. An action which involved a daylight military invasion with a fleet of boats, WWII era landing ships and landing craft, tanks, heavy weapons units – something that in no way could have matched the original parameter of "avoiding any appearance of U.S. intervention" and an action which could only be perceived inside Cuba as a literal American backed invasion. David Phillips described the change in strategy as "madness."

> "What had been conceived as a classic guerilla warfare operation with individual fighters carrying their own weapons had been converted only a few days before D-Day into an amphibious landing of tanks on Cuban beaches."

Phillips' comment is incorrect in regard to timing; as we will see the shift in focus from guerilla tactics to an amphibious invasion had happened considerably earlier, certainly by November 1960. Still, his description of his own personal response is telling: "*We're going to mount a secret operation in the Caribbean with tanks?*"[64]

Phillips' reaction is an interesting indicator of changes that were taking place within CIA Operations, changes that had dramatically escalated in the early 60's. The Agency was engaged in tasks of such scope that "deniability" was becoming farcical. In Cuba, in Laos and in Vietnam they were taking the responsibility for actual military operations with large forces, and wrestling with logistics, supply lines and all the other details normally handled by the military services. It was a trend very much at odds with the "covert and clandestine" charter of the CIA's Operations division.

Initially the staffing for the entire Cuba Task Force (WH/4) was set at only some 40 people, with 18 in Washington, 20 at the Havana station and 2 in eastern Cuba. But by April 1961, its roster had mushroomed to some 588 people, making it one of the largest CIA branches, larger than some of the CIA's global divisions. Eventually, the Miami JMWAVE station itself would come to have a huge "shadow" staff of Cuban exiles. The station was estimated to have had something like 200 case officers who in turn handled 4-10 Cuban exile "principal agents." In turn, each principal agent handled another 10-30 exiles, creating a CIA reach that touched literally thousands of exiles. But the station's reach was beyond even the Miami exiles. Every foreign CIA station had at least one officer assigned to Cuban affairs and reporting to JMWAVE, the watch on Castro's Cuba and its activities was global.[65]

The initial plan, as drafted by Esterline (January 18, 1960) called for exfiltrating a very select group of Cubans, training them and putting them back on the island (in the Trinidad area) and supporting them in an effort to ignite a major anti-Castro movement. The plan was conceived as safe because the cadre would have easy access to the Escambray Mountains where an active anti-Castro network was already in existence. But, as Esterline would tell Bohning, the Trinidad Plan (approved by Eisenhower on March 17, 1960) never had a chance to evolve: "It was taken away by Bissell's decision to go for more, much more, and create an invasion force."[66]

The basic components of the original Trinidad Plan involved formation of a Cuban exile organization, a major propaganda effort, creation inside Cuba of a clandestine intelligence and action apparatus, and development of a small paramilitary force to be introduced into Cuba to organize, train and lead resistance groups. A briefing paper presented in August for Eisenhower and the Joint Chiefs stated that the paramilitary force was to consist of some 500 trainees and 37 radio operators and that they would be "available to use as infiltration teams or as an invasion force." The paper did note that any successful large-scale paramilitary operations would be "dependent upon widespread guerrilla resistance throughout the area."[67]

The Taylor Commission, charged with evaluating the Bay of Pigs disaster, could find no specific date nor set of orders which changed the original Trinidad plan into something very different. However, they did find that by November 1960, a cable from Washington directed a reduction in the guerilla teams in training to 60 men and the formation of the rest into an amphibious and airborne assault force. That directive seems to have been the turning point for the Brigade and the project.

Events in Cuba had also taken the target environment into something far different than had been encountered with PBSUCCESS in Guatemala. Fidel Castro had been ruthless in taking control. In September of 1960, he had organized "Committees for Defense of the Revolution" (based on the highly successfully Soviet model) and they had instituted neighborhood spy networks against "counter revolutionaries." There had been hundreds of executions and a great number of professionals, including teachers, had either been jailed or had fled the island. By the end of 1960, all opposition newspapers had been closed and both radio and television stations were under strict state control. As a finishing touch in consolidating power, Castro had either jailed or executed a good number of his own revolutionary comrades.

The CIA Havana station had been put under heavy pressure; the U.S. Embassy had to be closed and the CIA infiltration program was encountering a great many problems – facing an extensive and highly effective Cuban counter intelligence program, one modeled on similar programs which had taken Eastern European nations behind the Iron Curtain and totally defeated CIA penetration efforts there.

There were also growing problems with the various on-island anti-Castro groups and exile groups in the U.S., with aggressive struggles for power and even violence among the groups. Worse yet, Castro had begun to jail tens of thousands of suspected opponents (some 50,000 would be in prison by the time of the Brigade landing). At first, efforts to insert CIA infiltrators onto the island had been somewhat successful. And documents show that by March 1961, the largest on-island group, UNIDAD, was preparing for local uprisings, a rebellion within the Cuban Navy and a coup of some military officers. However, UNIDAD advised that it was not yet ready to support any major military actions and had communicated that message to its own network inside Cuba. In his memoirs, *Reflections of a Cold Warrior*, Bissell wrote about some of these problems, including the effectiveness of Castro's repressive moves and about the lack of effectiveness of anti-Castro propaganda.[68]

Although the details of the shift are unclear, there is no doubt as to what the Trinidad Plan evolved into; Bissell himself wrote of "a metamorphosis" shifting to reliance on an invasion force of some 1,500 men." And Col. Hawkins was directed to revise his plans accordingly. Hawkins responded with a January 4, 1961 memorandum on "Policy Decisions Required for Conduct of Strike Operations against Cuba," pointing out that the incoming President, John Kennedy, would need to concur with an action before March 1 for a variety of reasons, including the fact that Castro was arming and training at an increasing rate and that trained Cuban jet pilots were quickly coming on board – along with the reality that Castro's efforts were quickly turning the island into an effective police state.

Hawkins placed particular emphasis on the amount of air support required for success, including the amount of aircraft and number of missions. He specifically stated that if policy considerations did not permit an aggressive tactical air campaign, the project should be abandoned.

The Taylor Commission inquiry determined that while Esterline did forward Hawkins memo to Bissell, there was no evidence found that it had ever gone beyond Bissell's office. There is no evidence that it was presented to or read by either the President or his national security advisor.[69]

What has become clear from Bohning's work with Hawkins and Esterline is that there was an ongoing disconnect between the demands of "deniability" (which the Kennedy administration demanded) and the metamorphosis of a PBSUCCESS-style campaign into a full-fledged sea borne invasion. And Richard Bissell was at the center of that disconnect. Hawkins felt that Bissell had made his own military decisions about dramatically increasing the side of the landing force, adding a parachute battalion and even a tank platoon – changes not recommended by either Hawkins or Esterline. In fact Col. Hawkins had specifically warned that the use of parachute troops and tanks would unquestionably brand the invasion as a U.S. undertaking; Bissell remained firm in his decisions and there was no further discussion of the point.[70]

Esterline also eventually learned that it was Bissell who had banned him from high level Washington meetings and came to the conclusion that Bissell was giving the President assurances and commitments on deniability that were not being shared with his force commanders. Esterline also concluded at some point, possibly even before the transition to the Bay of Pigs landing site, Bissell had given a commitment to President Kennedy that the operation would indeed be low key and would use absolutely minimal air power – an agreement not communicated to Esterline or Hawkins. Bohning notes there is reason to think that private agreement was indeed made; he points out Secret Service logs show that, in the first three months of 1961, Bissell had some 13 "off the record" personal meetings with President Kennedy. Hawkins also remarked that not once did Bissell pass on any feedback or direction from the Presidential meetings to him or Esterline.[71]

Both Hawkins and Esterline did make one final, last minute effort to express their objections, after working furiously to prepare a new plan and relocating the landing site from the Trinidad location to the Bay of Pigs. The two military officers had concluded that while they might seize the beachhead, it would be virtually impossible to extend the force beyond the beachhead operations and that such an operation could not achieve the goals of the project.

The following day both officers drove to Bissell's home and in some three hours gave him a detailed account as to why the invasion plan was not adequate to ensure complete destruction of Castro's air force and that if "any" of his fighters and bombers survived the first attack they could defeat the Brigade. In particular, they were concerned that the Brigade air support was not even under their operational control. Any surviving Cuban planes would make beachhead operations of the Brigade's B-26 bombers virtually suicidal. *Both officers then stated they would resign if the invasion were not cancelled - Bissell responded by saying that was impossible but made a firm promise that he would gain Kennedy's authorization for more aircraft and more strikes.* Esterline would tell Bohning that Bissell "solemnly pledged to Hawkins and I that he would ensure we would get the total number of planes, he would go to the President and explain why it simply had to be."

Within two days, completely unknown to the two officers, Bissell actually committed to Kennedy that he would cut the attacking B-26 force in half! Bissell was aware that both officers had expressed their concerns that if any of Castro's air force survived the first strike, the effort was likely doomed. And post-strike intelligence had confirmed that only something like half of the Cuban fighters and bombers were taken out in the first B-26 strike; that news made no apparent impact on Bissell's decisions. Hawkins and Esterline had a firm grasp of the reality of the situation and continually worked at making that clear. But, based on their interviews with Bohning, nothing of that ever passed beyond Bissell.[72]

WE WERE SCREWED BY KENNEDY!!!

It took decades and the ongoing release of key documents before Esterline and Hawkins reached the conclusions they shared with Bohning. At the time of the invasion they simply had no idea of the situation, no suspicion that Bissell had gone his own way, made his own agreements, and in the end possibly bet the lives of the Brigade on a last ditch secret effort to kill Fidel Castro. They didn't know that both Bissell and Air Force General Cabell had declined a last minute invitation from the President to present the case for more air support, another strike, to state flat out that without it the invasion was doomed. *What Esterline found "most unacceptable" about the whole thing was that even while the Brigade was going in, Kennedy offered Bissell and Cabell an opportunity to talk with him about additional air support – and "they elected not to."* In fact, at that point Bissell did not even personally communicate with the task force officers. He sent General Cabell to deliver the bad news and greet the firestorm it generated.[73]

The Bay of Pigs fiasco produced passionate reactions among a great number of the CIA staff. Hawkins called the decisions on the air strikes "an act of criminal negligence." Jake Esterline, in a tremendous show of courage, took personal leave and went to Miami to meet with families of Brigade members, by then either dead or in Cuban prisons. In the emotionally charged meetings he could only say that he had tried to call it off. That it was not his fault. That they had all "been screwed by Kennedy" and that he had "been made to send the men off to slaughter."

Others, further from the Washington scene – and not knowing of Hawkins and Esterline's efforts – assumed that the plan had been fully communicated, assumed their commanders had no outstanding concerns and that the Bay of Pigs invasion had been fully endorsed at all levels. Given that, the only explanation was a last minute failure of courage on the part of the President, or worse yet; a conscious decision to simply "dump" the Brigade into Cuba, taking care of what could have been something of a political problem.

As late as 1998, Grayston Lynch, who along with William "Rip" Robertson had been the only American military personnel to actual participate in the invasion, authored a book with the title: *Decision for Disaster: Betrayal at the Bay of Pigs – A CIA Participant Challenges the Historical Record.*

Lynch and Robertson had come into the project at a point in which the Trinidad plan had already morphed into a full-scale sea based invasion, complete with tanks, trucks, heavy weapons groups and a variety of military landing craft. Lynch provides a unique insight into what he believed the Brigade was capable of if it had been wholeheartedly supported, regardless of the foolish issue of deniability. The problem is that Lynch's view is totally at odds with the final assessment made by Hawkins and Esterline; the one which compelled them to call for a cancellation of the invasion.

Of course a commitment to extensive air support was a vital factor in Lynch's beliefs. If the B-26's could have operated unopposed for two to three weeks, not only sealing off the beachhead but going on to seriously damage much of Castro's military force and even prevent landing of Soviet support, then "the majority of the Cuban citizens must, in the end, lose." The Brigade would have been built up on the beachhead to a force of some 15,000 (with recruits from the local area and volunteers flown in from Miami). Castro would have been faced with a force he could not dislodge and one that totally ruled the sky above Cuba. With open support from the U.S. and other countries, the provisional government would result in Castro's regime simply "throwing in the towel."[74]

There is no doubt about Lynch's conviction; but there is also no doubt that his superiors believed something entirely different, even as the Brigade ships neared Cuba. However, their concerns were simply not making it beyond the Cuba Task Force leader and were definitely not being shared with the President. It is now clear that the size and scale of the air support Lynch envisioned had truly never been part of the agreement between Bissell and Kennedy.

There was no way for Lynch to know, just as there had been no way for Esterline and Hawkins to understand the true situation as the Brigade went on shore.

The only conclusion they could all draw was that they had been betrayed by the President of the United States. The words Lynch uses for Kennedy go beyond "criminal negligence and "screwed." He states explicitly that it was a lack of courage and leadership – and implies something even worse, that it was a conscious effort to dispose of the troublesome exiles by "dumping them into Cuba." However, it was CIA Director Dulles who had pointed out to Kennedy that with the Brigade in Guatemala, he simply could not cancel the whole thing as it would represent a huge "disposal problem." They would have to be brought back to the United States and that would be a security and political nightmare. At that point it appears that Kennedy simply concurred and introduced the choice of selecting a lower profile invasion site than the Trinidad area.[75]

Lynch concludes his book with a chapter on "Rewriting History" in which he argues that the Kennedy administration "feared exposure more than they feared defeat" and that *Kennedy himself made the "decision to sign the death warrant of the Cuban Brigade."*

With the publication of Bohning's 2006 book and the inside information from Esterline and Hawkins, it is clear that matters were not as black and white as Lynch still believed in 1998. But the subject of this book relates to what the CIA officers believed in 1963 and virtually to a man they felt that they had been betrayed. The new President lacked courage; he could not be trusted and that, in some sense, he had already committed treason in allowing a Communist regime to take full power 90 miles off American shores.

We have further insight into how strong these feelings were from friends of David Morales, the Cuba Project Counter Intelligence and Training officer who had prepared the very special groups, which were to administer and sanitize a liberated Cuba. Interviews with his closest friend and his personal lawyer give confirmation that Morales was an intensely patriotic individual and violently anti-Communist. Ruben Carbajal, who grew up with Morales and was as close as a brother, described Morales as the biggest patriot he had ever known, "He didn't want anybody to even talk against the United States. I never saw a man so dedicated to his country." Morales came away from the Bay of Pigs with a tremendous anger, and he spoke to Carbajal of his Cuban exile friends being "slaughtered on the beach."

At one point, in Bob Walton's (Morales' lawyer) office, Morales noted a small ceramic Kennedy campaign piece – his reaction was to tell Walton to either remove it or that he would personally break it into pieces for him. Another incident occurred when Morales was involved in business with Carbajal and Walton. They broke for drinks in a motel room. While talking, Walton mentioned doing volunteer campaign work for Kennedy. At that point Morales flew off the bed, screaming curses on Kennedy and going on at length about the fact that Kennedy had been personally responsible for his having to watch all the men he had recruited and trained wiped out, an exaggeration since the majority of his particular groups, did eventually make it back alive to the United States. Still, Morales' trainees did take losses and their senior field officer, Vincente Leon, reportedly killed himself on the beachhead rather than be captured.[76]

Clearly, President Kennedy was an intensely personal and violently emotional subject for Morales. After his tirade, having worn himself out, (they had also been drinking for some time), Morales just sat back on a bed and, talking to himself, remarked, "Well, we took care of that SOB, didn't we!"[77]

The meaning of Morales' remark will be explored in considerable detail as we proceed, for the moment it is safe to say that following the Bay of Pigs, there were a number of officers, in CIA Operations and the Cuba project paramilitary group, who felt very strongly about the President. Without a doubt they felt he was weak, that he could not be trusted, that he had betrayed the country – and over the next two years, some of them came to feel even more strongly.

8   EXTREME DYSFUNCTION

The CIA Operations officers in the Cuba Project were not the only ones to have lost their trust following the disaster at the Bay of Pigs. Certain of the most action oriented Cuban exiles (primarily those not directly involved with the Brigade) came to deeply distrust both the Kennedy administration and the CIA itself. The next two years would see those individuals launch a number of successful military attacks into Cuba, at times apparently with at least tacit support from elements of the CIA but later (following the Cuban Missile Crisis in the fall of 1962), with active opposition from the Kennedy administration. Government actions to stop "un-sponsored" Cuban attacks eventually highlighted what would become a state of extreme dysfunction between the administration, the CIA and many in the exile community. This dysfunction was so severe that by 1963, the Agency would be devoting a good percentage of its energy and efforts determining just what those exiles not in favor (and not being supported by the agency in its "autonomous" group efforts) were doing. The Miami stations' counter intelligence effort would generate more reports on exiles and exile groups than on what was going on inside Cuba itself.

Beyond that, the Kennedy brothers (both John and Robert) most definitely felt that they could not trust what they were being told by senior CIA officers – and as we have seen in regard to Richard Bissell and the JMARC project that was certainly a legitimate concern. They were still very much troubled by Cuba and focused on Castro (the Cuba problem became not only a national security concern but a significant political issue for the 1964 election). For the next two years, they would kick off a host of separate initiatives in an attempt to bring down the Castro regime. In doing so, they would never again rely solely on the CIA and would involve themselves (especially Robert Kennedy) directly in a host of different anti-Castro activities, conducting what could be called excessive micromanagement. Cuba operations would develop into an environment that would do nothing but drive professional CIA operations officers to drink (if they already had not been following the Bay of Pigs).

At the core of this dysfunction was a simple refusal to accept the reality of the evolving situation inside Cuba. As early as December 6, 1960, the American Embassy in Cuba had sent a lengthy cable to Washington, noting that Castro's executions (some 600) were troubling for the general Cuban population (regardless of the fact that many were Batista regime members who had indeed committed serious crimes) and Castro's initial popularity had significantly declined. Regardless of that, Castro himself was clearly in control and "the government is determined to suppress the opposition at any cost." It has accumulated a substantial quantity of military hardware from the Soviet bloc and is making great efforts to train the military in their use...It is not likely that the Castro regime will fall without great bloodletting and destruction of property."

Two days later, a Special National Intelligence Estimate stated that Castro "remains firmly in control in Cuba. His overall popular support has declined ...but as a symbol of revolutionary change in less than two years the Castro regime has consolidated its hold over Cuban society...any major threat to the regime was likely to be offset by the growing effectiveness of the state's instrumentalities of control."

On November 3, 1961, the head of the National Estimates Board reported that "The Castro regime has sufficient popular support and repressive capabilities to cope with any internal threat that is likely to develop within the foreseeable future. The regime's capabilities for repression are increasing more rapidly than any potentialities for active resistance."

Further national intelligence estimates in March, 1962 and June 1963, continued to stress that the Castro regime, aided by the Soviets, had developed truly substantial forces to suppress insurrection or repel invasion, noting that there was active resistance in Cuba, but it was "limited, uncoordinated, unsupported and desperate." The 1963 report specifically noted that "the mere passage of time tends to favor Castro, as Cubans and others become accustomed to the idea that he is here to stay and the regime gains in experience."[78]

Essentially then, the best objective view of the entire American intelligence community, throughout virtually all phases of the "secret war" against Cuba was that only an external intervention would be successful in toppling the Castro regime. Castro's aggressiveness, his adoption of Soviet style "repression" tactics and an internal spy network, as well as the ever-growing Soviet bloc military support, consistently outstripped the potential for any internally generated coup. The same fundamental National Intelligence Estimate remained in effect for four years, as the secret war continued through several iterations. A major military intervention would repeatedly be addressed in military planning; it would be within a hairs breadth of happening during the 1962 missile crisis. But as far as the CIA was concerned, from the summer of 1961 through 1963, Agency Operations officers would increasingly see their own "span of control" dramatically reduced, while continuing to bear the heat of repeated failures in their own ongoing efforts targeting Cuba.

Following the Bay of Pigs failure, Bissell actually remained in charge of the Cuba Project (Phase 2) and continued in that position until early 1962. Documents reflect that the immediate post-invasion activity in the project was to reorganize and focused primarily on counter intelligence activities "post strike." A memo of April 20, 1961 specifies that the AMOT organization (developed and trained by David Morales) was to be developed into an "Intelligence and Security" service based in Miami. The AMOT personnel were to be reinforced from members of a second group, which Morales had prepared as future Cuban counter intelligence and government officials.[79]

Additionally, after the disaster, AMOT personnel remaining in Cuba were used for further intelligence collection and covert action assignments. Some, such as Victor Hernandez, were actually sent back into Cuba on highly dangerous missions. Others were used to "increase counter intelligence operations run into Cuba in conjunction with liaison services of friendly countries" and to perform counter espionage, subversive and sabotage operations directed by the Castro services against other States within the Western Hemisphere. It appears that a good number of AMOTs were retained as domestic "assets" in Florida and elsewhere, working directly for the Miami station, in projects ranging from technical and electronics intelligence to surveillance activities.[80]

Their expanded role also resulted in the creation of a JMWAVE function as an adjunct to the Mexico City CIA station activities. AMOT personnel performed training for certain of the Mexico City wire tap and surveillance staff. Reportedly, Morales himself frequently traveled to Mexico City in support of the expanded counter intelligence effort. Other documents reflect a growing presence of JMWAVE staff in Mexico City during the period of 1962 and 1963, as JMWAVE officers performed activities targeting the Cubans in Mexico and the Communist Party of Mexico.[81]

This restructuring of Morales' AMOT personnel appears to have been performed under the oversight of James Angleton, head of CIA Counter Intelligence. A May 4 policy paper tasked Angleton's CI group with "creating, training, a highly motivated and competent" intelligence service which would support the Cuban Revolutionary Council and the Cuba Project. Angleton was to ensure that carefully selected and qualified Agency personnel were to work with this group. The same paper remarked that, "If Fidel Castro were to be eliminated from the scene, the regime might collapse for lack of a central rallying point."

In the fall of 1961, Angleton presented an assessment of Cuban intelligence including the effectiveness of Castro's own counter intelligence effort (which was highly rated). The assessment was circulated to the Special Group and it seems clear that the major source for Angleton's material would have been the new, AMOT based intelligence group still operating under Morales through 1961. That group would remain active, later going under the supervision of CIA officer Tony Sforza after his successful exfiltration from Cuba and David Morales' reassignment under William Harvey in 1962. Sforza (crypt Henry J. Sloman) had been one of the most successful deep cover covert agents in Cuba. He maintained a cover as a gambler. He was reported to be a close personal friend of David Morales and his Cuban efforts were highly respected. Sforza had acted as a "handler" inside Cuba, working with the sister of Fidel Castro, and assisting in her defection. Documents suggest that Sforza was also associated with a Castro assassination plot unknown to the Church Committee.

Following the Kennedy assassination, Sforza and the AMOTs were assigned to conduct a secret inquiry into the possible involvement of Cubans and Cuban exiles in the assassination; that inquiry has been confirmed by other JMWAVE staff, but no information from that inquiry can be found in available records. Shackley's apparent failure to debrief JMWAVE sources had been noted by the HSCA, before information on the secret inquiry became available. He was never questioned on that point but in general his testimony to the HSCA was vague in several areas; he also failed to remember certain events actually confirmed in related CIA documents.[82]

David Morales' work with counter intelligence had received praise in post-invasion internal CIA reviews (one of the very few areas of the project to do so) and he continued in his counter intelligence role until November, 1961 when the CIA portion of the Cuba Project began to assume new roles under a new designation of Task Force W, led by William Harvey (replacing Bissell as CIA Cuba project head). Contrary to popular perception, Bissell was not fired immediately after the Bay of Pigs and continued in his role through most of 1961. He was not formally replaced by Harvey until February, 1962 although Harvey was being approached internally within the agency in regard to Cuba in December, 1961.[83]

Morales was assigned to JMWAVE operations at the direct request of William Harvey; Morales had worked under Harvey in Berlin while Harvey was head of the CIA Berlin Station. Henry Hecksher (alias Nelson L. Raynock, Henry Boyson, and James D. Zaboth), another individual formerly attached to the Berlin Station (Berlin Operation Base), had worked with Morales both in Berlin and in Guatemala/PBSUCCESS and was also brought into Harvey's Task Force W. Both Henry Hecksher and David Morales would play a number of roles in ongoing anti-Castro activities, including activities in Mexico City. Their former PBSUCCESS fellow officer, David Phillips, had been reassigned to Mexico City, operating under State Department cover as part of the CIA's Mexico City station staff.[84]

Harvey's assignment and the creation of the reorganized Task Force W were part of a general rework of the Cuba Project (Phase 3). Following the Bay of Pigs, the President's unhappiness with the CIA's performance had led to the creation of a new, multi-agency effort to oust Castro. A Special Group was formed, with members from several agencies to oversee those efforts. When Robert Kennedy and General Maxwell Taylor (head of the Joint Chiefs) joined the group for meetings, they were referred to as the Special Group Augmented (SGA). During the remainder of 1961, further anti-Castro efforts could only be described as "disorganized and uncoordinated." In fact, they were characterized in that fashion in an early November 1962 memorandum to RFK, from the titular head of the effort, Richard Goodwin (assistant to the special counsel to the President, who was serving as temporary Chairman of the Cuba Task force in the months following the Bay of Pigs.).[85]

Goodwin's memorandum apparently served as the stimulus for a November 3, 1962 meeting convened by President Kennedy, authorizing a new covert program which would be headed by Air Force Brigadier General Edward Lansdale; Lansdale had developed a significant reputation as a counter insurgency specialist in SE Asia, especially respected for his psychological operations against a Communist insurgency in the Philippines. Lansdale's assignment to the secret war against Cuba (he would designate the new project as "Mongoose") is detailed in many other works and will not be repeated here. It needs only to be said his previous experience in counter insurgency did not translate well to actually overthrowing the Castro regime and that his various proposals (many of which have been described as "zany," at best) as well as his extreme micromanagement of operations, seem to have served primarily to frustrate and further antagonize the CIA operations personnel assigned to support him, especially those at the Miami Station.

During this same period, the Army would be instructed to maintain its contingency/OPLAN (operational planning) work in preparation for an actual invasion of Cuba. In April 1962 a 40,000 man Marine and Navy force engaged in exercises over an area ranging from North Carolina to the Caribbean – concluding with a full scale amphibious landing exercise on the island of Vieques off Puerto Rico. In conjunction with its assignment to the Cuba project, the military also developed a series of contingency tactics for "provoking" military action against Cuba (known as the "Northwoods" proposals). Within the Special Group and the Administration, talk of both military invasion and provocations would continue up until fall. At that point, massive Russian forces and ballistic missiles in Cuba would deliver a much more dramatic provocation than anything considered by the "Northwoods'" planners.

ZRRIFLE AND THE CUBA PROJECT / CASTRO ASSASSINATION ROUND 3, OR MAYBE 4?

William Harvey had come back from Berlin in 1960; taking over operation of Staff D. Staff D (along with Counter Intelligence, originally Staff C) was one of the most secret areas of the CIA. Its charter was supporting technical intelligence collection, which included efforts ranging from wire taps (both within the United States in support of domestic operations and at foreign stations including Berlin and Mexico City) to supporting the global collection efforts of the National Security Agency. Staff D frequently received support from the Audio section of CIA technical services.

Readers may be familiar with the story of a CIA technical services team, apparently working for CIA Staff D in Cuba in 1959. Those individuals had installed bugs at the Chinese offices in Havana and later returned to collect tapes; they also made an effort to actually steal Chinese code books. The head of the team, David Christ, was the founder and chief specialist in the Technical Services audio section and when the entire team was taken prisoner inside Cuba, the Agency was desperate that the Cubans might discover the true value of their catch. Efforts were made to recruit Cuban criminals to break them out of jail (to no effect) and later lengthy legal negotiations managed to free them along with other Americans being held.

James Angleton was directly kept informed of those Christ team efforts by Richard Helms. The legal extradition efforts publicly focused on an individual named John Martino (another American imprisoned in Cuba). Martino himself is of great interest to our overall inquiry and would later admit to his actual involvement in the Kennedy assassination. The negotiations for Martino's release served as a cover for including the Christ team with him. Recent document discoveries suggest that David Morales, while under State Department cover in Cuba, had been responsible for arrangements on at least one of the initial Christ team (Staff D/TSS) trips to Cuba.[86]

One of Staff D's most interesting assignments was to literally steal code books, crypto lists and related materials from foreign sources (including couriers). Staff D personnel at headquarters and at field stations supported collections from wire taps through "black bag" jobs. Some of staff D's professional safe crackers and burglars were true criminal professionals, well known to the FBI. This called for close coordination between the head of Staff D and the Bureau; some Staff D "professionals" even had to be reported to the FBI when they traveled.[87]

A number of months after returning to Staff D, Harvey had made a recruiting trip to Europe (October, 1960) with a primary interest in making contacts with and vetting potential criminal recruits in support of Staff D operations. In *Flawed Patriot*, Bayard Stockton provides a copy of Harvey's notes from the trip; Harvey mentions finding experienced criminal contacts for safecrackers and document forgers in Italy as well as leads to safecrackers in France. He also identified a potential referral candidate in Antwerp. The last contact would apparently lead to two individuals who did become of some use to Harvey. The first, designated WIROGUE was a young "hood" with certain skills but limited contacts. We have previously discussed his failed mission in the Congo. Although WIROGUE proved to be less than useful, the second individual, recruited by Harvey in Luxemburg, proved to be more seasoned and apparently did support certain Staff D sensitive projects in Europe. The individual, designated QJWIN was a seasoned criminal, with an apparently successful smuggling record and a great many contacts across Europe. At the time of the Lumumba assassination effort, both men appear to have been thrown into the Congo along with Sidney Gottlieb, possibly because they were the only foreign individuals Harvey had tagged at the time. Given the lack of coordination between the two men, handled by different CIA case officers, it seems unlikely that Harvey was actively involved with them on the Lumumba project.[88]

Things were quickly going to get much more interesting for William Harvey. As can be best determined, by the early fall of 1961 Richard Helms had already begun to talk to William Harvey about formalizing a project that would place political assassination with Harvey. *Harvey was to formalize the deniable political assassination of foreign leaders.* As we have seen, this was not an entirely new tactic or subject for the Agency, and certainly not for Bissell (who was clearly on his way out due to the Bay of Pigs and his ongoing failure to do anything more substantive against Castro). Later Harvey would testify that he had simply been given the responsibility for an "ongoing" task and to some extent that would certainly be true – especially as he would quickly begin to focus the program on Fidel Castro. *Although Harvey would single-handedly take on the intensely secretive assignment from Helms, it now appears that he received at least some level of support from the head of CIA counter intelligence, James Angleton.*

In *Flawed Patriot*, Bayard relates the details of two October, 1961 meetings during an NSA conference in Washington, D.C. William Harvey and James Angleton met with a British Counter Intelligence officer for dinner and then for a luncheon. During the meals, the two men began directing questions to the British officer as to his professional opinions on Castro, including options for killing the Cuban leader, including the necessity for deniability and deniable "delivery mechanisms." Harvey expressed considerable interest in poisons and improved materials and systems, which were becoming available. Recall that both Angleton and Harvey, as Counter Intelligence chiefs had been heavily involved with aspects of non-lethal drugs and toxins from the earliest days of the Agencies' involvement in "Bluebird" and "MKULTRA." Both were familiar with the work and resources of Technical Services and Sydney Gottlieb. Harvey told the British intelligence officer that the CIA was "developing a new capacity within the Company to handle these kinds of problems" and "were in the market for requisite expertise." Angleton sat quietly and simply made notes.

Further corroboration that Harvey had determined to involve Angleton in the executive action program can be found in Harvey's own notes of his original meeting with Helms. Those notes include several points:

> "Never mention word 'assassination'...no projects on paper...strictly person-to-person, singleton ops, planning should include provisions for blaming Sovs or Czechs in case of blow...should have phony 201 in RG [Central Registry] to backstop this, all documents therein forged and backdated...should look like a CE [counter-espionage/counter-intelligence] file... [executive action

would] require most professional, proven operationally competent, ruthless, stable, CE-experienced ops officers."

Finally, Harvey concludes his action item list with a final note:

"[talk to] Jim A [James Angleton]"

There seems little doubt that Angleton was aware of the assassinations project and was prepared to assist Harvey as he could. And his support would extend inside Cuba itself. Angleton himself admitted that he had quite independently activated an agent in Havana, "to watch Harvey's back." Angleton would even tell the Church Committee that because he and Harvey were such good friends he felt it best to get him a source in Cuba, unknown to anyone else in the Agency. "No one knew of his existence except Harvey, myself, and, of course, Dick Helms."[89]

The origins of a more formalized CIA assassination project are murky at best. There may be a reference to it as early as May 1961, but the first document attributed to Harvey is dated January 1962. The project's ZRFIFLE crypt itself was not officially assigned until February 1962 and in what references we do have, it seems as if Harvey initially applied ZRFIFLE to himself personally. Certainly by the time of Harvey's replacement of Bissell as the new man in charge of the new Task Force W, the project most definitely had become focused on the elimination of Fidel Castro.

By the time he began to document the parameters for the project in an official document, he had developed a cover for it; ZRRIFLE would then appear as another Staff D effort to recruit foreign agents to procure code and cipher materials abroad. It was a masterful cover and even at this late date a great many writers confuse the real ZRRIFLE (William Harvey and a program focused on the assassination of Fidel Castro using criminal assets) with WIROGUE and QJWIN. Harvey's biographer Bayard discovered documents retained by Harvey, which included an endorsement authorization for ZRRIFLE from Richard Helms. That February 1962 memo noted that the project was so sensitive that it will be handed on an "eyes only" basis outside all regular Agency authorizations – but is phrased in such a way that it is simply an employment authorization for QJWIN.[90]

As we will observe in events of 1963, such a well-designed Staff D cover may have served William Harvey quite well. Indeed few, including Robert Kennedy, would realize that Harvey's virtual first step in ZRRIFLE was to reactivate the earlier Bissell-era Castro assassination effort, using John Roselli and Cuban exile leader Tony Varona. Varona had been brought into play by Roselli when the first Cuban connections had failed to deliver. Several authors write about Varona as simply a gambling network conduit into Cuba. In doing so, they fail to realize the true impact of Roselli and Harvey's reliance on him.

Varona was definitely not simply some low-level former Cuban casino connection in Havana. Dr. Manual Antonio "Tony" De Varona Y Loredo was a major figure in Cuban politics and following the Castro revolution. Varona had become the virtual spokesman for the former Cuban President in exile, Carlos Prio Soccares. Varona served as head of the Cuban Revolutionary Council, the exile group that would have become the new provisional government if the Brigade invasion had succeeded. Varona did have extensive contacts inside Cuba and in Florida and maintained good relations with Manuel Artime, one of the Brigade military leaders and the man who would become Robert Kennedy's selection for one of the most important exile initiatives that would develop in 1963. Varona knew everyone in Cuban politics and in the exile military factions. In 1962 and 1963 he would be privy to the ongoing Castro assassination project and select individuals to work on it. He would receive supplies and equipment from JMWAVE although it is unclear that he personally had operational groups either inside or outside Cuba. Perhaps equally interesting is that HSCA investigative documents also record that Varona was at one time of "operational interest" to James Angleton.

In summary, by early fall, 1961, Helms had assigned William Harvey the task of formalizing a deniable assassinations program, and as Harvey moved into the Cuba project (Phase 2) the target for the project would be designated as Fidel Castro. Harvey used Staff D and the ZRRIFLE crypt as the cover for that project. As 1961 moved into 1962, Harvey was being groomed to replace Bissell as the overall manager of the CIA's portion of the Cuba project – which Harvey would designate as Task Force W.

One of Harvey's first requests, upon moving into the restructured Castro project, seems to have been a request for David Morales (November, 1961). This led to the reassignment and promotion of Morales from his counter intelligence role into assuming management of all operations at the Miami Field Station (JMWAVE). In that position, he was effectively second in command, reporting to Theodore Shackley, when Shackley came into Miami in 1962. But reports from JMWAVE staff suggest that Morales operated with a great deal of autonomy.

In fact, Shackley himself confirmed Morales' autonomy and the effective compartmentalization of his relationship with Harvey. Shackley testified that when Harvey would come to Miami, he would meet only briefly with him. The purpose for Harvey's Miami visits seems to have been meetings with Morales, Roselli, and possibly others of Morales' special operations officers. Shackley stated that he made no inquiry with Harvey about the purposes of his visits or his other meetings – it appears that Shackley viewed himself primarily as running the station, focusing on its huge administrative demands. Given what we have previously reviewed about assassination projects, it simply isn't in the cards that we would turn up actual documents recording the interactions and activities of Harvey, Roselli, Varona and Morales in 1962 and 1963.

A review of JMWAVE documents does show that for normal operations and activities including authorized Cuba maritime missions, Shackley and Morales often signed off and approved various elements of the actions – actions that were authorized by Task Force W (Harvey) or under the Mongoose program umbrella sign offs. However, in one area, the ZRIFLE Castro assassination activities (totally compartmentalized from JMWAVE and apparently even Shackley), it appears that Harvey must have coordinated strictly with Morales.

In regard to his higher-level Task Force W role, people who knew Harvey and worked for him describe his activities as very professional and methodical. Harvey was obsessive about intelligence collection and network building, paramilitary affairs were not his forte and he appears to have left that to subordinates like Morales and the JMWAVE paramilitary and maritime operations officers. In fact Harvey's conservatism, obsession with security and professionalism appears to have been at the heart of many of his problems with Robert Kennedy.

In regard to Castro assassination activities, it must be remembered that the Roselli project had actually started some two years earlier, initiated by Bissell, Maheu, and with Roselli's recruitment. Harvey was simply taking over an existing effort in regard to Castro; he was personally briefed by Bissell in November 1961 and given a heads up that he would likely inherit Cuban operations. And it appears that one of the first things that Harvey did, once he had control, was to use Sheffield Edwards of CIA Security to get in touch with Roselli and arrange a private meeting. In a transitional meeting, on April 21, 1962, Harvey made it perfectly clear that he and Roselli would be the new team – no Trafficante, no Giancana, no Maheu, just the two of them. Roselli would maintain his Cuban contacts. Amazingly the two men went on to become fast friends, with Harvey displaying an immense long-term loyalty towards Roselli. Harvey would buck both the FBI and his own agency over his relationship with Roselli and in the end Roselli would be found murdered; only a couple of months after Harvey himself had passed away.

Beyond that, as Bayard writes, there are a number of reports that the friendship was really a three way affair, with both Harvey and Roselli becoming very close to a CIA officer named "Dave M" (it requires no major effort to translate this to David Morales). "Dave M." would provide covert support for the assassination project, entirely compartmentalizing it from routine JMWAVE operations – and from Miami Station boss Shackley.

Given the lack of documents, the Castro assassination activities of 1962 and 1963 become virtually impossible to track in any real detail. Harvey and Roselli both gave extensive testimony on the subject but in Harvey's case it was focused on how he came into the effort, who had approved it and who knew about it. He provided virtually no operational details on how it was actually conducted during his time with it. Roselli spoke at much more length – but primarily about the first phase, the poison pills, the efforts to get them into Cuba and various problems with making the plans work. Reportedly he enthralled his listeners during his first HSCA appearances. But later they realized they had failed to follow up on his remarks suggesting that the assassination attempts had evolved during 1962, from poison to rifle teams. They had begun to consider the possible association of Castro assassination activities with the Kennedy assassination. Roselli was called back to testify again – but before he could appear, someone killed him in a highly brutal and demonstrative fashion.

We are left with anecdotal stories about the final phase of the efforts, with information from Roselli and a number of reports that cannot be fully verified. Some authors even have Roselli spending months in military camps and leading boat missions into Cuba (at the age of 60 and with no military experience). Fortunately, with the relatively new availability of extensive FBI Roselli surveillance documents from the period in question, we can now be a bit more specific. The reason for the heavy FBI surveillance is in itself a story — one covered in *Someone Would Have Talked*.[91]

In April 1962, Roselli was called to Washington, informed that there was new energy in the Castro assassination effort and that he would be meeting with the new man in charge.

Nothing had really happened on the project during the latter half of 1961 and Roselli had been very much involved in his own business and personal affairs – dividing his time between Los Angeles and Las Vegas. Harvey met with Roselli and made it clear the game would be played differently, just he and Roselli. Roselli is to handle the Cuban connections and personnel and Harvey will ensure he has what support he needs. The next step was an April 21 meeting in Miami, where Roselli brought Varona back into play as the key Cuban contact.

During the period of April through early July, Roselli fell off the FBI's radar screen: he went missing from his normal haunts; he was absent from his apartment in LA. It appears that he was indeed in Florida, working with the Cubans and with his CIA operations support people. There are rumors of a special camp for those activities; Bradley Ayers (an Army paramilitary trainer for the Agency at JMWAVE) reports visiting the camp; it was managed by one of David Morales' senior action officers, a Guatemala and Bay of Pigs veteran, Rip Robertson (alias Irving Cadick). According to Ayers, the Cubans in the camp were devoting themselves to weapons training and were quite proficient shooters. However, the camp and its personnel were kept very much at arms length from regular JMWAVE activities.

Roselli returned to LA and his regular business affairs for most of July but he went "missing" again in August, most likely going back to Florida and very possibly working directly with the assassination team. That trip marks his last extended time away from Los Angeles and Vegas. He was off surveillance in September but only for three days. According to Roselli, the Cubans made at least two major efforts against Castro in 1962, with poison and with rifles – both failed.

In mid October, Roselli left Los Angeles and was either in Washington DC and/or in Miami for a full week, (Oct. 19-26). This was at a time when the missile crisis had not become fully public and at a point where the Kennedy administration reaction to the missiles had not yet jelled. October 18 was one of the most crucial dates in the crisis, when the extent of the Russian deployment had been confirmed by U2 photography and it had become clear that a quick decision must be made – either for invasion or blockade. Given that JMWAVE has been heavily involved in intelligence collection on the missiles for some weeks, the question rises as to why Harvey would be calling in Roselli at that time. On the other hand, we know that at this approximate time Harvey did dispatch three undefined boat missions into Cuba, ones that later appear to have helped cost him his job and ones he never attempted to explain in any detail, even in his defense. Perhaps they were intelligence collection missions; perhaps one or more were high-risk assassination missions using Roselli's people?

When Robert Kennedy became aware of the boats going into Cuba (how he would get that tactical detail when he was totally focused on the high level missile crisis is unknown), he was irate, ordering the boats back; he was told that was impossible yet we know that the average JMWAVE mission involved positive control via coded radio messages. That at least suggests the missions may have been something special, compartmentalized from normal WAVE maritime operations (again, suggesting possible assassination missions).

Given the impact of the boat missions on Harvey's career (and his emotional confrontations with Robert Kennedy over the issue); his biographer explores the October boat missions in some detail. He cites October meeting notes in which General Lansdale denied any knowledge of the dispatch of any covert teams into Cuba. General Taylor denied that the military had requested any missions or even specified requirements for them. Harvey was backed up by McCone, admitting that the three teams had not been requested by the military but maintaining that they had been dispatched as part of previously approved operations. Yet there is no sign that they were able to prove that contention or that they offered any specifics on what missions those involved. Harvey only noted that the missions did not use existing assets.

In the end it was clear that Robert Kennedy felt it was an "end run" at the most sensitive time in the crisis and that Harvey was out of control. That leaves us with even more reason to speculate as to whether the missions might have been something that Harvey simply could not defend in detail without exposing the Cuban application of ZRRIFLE. If so, it would reinforce the Harvey and Roselli teams were very much compartmentalized from everyone, perhaps even Director McCone. Certainly it also leaves a number of questions as to why Roselli would be operationally involved at such a sensitive time.[92]

In regard to further ZRRIFLE Cuban missions, it seems that following the missile crisis, after some 12 months of effort, Harvey reportedly shut down the project late in 1962 (although records confirm that Helms funded ZRRIFLE through 1963). By the beginning of 1963, Harvey was effectively gone from the Cuba project. Task Force W was shortly to be given a more bureaucratic designation and the final phase of the Cuba project was coming into being; Task Force W and Harvey would be replaced by Special Actions (SAS) and Desmond Fitzgerald. After an interim period, Harvey was assigned as Chief of Station for Italy but he did not actually relocate until late June, 1963. During that spring he met with Roselli in Florida in April (supposedly a termination meeting) and again in Washington just prior his move to Rome. Prior to the move, Harvey remained at CIA headquarters in D.C.

9 TAKING STOCK

A fundamental question underlying this study is how could an action against the President of the United States originate within the CIA, within a "nexus" of officers directly involved in clandestine intelligence and covert special operations. Up to this point we have examined the background of the Agency itself, its birth and activities within the context of an actual state of undeclared warfare. We have seen "national security" develop as a primary concern for its officers and a culture of "whatever it takes" emerge in support of its declared mission to stop (or better yet "roll back") the expansion of Communist control. Under no circumstances was any country going to be allowed to fall under Communist influence without aggressive confrontation. Even somewhat unwitting (possibly well intentioned but obviously terribly naïve) individuals such as Arbenz and Lumumba had to be removed simply because they offered the Communist's an opportunity for expansion.

We have also followed the emergence and evolution of political assassination as an accepted tool within the Operations arm of the Agency. It began simply enough, suggested in Guatemala by the Agencies' surrogates, the anti-Communist rebels. The surrogates came up with the idea themselves and the CIA project officers simply responded, using Agency intelligence capabilities to refine "black lists" for targeting, to training in the actual skills (professionally supported by the creation of an "assassinations manual") and logistics support to move the right people to the right places. That pattern would continue, from Guatemala to Cuba to Vietnam. As we will see, often the same operations personnel would be involved.

The Agency eventually reached the point at which it would accept what amounted to "political cleansing" by its surrogates; in Guatemala and Cuba the "black lists" contained dozens or hundreds of individuals that would need to be "removed" to protect new regimes. But over the next two decades, Agency supported regimes would field actual "death squads" to protect themselves, with murders and disappearances escalating into the tens of thousands throughout Latin America alone.

But Agency personnel were never involved (or approved to be, at most they would be trainers or perhaps "advisors") in the acts themselves – that would have compromised the other aspect of CIA culture which had involved, complete and total deniability. After Guatemala there were no more documented "black lists," or at least none that went into the files. There were no more meeting minutes which discussed options such as assassination – or if there were, as occurred in one meeting involving Defense Secretary McNamara, William Harvey would move aggressively to stop any such talk.

But political assassination had evolved beyond the tactical level as well. It began to be seen as the "Magic Button," the act of last resort even for political leaders. And in that case, deniability became even more obsessive. In fact, as deniability became more institutionalized and more obsessive, the chain of command for such actions became far more nebulous - and far more dangerous. The instances of approved political assassinations recorded by the Church Committee reveal no paperwork nor do they suggest that there was a definite process and a final point of operational approval. For example, it now seems clear that Barnes and Bissell were willing to authorize high risk actions including murder, which were in line with Allen Dulles's own views but in which he (and certainly not the President) was ensured full official deniability.

To some extent it seems to have become a matter of senior operations officers literally interpreting their superiors concerns and peripheral remarks – raising the question of exactly which words or remarks would become "triggers" for something apart from official projects. A second point is the switch to "deniable" wording had added a totally new element to the situation – "interpretation." Words used loosely (perhaps intentionally) could take on a whole new meaning when translated at different levels within the Agency. On August 26, 1960 Allen Dulles had cabled the CIA station chief in the Congo that, "In high quarters here, it is the clear-cut conclusion that if [Lumumba] continues to hold high office, the inevitable result will at best be chaos and at worst pave the way to Communist takeover…His removal must be an urgent and prime objective." The station chief later testified that he was amazed when Gottlieb showed up with poison as he had interpreted Dulles cable in terms of political action, not murder.

Following the murder of the Diem brothers in Vietnam, President Kennedy would be stunned by how words became translated to action as they passed down levels within the Agency. Matters could clearly move far beyond expectations, totally out of control, especially when aggressive "meeting" language made it down the level of field officers, working in volatile situations and with emotionally charged surrogates and third parties (rebels, coup leaders, exiles).

The Church Committee appears to have been a bit cautions with its conclusion

> "…the system of executive command and control was so ambiguous that it is difficult to be certain at what levels assassination activity was known and authorized. This situation creates the disturbing prospect that Government officials might have undertaken assassination plots without having it uncontrovertibly clear that there was an explicit authorization from Presidents."

It would have been more accurate to say that it was often unclear not only as to who had given an explicit authorization, but whether one had been given at all.[93]

If that view sounds overly dramatic, even the Committee documented that fact that in one case Tracy Barnes, on his own, approved an assassination attempt on Fidel Castro, Raul Castro and Che Guevera. He was ordered to cancel the attack, so he proceeded to do so, but it turned out to be moot only because the foreign agent involved did not receive Barnes approval in time to carry out the bombing. The Church Committee apparently was not told of other attack plans against Castro, which involved systematic tactical planning but which were totally un-documented and where authorization is still totally unknown.

One final lesson has to be drawn from the preceding study of Agency activities and that is the CIA never acknowledged responsibility for a single political assassination of any sort. In a number of cases, it was forced to admit that third parties, with whom it was associated, might have been trying to murder someone, but since they had not succeeded, the Agency could not really be held at fault. And even in those cases where Agency employees were directly associated with individuals who did conduct an assassination – Lumumba, Trujillo, the Diem brothers – it could be classified as a simple misunderstanding. Nobody in the Agency had actually given the order for the murder; there was no hard and fast evidentiary line between the killer and the Agency. CIA employees were never found administering the poison, pulling the trigger, planting the bomb. And if at all possible, as described in William Harvey's ZRRIFLE notes, the murder would be to a third party, if at all possible, the Soviets.

We can regard this all as a lesson learned in being able to detect the hand of CIA involvement in political murders. No fingerprints would be left, no employees would be present, surrogates would be involved and any obvious leads or evidence would point to the enemy, the Russians or their fellow travelers. But now we need to return our focus. This study is following the premise that President Kennedy's murder was deeply embedded in the secret war against Cuba and the Castro regime. To go further, we need to return to that secret war, circa 1962-1963.

10 MONGOOSE BITES EVERYBODY EXCEPT FIDEL

It's critical to note that Harvey's Task Force W assignment was only the CIA's limited portion of the multi-agency effort designated as "Mongoose," named by its newly appointed leader, Air Force General Edward Lansdale. President Kennedy had become doubtful of the CIA's ability to engage in large-scale covert operations, partially because of their failure at the Bay of Pigs but also because of their similar failure in aggressive covert operations against North Vietnam. Kennedy himself had become highly interested in and supportive of special warfare and covert action, but he was skeptical that the CIA had the experience or personnel to be effective in it. His choice of Maxwell Taylor as his chief military advisor reflected those feelings; Taylor had been experienced in "behind the lines" operations in France during WWII and had organized counter-guerilla operations in Korea.

For an excellent survey of the transition in covert operations initiated by President Kennedy as well as a comparative benchmark for Cuba covert operations, readers are referred to *The Secret War against Hanoi* by Richard Shultz, Jr. The discussion which follows is based on his analysis and information.[94] It must be noted that while large scale covert operations against North Vietnam were ultimately transferred from the CIA to the military in 1963, over the long term (for a variety of reasons, largely matters of experience and political control), the Army's efforts in North Vietnam were no more effective than had been the CIA's. The Agency retained the responsibility for covert operations inside Vietnam and in Laos.

After taking office, Kennedy had requested an in depth review of the Vietnam situation and in January of 1961 he had invited General Lansdale, with years of experience in Vietnam and just back from a two week fact finding tour, to attend a National Security Council meeting. The meeting was being held as a review of a "Basic Counterinsurgency Plan for Vietnam" submitted by the U.S. embassy in Saigon. Kennedy was impressed with Lansdale's comments on the plan (which Lansdale supported) and felt Lansdale to be "in synch" with his own views. The plan itself was approved and the CIA was tasked with a major new, covert action effort against North Vietnam. During the following year, that effort would prove to be a total failure — as had the CIA's similar efforts against other "denied" areas in Eastern Europe, including East Germany, Albania and Poland (denied areas having massive police and intelligence forces, intense internal security and population control institutions). The Agency had lost hundreds of native agents sent into Eastern Europe; it would lose hundreds more trying to operate in North Vietnam.

Following the CIA's lack of progress against the Hanoi regime, Lansdale had been called back in to assess and make recommendations for a more aggressive covert campaign against North Vietnam. A Special Group (Counterinsurgency) oversight committee had already been created in January 1962; its charter was to focus on expanding interdepartmental participation in combating subversive insurgency and indirect aggression in targeted countries. Another group, the 303 Committee, was specifically assigned the responsibility for ensuring direct White House control of covert operations, including paramilitary actions. It held responsibility for both Vietnam and Cuba.

In June of 1962, following the Bay of Pigs failure, JFK had already begun the groundwork for a transition of covert military activities with a series of National Security Action Memoranda (NSAM 55, 56 and 57) which opened up denied area action to the military and attempted to limit the CIA to relatively small scale paramilitary operations. In July, 1962, Defense Secretary McNamara held a meeting in Hawaii to lay out a plan for turning over the CIA's paramilitary programs to the military; the transition process was designated "Operation Switchback."

General Lansdale impressed President Kennedy during the overall process of evaluating covert operations in Vietnam and the change in approach to a military/inter-agency to large-scale paramilitary operations making him the ideal choice to lead a reinvigorated effort against the Castro regime. In that new effort, the CIA was very much relegated to a support role. Even in its limited paramilitary operations, its officers would find their activities under intense scrutiny and their tactical control severely limited. Overall strategy, mission selection and final approval would come out of Washington.

Lansdale himself was highly enthusiastic, aggressive, a consummate "salesman" for his operations. He initially created a favorable impression with both the President and Attorney General. By February 2, 1962, Lansdale had submitted a firm timetable and a thirty-nine page action plan, in six sections. Phase 1 started on March 1 and Phase VI, scheduled for October, dealt with the establishment of a new government in Cuba.

Unfortunately both Lansdale's "out of the box" psychological warfare plans and his generation of minutely detailed "task lists" and "action schedules" would lead to his being viewed with disdain by participants from virtually all the agencies involved.

The State Department's representative wrote that "the entire operation was pathetic and I ruefully longed for a way to turn it off." When asked for his view of Mongoose, Arthur Schlesinger, who served as a Kennedy White House special assistant, responded that once Mongoose was in progress (it only lasted some 9 months) "the CIA didn't like it anymore than we did." Still, while Lansdale may have borne the distain and dissatisfaction ultimately generated by Mongoose, the people bearing the real heat at the time were the CIA officers involved in Cuban operations.[95]

Initially, in Phase 3 of the Cuba project, the Special Group's focus was on improving intelligence. On March 2, they had agreed that "the immediate objective of the U.S. during March, April and May will be the acquisition of intelligence" and that mission was aggressively undertaken by JMWAVE. In early 1962, the Station had opened the Caribbean Admissions Center, a refugee interrogation facility near Miami. The center operated seven days a week and contained both a filter center and actual interrogation team for exiles who appeared to have significant information. The Cuban Intelligence Service (evolved from and using AMOT personnel) was heavily involved with those collections, as well as other sources across the exile community in Florida.

Beyond that, JMWAVE was broadening its reach outside the U.S., both with assets on the island and across Latin America. The centerpiece of the Agencies' Latin American collection activities was the Mexico City station. While most studies of the "secret war" focus on JMWAVE in Miami, it is critical to realize how important the Mexico City station was throughout the period. Beginning in 1960, at the start of JMARC/JMATE, all the stations' investigative assets were directed against the Cuban community in Mexico as well as the Cuban embassy and its staff. A JMWAVE presence was established (separate from the regular Mexico City CIA station) and JMWAVE staff would routinely travel from Florida to support covert actions in Mexico. David Phillips, alumnus of Guatemala and the failed Bay of Pigs effort, was reassigned to the Mexico City station, going under State Department cover at the U.S. embassy there, eventually taking charge of anti-Cuban covert activities efforts across Latin America.

As early as 1960, virtually all of the Mexico City stations' investigative assets were directed against Cuban targets. Covert action (CE) staff were used and it was at that time that a totally deniable staff was formed outside the normal station to provide additional CE staff and support functions. According to the official CIA Mexico Station history, AMOT personnel conducted special training for the Mexico City covert staff.

Covert activities included intensive technical services, electronic and photographic surveillance of the Cuban, and other, embassies. Specially equipped cameras monitored all individuals traveling to and from Cuba as well as any related travelers coming into Mexico from the United States. That work was supported by an effort to recruit not only Cuban embassy staff but members from the local Cuban exile community who had routine embassy contact. Photographic surveillance was extensive and sophisticated; the camera monitoring the door to the Cuban embassy was equipped with a circuit that also allowed audio monitoring of visitors. The camera and audio circuit was activated as people neared the door between the technical and human intelligence, so virtually all visitors to the embassy were identified and select visitors were then targeted for surveillance and possible recruitment. Embassy surveillance photos were taken to agents inside the Cuban embassy who identified the individuals and some of the visitors were exploited. The station ran 11 access agents into the Cuban embassy from the local pro-Castro Cuban colony. Related Mexico City collections programs included:[96]

- LIKAYAK – access to international passenger lists, air shipments, spot photographer of travelers, mobile photo truck, camera installations at the airport and apparently some government files and mail.

- LIFIRE – travel monitoring operation with focus on all travel to and from Cuba; the Cubans were also found to be shipping arms to Latin America through MC and also sending cash for arms deals in MC.

- LIFEAT and LIENVOV – telephone taps

- LIEMBRACE – physical surveillance with multiple teams

By 1964, the CIA station had some 50 agents working specifically on Cuba, including mobile surveillance teams with photographic capability.

SOMETHING'S HAPPENING HERE:
Starting in the spring of 1962, while not directly involved with Mongoose, things began to occur in Cuba that, while unclear at the time, would eventually bode ill for all parties involved. The activities involved Russians in Cuba and would lead to major grief for certain CIA officers involved in Mongoose. Certain acts carried out against the Russians also suggest that "pushback" against Kennedy administration policies had begun to occur from certain CIA officers assigned to the "secret war." We will examine all three aspects of these events.

By the summer of 1962, the aggressive JMWAVE intelligence effort had begun to produce information about an escalating Soviet presence in Cuba. That information was not making anyone in Washington D.C. happy and the well-known tendency to either reject (or "shoot") the messenger" seems to have come into play.

First, as spring turned to summer in 1962, it became quite clear that Soviet personnel were becoming militarily involved in Cuba. For one thing, the huge influx of young Soviet citizens, all dressed in similar civilian attire, was quite noticeable; it really was not possible to pass off thousands of young men as tourists and agricultural advisors. Beyond that, the dramatic escalation in Soviet merchant traffic going into Cuba was detected by the National Security Administration's (NSA) communications monitoring posts, which had the capability to effectively track positions and movements of virtually all of the 85 Soviet bloc merchant ships that began to move towards Cuba. The NSA also monitored them acoustically as they passed through "choke points", later they would use the ocean bed emplaced Sound Surveillance System (SOSUS) to track the submarines that were eventually dispatched to accompany missile and atomic warhead shipments to Cuba.

The NSA technical intelligence was effectively supplemented by field reports from CIA agents inside Cuba as well as Agency contacts with diplomats, reporters, and business travelers from across Latin America. In addition, the new refugee processing facility outside Miami (in Opa Loca) was very aggressive in collecting information from the hundreds of refugees that Castro's immigration policy was still permitting to flee Cuba.

It was literally impossible for the Cubans (regardless of sealing off docks, emplacing barricades and setting up security control zones) to conceal the dozens of Soviet ships that began unloading cargo. By June, it was equally impossible to totally conceal the shape of some of their larger items of cargo – which ranged from patrol boats and bomber parts, to larger and larger rocket shaped assemblies. Reports of convoys carrying missiles began to come in from all over the island. First to arrive were the surface to air batteries.

By August, the CIA was officially advising the President not only of the deployment of an island wide surface-to-air missile defense but raising issues about "the speed and magnitude of this influx of Soviet personnel and equipment into a non-bloc country in Soviet military aid activities." It would be decades before the planned disposition of Soviet military forces in Cuba was fully known. It consisted of four motorized Soviet infantry regiments equipped with tactical nuclear weapons, 40 MIG 21 jet fighters, 56 medium range bombers, 24 medium range ballistic missile launchers and 16 intermediate range missile launchers. Forces also included a comprehensive radar/surface to air missile network covering the entire island, four guided missile patrol boats and several short range tactical nuclear missile launchers for coastal defense. At least 162 nuclear warheads were also deployed to Cuba.[97]

By the end of August, the President was facing public Congressional pressure over the issue of a Soviet military presence in Cuba and the Kennedy administration was in a real bind, alternatively sensitive about being called weak on Cuba and exposing the Mongoose effort and sabotage missions into Cuba. Mongoose staff had every right to be proud of their intelligence collection efforts and their contribution to revealing the Soviet's build up on the island. However, their second role in Mongoose was another story. Former JMWAVE personnel cite the fact that Lansdale "drove Harvey up the wall;" he would demand detailed operational schedules months in advance, leaving no room to adjust for variables such as personnel, weather, condition of the beaches, etc. General Taylor wanted to see the sort of staff detail produced for major military operations – detailed plans of 30 to 40 pages were required for a single mission. And given what was going on in Cuba with the Soviet military build up, conditions could change in a matter of days.

Still, it appears that one of the most fundamental areas of conflict within Mongoose was directly between William Harvey, as head of Task Force W, and Robert Kennedy, acting leader of the Special Group Augmented. The matter was both a clash of personalities and a clash of cultures. Harvey was an Intelligence professional, operating by the book and with an overriding commitment to adequate intelligence before launching missions – and a fanatic dedication to security on operational matters. RFK, according to virtually all the Mongoose participants, was far more spontaneous, emotional and hands on; beyond that, he simply had no training in or feel for standard security constraints. Harvey's biographer provides numerous interviews that cite RFK's tendency to take things into his own hands, to work directly with Cuban exiles and to personally micromanage activities where he truly had no experience.

But far worse that than that, the conflict between the two men grew to the point where Harvey considered that RFK's "amateur" actions were endangering operations and lives. Stockton quotes sources relating that *Harvey came not only to hate RFK but also to suggest that certain of his actions bordered on being traitorous.* He became adamant that the Kennedy's should not be personally involved in covert operations such as Mongoose.[98]

Although no single incident seems to have finished Harvey's assignment to the Cuba project, Mongoose itself morphed once again after the Cuban missile crisis (with Task Force W being reorganized and re-staffed). One confrontation does seem to have played a major role in Harvey's essential "firing" by Robert Kennedy. As previously discussed, during the missile crisis, Harvey had dispatched boat teams to Cuba. When challenged, Harvey would take the position that it was done to provide intelligence in support of the anticipated U.S. military invasion of Cuba. When he learned of the mission, RFK ordered the boats recalled. Reportedly he considered it an attempt to operate behind his back and a flaunting of both political control and the authority of the Special Group. Within two to three months, Helms had reassigned Harvey, sending him to Europe as Chief of Station in Rome.[99]

For reference, readers should note RFK's emotional reaction to this 1962 boat mission and to the violation of Special Group approvals. We will return to the subject in a future discussion of what appears to have truly been a much more serious "end run" in June of 1963. A mission conducted by Shackley and Morales, one with explosive political implications and one with no indication of approval by the Special Group, RFK or the President (who by that time was personally signing off on all major Cuban missions).

But another and equally serious "end run" seems to have begun towards the end of the Mongoose era, something apparently triggered by the early lack of Administration response to the Soviet build up; something involving one or more CIA operations offices and acts which were intended specifically to provoke a confrontation with the Russians. These actions failed in that objective but were a key element in what became a fundamental break between Cuban exiles and the Kennedy administration.

PUTTING KENNEDY'S BACK TO THE WALL!

At the end of 1961, Antonio Veciana was forced to flee Cuba, following fears that Cuban intelligence had learned of his involvement in a planned October heavy weapons attack on Castro. That attack would have used automatic rifles, grenade launchers and a bazooka. He had been encouraged to organize such an attack by a man who had approached and trained him in Havana, before the Bay of Pigs invasion. That man spoke excellent Spanish and had connections at the U.S. Embassy in Havana. Most importantly, the man knew of Veciana's anti-Castro feelings, which Veciana had only expressed to two people, one being the Minister of the Treasury and also the CIA's channel into the Castro government. Veciana assumed that the man was working for a U.S. government agency (although the man refused to verify that). He trained Veciana over a period of a few months, focusing on propaganda and psychological warfare; he also constantly pressed Veciana for information on what anti-Castro elements were doing. The man had left Cuba well before the Bay of Pigs invasion but returned briefly afterwards to meet with Veciana in Havana. *Veciana described him as extremely frustrated – saying that the Bay of Pigs disaster was the fault of President Kennedy who had withheld air support for the Brigade.* With no other options left, he told Veciana that the only thing that could be done was to kill Castro. The man did not stay long in Cuba but he and Veciana determined the best opportunity would be to stage a major attack on Castro during a planned public ceremony in October.

An extremely strong case can be made that the "man in question" was David Phillips, first operating under cover in Havana and then assigned to Phase 1 of the Cuba project. Readers are referred to the work of Anthony Summers (*Conspiracy*) and Gaeton Fonzi, HSCA staff investigator (*The Last Investigation*) for the identification of the man (using the alias Maurice Bishop) as David Phillips. Additional information corroborating the identification is provided in Chapter 10 of *Someone Would Have Talked.*[100]

Not long after Veciana's arrival in America, he was contacted again by the man he had known in Havana. The man had a proposition for him; he would help him with funding for the formation of an aggressive new exile organization – one that would be named Alpha 66. Veciana would be the chief executive officer, spokesman and fund raiser. He would recruit a proven and capable combat leader. Veciana did just that, selecting Major Eloy Menoyo (at first this worried the American, who was concerned that Menoyo had socialist tendencies but Veciana convinced the man he could be trusted). Veciana did go on to raise a considerable war chest (over $100,000), much of it apparently from old line New York Cubans who formerly had major businesses in Cuba. In that regard it is interesting to note that David Phillips had extremely strong connections with American companies doing business in pre-Castro Cuba, companies in New York and in Texas. Phillips had leveraged those connections to fund one of the very first late 1960 Cuban infiltration vessels used by the CIA, with complete deniability. Crewman on that vessel, the Tejana (Tony Cuesta and Eddie Bayo) would go on to join Alpha 66, running daring and successful attacks into Cuba. Like their vessel's Captain, Alberto Fernandez, following the disaster at the Bay of Pigs, neither man wanted anything directly to do with the CIA – but Veciana had made sure that nobody, including his military commander, Menoyo, knew anything about their shadowy American organizer.[101]

But perhaps the most important thing about the origins of Alpha 66 was that the man behind Veciana was very specific in directing the overall strategy for the group; *it was to conduct attacks that would create "headaches for President Kennedy."* Raids conducted during the Cuban missile crisis were deliberately planned by the American (Bishop); the timing of the raids was synchronized with events in the crisis. The purpose of the Alpha 66 missions *"was to publicly embarrass Kennedy and force him to move against Castro." Raids specifically targeted Russian ships and installations with the intention of provoking confrontation.* This continued on into 1963, following the negotiated missile agreement.

In one instance Alpha 66 attacked a Soviet ship and engaged in a firefight with Soviet troops – again the strategy was to force Kennedy to act against Castro, to "put his back to the wall." Following the ship attack and firefight, Veciana was instructed to hold a high profile press coverage and was impressed by how much attention he drew. In fact, his American backer had even arranged for two high-ranking government officials to attend, in order to suggest American backing for Alpha 66 and its activities. The story made headlines across the nation, provoking a highly irritated response from the President and leading him to issue orders to stop all exile missions from U.S. soil.[102]

Earlier in the fall of 1962, JMWAVE had been tasked with improving its control over exile groups, mounting an increased intelligence effort against them and ensuring that only "approved" missions with CIA trained and supported personnel were going into Cuba. That had started when one of the Agencies' own sponsored groups, the Revolutionary Student Directorate (DRE), provoked by the increasing Soviet presence in Cuba, had sent a two boat mission directly into Havana harbor. They had opened fire on a section of the city for several minutes before successfully fleeing back out to sea. Cuba had protested at the U.N. and in the end, President Kennedy issued a statement deploring such raids as counter productive and warning against future raids. Still, the U.S. would continue to sponsor all elements of the DRE including its military section (with David Morales as its liaison), paying a monthly subsidy of some $51,000.[103]

JMWAVE faced the problem that many of its exile military trainees would participate in both sanctioned and unsanctioned missions. By 1963 a number of them were beginning to participate in what were not only un-sponsored but illegal anti-Castro missions, funded by virtually anyone with money. Of course this made for some extremely complex relationships, especially with the more aggressive groups such as the Student Directorate (DRE) and with JURE (Manolo Ray). The Agency had several levels of official contact with the DRE (AMSPELL), run by Ross Crozier (alias Harold R. Noemayr) and later George Joannides (alias Walter Newby and Howard), but they also had a series of trained personnel within the organization (AMHINTs.)

An example of this can be seen in the activities of John Koch Gene (AMHINT-26). John Koch Gene had come out of Cuba in 1961 (his brother Herman had been killed in the Bay of Pigs landing), had been recruited as an asset and received advanced military training for infiltration into Cuba. He was assigned to and involved in sanctioned DRE military operations, but apart from his Agency and DRE activities, by 1963 he was also participating in independent actions including two different anti-Castro operations organized by former Havana CIA operator Mike McClaney.[104]

By the fall of 1962, JMWAVE was definitely on notice that unsanctioned, exile raids were something to be prevented. And officially they became ever more increasingly involved in intervening and preventing them. Yet we now have CIA documents which reveal that Alberto Fernandez, formerly of the Tejana, continued to provide spot reports on exile group activities and missions, including those of Bayo (Alpha 66) and Cuesta (an Alpha 66 spin off group, Commandos L). One memorandum notes that "the Alpha 66/Commandos L raid on the Soviet vessel Baku and…the raid on Cayo Blanco were reported pretty accurately in advance…" This indicates that JMWAVE was fully aware of the Soviet attack mission before it was launched and did nothing to preempt it or apparently to inform higher authority.

It was that mission that generated the Veciana press conference and the Kennedy administration directive mentioned above. The memo goes on in veiled language to suggest that actually, some element of the Agency was interested in supporting such missions if absolute deniability could be obtained. It states that to do that, Commandos "L," would have to be unable to trace such support to the CIA. The memorandum describes such a relationship as "unwitting" utilization. One can only wonder if the memo's author had any idea that at least one CIA officer, who already had such an arrangement, was already in place with Alpha 66 – an arrangement, and a strategic objective very much at odds with the President, Robert Kennedy, and the Special Group in Washington.[105]

By the spring of 1963, there were even doubts emerging in Washington as to whether or not all parts of the Agency might be pursuing official U.S. government policy. As the aggressive, independent exile attacks into Cuba continued, the President was asked who was supporting the exiles involved in them. This was at a point in time in which the Special Group was deeply involved in every authorized mission into Cuba, down to the level of placing supply caches and President Kennedy himself had to approve all major military and sabotage missions. His answer seems to suggest that even with the system in place, he himself was not totally certain of what might be going on – "We may well be…well, none that I am familiar with…I don't think as of today we are."[106]

And neither were others. As early as February of 1963, Paul Rogers, a Democratic Congressman from Florida had called for a Joint Congressional Committee to oversee the CIA. As part of that call he had asked, "What proof have we that this Agency, which in many respects has the power to preempt foreign policy, is not actually exerting this power though practices which are contradictory to the established policy objectives of the Government."[107]

11 ELATION! — THEN BETRAYAL

While many of the initial Cuba project operations officers, from Bissell and Barnes down to field personnel such as Morales, Phillips, Lynch, and Robertson, became extremely bitter towards President Kennedy as a result of the Bay of Pigs, it seems that a number of the Cuban exiles did not reach that same level of emotion until the months following the late 1962 resolution of the Cuban missile crisis.

After all, in Miami, JMWAVE remained a huge and active influence through 1961 and 1962; it was clear that the CIA was still involved with and funding groups such as DRE and JURE. The build up of the CIA boat fleet, training bases in the Keys and other spots in Florida, the continued recruitment and training of selected young exiles, continued intelligence collection and rumors of missions into Cuba – all seemed to show that the U.S. was still very much targeting the Castro regime and, of course, it was – Mongoose, was in full swing and active, even if inept. Even RFK was constantly involved in contact and encouragement of individual exiles and heavily involved with efforts to ransom the Brigade members held in Cuba. Then in the summer, the U.S. Navy and Marines staged a huge military exercise, very openly training for an amphibious invasion on the Caribbean island of Vieques. The "hypothetical" enemy for the complex war game was a regime designated as "Ortsac" – "Castro" spelled backwards. The Joint Chiefs had been pushing a military solution for several months, being totally skeptical of the Mongoose project. The Ortsac exercise was to have landed 4,000 marines on the island, to occupy it and dispose its "imaginary" dictator, in some two weeks. Some 40 warships were involved and only the intervention of a hurricane prevented the landing portion of the exercise from actually occurring.

The military exercises reflected operational plans developed by the Commander In Chief Atlantic, Robert Dennison. He had been in command of the Navy ships in international waters off the Bay of Pigs and had watched the Brigade go down to defeat in extreme frustration. His staff had prepared OPLAN 314 and 316 to ensure that if the word were given, a full-scale American military operation would surely oust Castro. In an ironic coincidence, the plans themselves had a working target date of October 1962. That month would turn out to be the actual month in which an invasion came within a hairs breadth of being ordered.[108]

All signs indicated that the Kennedy administration had indeed not given up on ousting Castro, and then the rumors about a massive Soviet build up in Cuba began to circulate. Of course many of the rumors were just that, and sightings reported to the new Caribbean Admissions Center included things which turned out to be telephone poles, torpedoes, fuel tanks, industrial piping and maritime marker buoys In *Eyeball to Eyeball*, Dino Brugioni described the difficulty in isolating the few truly significant reports and the verification of reports using U2 photography. Still, all the rumors, the reports, the intelligence collection indicated that the pot was boiling in regard to Soviet involvement in Cuba.[109]

Surely the Americans would not tolerate that, not 90 miles off Florida! And surely they would not tolerate more provocations such as the August incident in which Cuban patrol boats fired at a Navy antisubmarine aircraft in international waters some 15 miles off the Cuban coast.

The Navy plane was manned by three reservists who were from a unit stationed at Andrews outside of Washington, the flight originated out of Boca Chica Naval Air Station in Florida. Reportedly the President was unsure that the flight was in reality a training exercise – "What in the hell are reservists doing so close to Cuba…have we run out of training space in the United States?"[110]

And then the rumors got even more serious; the Russians were bringing in missiles. Word was passed to the CIA and anybody else, including Congressmen that the exiles could reach. And the old line, influential Cuban businessmen did have considerable reach into the U.S. Congress. This was especially true of Congressmen increasingly attuned to the upcoming elections and seeing the Cuba issue as a golden opportunity to challenge the Kennedy administration. The President had already been charged as being soft on Communism and on Castro, of pursuing a "do nothing" policy and was pressed by powerful Senators to enforce the Monroe doctrine.

On August 27, Senator Homer Capehart charged that the President was allowing thousands of Soviet military to enter into Cuba and concluded with a call for invasion. On August 31, Senator Keating of New York (a center of old line Cuban business interests) issued a statement with considerable detail, describing 10-12 Soviet cargo ships at the Mariel docks (which had been surrounded by a new cinder block wall) offloading over 1,200 Soviet troops in fatigue uniforms. Five torpedo boats had also been offloaded and moored at a nearby base. Another 1,000 Soviets in uniform had been reported working at a probable missile base near Finca La Guatana and on August 3, a large convoy of military vehicles manned by Soviet personnel had been observed in Las Villas, carrying tracked and amphibious vehicles as well as trucks and jeeps.

The Senator went on in more extensive detail with information about convoys, missile transporters, and other equipment suggesting missile installations. Clearly Capehart had been fed a good deal of accurate information; the details and breadth of that information suggest that it was not simply random reports from exiles but that someone had leaked actual intelligence data being collected by JMWAVE. That seems further corroborated by Brugioni, who evaluated each element of the Keating information and largely verified it from NPIC photo analysis. Capehart and Keating would shortly be supported by Senator Smathers of Florida and others. Keating himself would consistently refuse to identify the sources of his ongoing and highly accurate information – which looks very much like yet another effort to "put Kennedy's back to the wall," especially given the fact that similar information began to be leaked in media circles.[111]

Given aggressive Congressional support for military action against Castro, the escalating Soviet presence and finally, Administration confirmation of ballistic missiles in Cuba, one can only imagine that the exile community was totally convinced that Castro's regime was in its final days. They certainly had ample indication of that, right in front of their eyes. At the height of the missile crisis, the full might of the U.S. military spread over the southeastern United States, largely concentrated in Florida. Troop and Armor convoys jammed both roads and rail lines, virtually every airfield jammed with fighters and bombers, Hawk anti-aircraft missiles deployed on the beaches at Key West. The exiles could only have been elated at the assembled might aimed directly at the Castro regime. And in fact the planned invasion called for the largest amphibious landing since Okinawa during WWII, with over 100 Navy vessels participating. All dependents were evacuated from the Guantanamo Naval base in Cuba, and Marine forces flown in to replace them.

Clearly the elation and certainty of both the American military and the Cuban exiles might have been tempered if they had fully understood that by October, 1963 the Soviets had managed to place a vast force inside Cuba, including armored Soviet Army brigades and a mix of tactical nuclear weapons ranging from mobile missiles to anti-ship atomic rockets placed near the anticipated invasion beaches. It was not until 2008, with the publication of *One Minute to Midnight* by Michael Dobbs, that it became widely known that multiple atomic tactical weapons had been successfully deployed in positions around Guantanamo and that several of the Soviet submarines being harassed (with dropping of small depth charges) by he Navy had been equipped with atomic torpedoes.[112]

THEN BETRAYAL!

Gaeton Fonzi interviewed a number of key anti-Castro exiles in Miami during his work for the Church Committee and later the HSCA. They all told him virtually the same thing. In September 1962, they had heard Kennedy declare that the United States would "use whatever means may be necessary" to prevent Castro from exporting his aggressive purposes. Then the missile crisis exploded, the U.S. military was massed and – and nothing happened. What followed was described as a "bombshell," something terrible and totally unexpected – *Kennedy made a "no invasion" pledge in his settlement with Khrushchev. Fonzi was told that wherever exiles gathered, including in CIA safehouses and training camps, the word "traitor" was heard. It was described as "soul shattering"* – not only had Kennedy bowed to Castro but within months virtually all agencies of the U.S. government were beginning to crack down on exiles operating on U.S. soil. Groups that had a "green light" for missions into Cuba were condemned. The exiles felt that Kennedy had "become the victim of a master play by the Russians."[113]

There is no doubt that the "crackdown" that so infuriated a great number of the exiles was real. Mongoose essentially disbanded after the missile crisis; Lansdale was sent elsewhere and it took a few months for yet another Cuba project reorganization to occur. Not until January 1963, did a National Security Council memorandum address reorganization, while noting that future activities would have to consider the "no invasion" pledge while attempting to still bring pressure on the Castro regime. That would lead to a somewhat schizophrenic approach, focused more on economic pressure and Cuban internal political opportunities than military action. Sabotage of clearly defined economic targets was still to be part of the program – if it could be done without too much press visibility. This approach led the CIA operations officers into Catch 22 situations such as *How do we blow up a key power plant that drives the economy without everyone noticing the lights just went out?*

In order to live within the non-invasion pledge, it became absolutely necessary to stop highly public exile military missions from U.S. soil. The solution to that would become obvious, if difficult. Select exile leaders/groups would be supported but only if they moved their operations off shore and publicly broke any connection to the U.S. government. That approach would come to be described as the "autonomous" group strategy. By extension, that meant the CIA intelligence effort in Florida needed to heavily concentrate on the other groups (the outsiders), groups like Alpha 66 and their spin off, Commandos "L." Once a new Cuba project leader, Desmond Fitzgerald, was appointed in January, 1963, (Phase 4 of the Cuba Project) one of his first acts was to go to Miami and bring in all the relevant agencies (Coast Guard, Air Force, Navy, Immigration, police, FBI etc.) into an orchestrated effort to block exile group staging of missions from the U.S. Of course that was a bit tricky because in reality it meant the individuals and groups which were on the "insider list," would have to be given special permissions until they could move their operations off shore. It also meant that special permissions and passes had to be given to the other "official," administration approved infiltration, intelligence collection and sabotage missions out of JMWAVE. Those missions would be authorized by the Special Group and the President. Needless to say this contributed to some confusion and a lot of tension within the exile community, not to mention the agencies supposedly policing them.[114]

The "approved" JMWAVE missions were focused tightly, planned in great detail, and not all that numerous. In April, Fitzgerald proposed three sabotage targets – a railroad bridge, some petroleum refineries, and a major molasses storage tank. They were selected to "meet the President's desire for some noise level" while representing targets which would not do extensive damage or casualties and they could be carried out fairly soon, in a matter of weeks. In approving those missions, much discussion was given to the need for cracking down on non-sanctioned exile raids. President Kennedy was not terribly impressed by the overall proposal, comparing it to what the Communists were doing in their effort to overthrow the Laotian government. Discussion continued and by late April the thinking seemed to be that refineries and power plants would be the best economic targets.

The strategy seems to have been that such attacks would complement a new project intended to locate military and civil leaders in Cuba who could be persuaded to join in a coup against Castro. That project was given the crypt AMTRUNK and was universally opposed by the old time Cuba project personnel such as Shackley and Morales. They viewed it as unrealistic, given Castro's immense power and the efficiency of his counter intelligence operations. CIA documents on the project through 1965 reveal that the pessimistic view was well deserved. Virtually all the individuals contacted inside Cuba responded that they would never participate unless Castro was eliminated, and virtually all the agents (AMWHIP crypts) recruited to make the contacts were revealed to have been "turned" by Castro intelligence, most very early in the effort.

As time passed, with little overt sign of American action against Cuba, the exile community in Florida was becoming more outspoken. The head of the Cuban Revolutionary Council resigned in protest of American inaction, and groups such as Alpha 66 managed to continue their own provocative attacks. It should be noted that magazine coverage of the exile raids was intense, with frequent *LIFE* Magazine, *LOOK* Magazine and even *Saturday Evening Post* photo coverage of the daring Cuban exile raiders. The coverage was ordered by *TIME LIFE* owner and publisher Henry Luce, himself a devout opponent of President Kennedy and a firebrand in regard to action against Castro.

The success of Alpha 66 seems to have drawn some operational interest by the Army if not the CIA. The Army had made intelligence contact with Alpha 66, motivated by access to field information about Cuban defenses and Soviet bloc weapons that Alpha 66 had encountered. That contact had been made as early as October 1962, and Lansdale had agreed to take a pass for the CIA, giving the Army sole access to Alpha 66 contact. The CIA and Army did share what information they managed to collect on the groups operations and, in February 1963, the Army (Cyrus Vance) drafted a memo to be presented to the Special Group for exploratory discussion of the utilization of Alpha 66 for very select missions. Apparently the proposal was to be presented in March but the draft is marked over with the annotation "Not Used;" it may well be that the Alpha 66 Russian strike and related press conference of March put an end to the Army's thoughts of exploring use of the group.[115]

With a specific strategy slow to jell in Washington, the Cuba project field staff was having little luck getting plans and proposals accepted. It would not be until June 1963 that the President approved a program of "sabotage and harassment" targeting power plants, fuel production and storage and manufacturing facilities. Fitzgerald committed to beginning sabotage operations in July of 1963; it didn't happen. Virtually no sabotage activities had been carried out during the first six months of 1963 and in reality it would not be until October 24 that the President signed off on 13 specific missions to start in November, involving a power plant, a refinery and a sugar mill among other targets.

Even for non-sabotage missions, the placing of supply and arms caches, infiltration and exfiltration of intelligence personnel, detailed plans had to be prepared and approval obtained from the Special Group. In testimony and in remarks to authors, Shackley would complain about how painful it was to get approval for even the most routine maritime operations.[116]

Given Shackley's remarks and what is known of the approvals process, it is extremely surprising to come across a very unusual mission that was fully supported by JMWAVE in June 1963. *In reality, the mission appears to have constituted a second, very risky, attempt to push back against JFK; indeed if it had produced the desired results it would have caused major political damage to the Kennedy administration and the Kennedy presidency.*

RUSSIAN DEFECTORS AND OPERATION TILT:

Beginning in the winter of 1962, following the Cuban missile crisis agreement and while Soviet equipment was still coming out of Cuba, a rumor began circulating within exile circles in Miami. Of course, there were already a number of reports that the Russians were cheating, hiding missiles in caves and playing a waiting game – and Castro's total refusal to allow any U.N. inspection, regardless of the American/Soviet deal, lent credence to such talk. But this rumor was much more specific, it was said that two Russian officers had contacted anti-Castro forces in Cuba and wanted to escape the island, to reveal details of how the Soviets were cheating on the missile agreement. They could provide specifics on hidden rockets and even atomic warheads. Word of their defection had been smuggled out in letters through Mexico City and Spain.[117]

It appears that the primary source for the original Russian officer story came from Alpha 66 members, in particular Eduardo Perez a.k.a. "Eddie Bayo." The group's success in attacks on Russian targets in Cuba lent some credibility to it having contacts, which might provide such intelligence. Of course it now appears that, from its inception, Alpha 66 was being stage managed with a focus on Russian provocation and a goal of "putting Kennedy's back to the wall." That suggests that from the beginning the "Russian missile officer" story may have been designed as a political propaganda device, reflecting the talents of David Phillips. That view is reinforced by the fact that the story was essentially "shopped" to certain conservative political figures. The point man in that effort was anti-Castro advocate John Martino.

Martino had been recently released from prison in Cuba. Arrested in Havana in 1959 and charged with anti-Castro activities, he had previously worked performing electronics services for a Havana casino and had a number of Cuban friends. His background is detailed at length in *Someone Would Have Talked*, but in regard to the TILT operation, Martino's recent release and the widespread media attention it had received in Miami is most important. His story served as a focal point for Castro's abuses, his imprisonment of innocent people, torture, executions – Martino served as a first hand witness to much of that and began working with a conservative ghostwriter, Nathaniel Weyl (who had previously produced *Red Star Over Cuba*). Martino's experiences would be published in a 1963 book, *I Was Castro's Prisoner* and his recounting of his experiences was also issued as a record.

Martino quickly became very much in demand as a speaker at conservative gatherings in 1963 and 1964 and was sponsored on book promotion and speaker tours by organizations such as the John Birch society. Equally important, his ghostwriter Weyl was also doing a book with William Pawley. Pawley was a significant political figure, having served as the U.S. Ambassador to both Peru and Brazil; he had owned major businesses in Cuba and had served as a personal liaison between the Eisenhower administration and Batista prior to the Castro revolution. He had high level contacts in Washington D.C. and within the CIA, including several of the Directors, Deputy Directors and Western Hemisphere chiefs.

It appears that Martino's contacts with conservative political staff resulted in word of the Russian defectors getting to Senator James Eastland, the highly active anti-Communist chair of the Senate Internal Affairs Subcommittee. Eastland in turn passed the word on to Pawley, well known for his own support of anti-Castro activities. Pawley's inquires convinced him that the matter should be aggressively pursued. If the Russians could be gotten out of Cuba and put before Eastland's committee, the political fallout for the Kennedy administration would have been immense. Kennedy's chances for re-election in 1964 would have become minimal if it was demonstrated that the Russians had fooled him, leaving missiles behind in Cuba, stored or even secretly emplaced.

Given Pawley's connections, he felt comfortable taking the matter both to CIA station chief Shackley at JMWAVE and to Marshall Carter, Deputy Director of the CIA. A variety of documents are available on the TILT project, although some stages of the dialog may have been "sanitized" for the record. It is clear that after discussions with Shackley and Carter, Pawley committed himself and his own private yacht to a Cuban mission to bring out the Russian defectors. Martino himself joined the mission and appears to have brought in a number of Alpha 66 personnel, including one of its most well known military leaders, Eddie Bayo.

After a complex series of discussions, Shackley and Carter allowed operational CIA personnel from JMWAVE, led by Rip Robertson, to join in the mission. CIA documents relating to the TILT mission, including an after action report, are available for review online; the documents use Robertson's alias of Irving Cadick.[118]

One CIA officer (alias Fortson) who could speak some Russian was also assigned to the mission so that he could do a quick debriefing of the officers. A considerable number of automatic weapons were provided to the party and it was even agreed that at least two of the exiles could stay behind in Cuba. The navigator and boat guide for the mission was Rolando Eugenio Martinez. Martinez was a virtual legend (along with Robertson) for the number and success of his missions into Cuba and would later become well known because of his participation in the Watergate burglary. Perhaps the most amazing thing is that in violation of all standard Agency security, an agreement was reached with LIFE magazine to allow a photographer to record the mission and a commitment made to eventually facilitate the transfer of the Russians to Senator Eastland's committee.

There was personal communication between King and George P. Hunt, the LIFE managing editor (with no indication that Hunt had any special security clearance for JMWAVE operations). A promise was made that LIFE would not mention the CIA in any form in coverage of the operation, essentially handing the Russian defector story off to LIFE Magazine – and Senator Eastland's committee. Of course LIFE was already active in showcasing the independent DRE and Alpha 66 raids against Cuba and Soviets in Cuba.

The LIFE staff member assigned to the mission and on the boat with Pawley, Martino, Bayo and the Alpha 66 personnel was Richard Billings. Billings would later play a key role in New Orleans DA Jim Garrison's JFK assassination investigation, at first appearing to work with Garrison and later spearheading what became a highly negative LIFE media campaign against the investigation. Even later, Billings was hired by HSCA head Robert Blakey to write an introduction to the HSCA final report and then co-authored a book with Blakey with the title Plot to Kill the President, presenting the assassination as an act by several organized crime figures.

The TILT mission finally came to fruition in June of 1963. It was a complex effort (supervised by David Morales), involving Pawley's yacht, an aircraft used to ferry in personnel for a rendezvous off Cuba and the shadowing of the entire operation (including provision of search radar coverage) by one of the Agency's two highly secret and specially equipped mother ships, the LEDA.[119]

A full shipload of heavily armed and supplied fighters, including Bayo himself, was sent in towards the beach; the boat never returned and from that point on no further contact was ever made with the team.[120] No reports ever came out of Cuba on Bayo or his team members; certainly if they had been killed or captured it would have been headline news within Cuba. Pawley himself later speculated that the craft might have been lost at sea not long after launch. An after action report from a CIA operations office on Pawley's yacht describes a smooth launch, no problems with the seas, and states that a radio check was conducted with the team's boat some 20 minutes after departure.[121]

However, William Turner has written, "In 1995, ex-Cuban security Chief General Fabian Escalante told him that Bayo's boat was found swamped near Baracoa, but there were no signs of its occupants."[122] In addition, interviews with Bayo's wife revealed that she was aware of the mission but that her husband had given her no indication that he would not be returning shortly; she felt sure that if he had intended to go into Cuba for an extended stay he would have told her.[123] The author's current belief is that Bayo's boat may have well foundered at some point, being overloaded both with weapons and people.

Eventually a CIA after action report concluded that the Agency had probably been the victim of a scam intended to place a well-equipped exile team on the island. Of course given Alpha 66's previous successes in Cuban missions, that avoids the question of why Martino and Bayo would hoax Pawley and Eastland (damaging connections with major anti-Castro figures who could help their cause), spend almost six months in the effort and produce no result – no Russians and not even any attacks inside Cuba.

Readers are referred to the extensive series of TILT documents on the Mary Ferrell Foundation website; one is a 250 page summary file collected during the HSCA investigation, while the HSCA was investigating Martino's eventual confession of involvement in the JFK assassination.[124]

Overall, the most interesting thing about the TILT mission, other than the involvement of persons of interest such as Martino, Robertson and Morales is that to this point the author has found no memoranda or even endorsements that would suggest the mission was discussed within the Special Group or the Special Group Augmented, that Robert Kennedy or the President were aware of it or that it had any sort of clearance below Western Hemisphere. There is no sign it was coordinated in advance with the new Cuban Special Affairs Staff under Desmond Fitzgerald. One document, from July 26, 1963 indicates that the SAS Chief was copied on TILT information, but only after the fact (the copy includes a full background review on how the project came about and all reference documents are dated post mission).[125]

Given the level of Robert Kenney's involvement, the firing of Task Force W leader Harvey for authorizing boat missions on his own and Shackley's comments about even minor missions requiring authorization, the lack of authorization and communication pertaining to TILT seems to be exceptional.

Especially so since the CIA was conducting the mission with a former U.S. Ambassador with past connections to the Prio regime; Pawley actually went on the mission himself and his possible capture or death at the hands of Cuban forces itself would have been a matter of international concern. Plus the mission itself had a major anti-administration political agenda: to provide Russian defector testimony to a Senator notoriously critical of the Kennedy administration actions on Cuba, as well as providing *LIFE* Magazine coverage which in and of itself would have had an explosive political impact.

All in all it seems impossible not to at least consider the entire TILT effort as yet another effort, possibly even instigated by David Phillips, to push back against the Kennedy administration and force a more aggressive policy towards Cuba.

12   GOING NOWHERE

We previously discussed the high level of emotions and anger produced by the Bay of Pigs, particularly with the CIA personnel involved. During the following eighteen months, the secret war simply went nowhere. Plans were made, and remade, some missions were launched, some people died but it was plain to virtually everyone that no real progress was being made. It's fair to say that most parties had reached the conclusion that without U.S. military involvement the Castro regime was in Cuba to stay. Worse yet, all the signs pointed to Cuba becoming more and more a front line Russian bastion – all the intelligence coming in showed a major escalation in Russian shipping, Russian weapons and Russian personnel. That point was being carried to the American public by the media coverage (*LIFE, LOOK, POST*) of the DRE, ALPHA 66 and Comandos "L" boat raids into Cuba – raids targeted on Russian facilities and producing fire fights with Russian troops and even the sinking of a Russian freighter. The Russian presence in Cuba had become a major strategic and political issue; the only question was what the Kennedy administration was going to do about it. Truly, as Antonio Veciana quoted his CIA mentor, Kennedy's back was against the wall (and both John and Bobby Kennedy knew it).

Then, what seemed to be a golden opportunity, appeared. The Russians pushed beyond tolerance, by placing strategic weapons in Cuba. The U.S. military, the CIA and certainly the Cuban exile community was convinced their time had come and Castro's time had come. But then – it didn't. And for the exiles, things actually got worse. Within a few months many of the most aggressive of them found their missions being blocked by the United States itself. It appeared to them that the administration had given de facto acceptance of the Cuban situation and (with the exception of those inside the highly secret "autonomous" effort that developed in 1963) that seemed validated by the new crackdown by virtually every government agency. Boat's and weapons were seized, the INS began to issue warnings and take legal actions; people like Felipe Vidal Santiago were ordered not to travel outside the Miami area. Pilots had their certifications taken away or removed by the FAA and the FBI began a major campaign to deny access to weapons or seize what the independent had.

Frustration and outright anger had escalated among all the parties involved in the secret war; when the Cuban brigade members were released and returned to Miami they were greeted by President Kennedy in Miami. And we now know that meeting was the first time active exile threats were made against the President. A Cuban rifleman was reported to be targeting JFK at the Orange Bowl stadium and a bomb was found placed alongside the President's motorcade route.

The growth of exile anger escalated throughout 1963 but it's more violent expressions were largely kept out of the press. Only decades later can we see some evidence of it, with a Presidential trip to Chicago cancelled in October, 1963 due to FBI warnings to the Secret Service of a possible threat to the President (details are lacking but it is seems clear that the FBI felt that the danger was posed by Cuban exiles traveling to Chicago in conjunction with the President's visit). Tensions were so high during the President's November trip to Florida that the Secret Service actively reached out to the CIA and the JMWAVE station and became involved, approaching selected Cubans to monitor community activities in an effort to prevent major protests, which might have turned violent. Documents showing that concern and outreach are now available, on the other hand, it appears that documents pertaining to the threat in Chicago and possibly other threats have been destroyed. In fact Secret Service files on the President's fall travels were destroyed as recently as 1993 following the passage of the JFK records act, the formation of the Assassinations Records Review Board and after directions had been sent to all agencies ordering that any JFK records' destruction cease.[126]

AND THEN...

Whether or not there was an official consensus, it was becoming increasingly clear as the months of 1963 passed, that the ongoing Kennedy administration efforts against Castro were unlikely to bring about a regime change. Castro was entrenched from both a military and an internal security standpoint. The Soviets had extracted a no invasion pledge and there were no longer any major resistance movements operational on the island, only small and isolated groups of fighters. Castro had purged Communist leaders within Cuba in 1962, as he had purged any other threats to his leadership; he was not at all happy with the Soviets (the Russians felt that Castro had even encouraged a nuclear exchange during the crisis) and he felt that the Russian leadership had backed down from its principals and revolutionary leadership. But in regard to the American covert threat, it seems safe to say its time had passed – and of course decades later, the Castro regime remains in power in Cuba, supporting that assessment.

The only significant leverage at hand was the continuing American economic embargo and associated efforts to undermine the Cuban economy. That was a serious problem for Cuba and we now know that Castro would like to have reached some sort of accommodation with the United States. That possibility surfaced during negotiations conducted by James Donovan, a New

York attorney who was involved in an effort to gain the release of American citizens remaining in prison in Cuba. At the end of January, 1962, as Donovan was departing Cuba, Rene Vallejo (Castro's personal physician and confidant) privately broached the possibility of re-establishing diplomatic relations with the U.S. Donovan was also invited back to Cuba, on a private visit with his wife, for extended conversations with Castro himself.[127]

Upon his return to New York, Donovan informed his State Department contact who in turn sent a confidential memo to Secretary of State Dean Rusk and a communication to CIA Director McCone as well. Word of Castro's outreach was passed to President Kennedy, who directed that no conditions should be set that Castro could not fulfill and that more "flexibility" was in order. Donovan did return to Cuba in April and, when back in the U.S., was debriefed by the CIA. *McCone himself wrote Kennedy that Castro knew that relations with the U.S. were necessary and that Castro wanted relations developed.* President Kennedy met privately with McCone and expressed great interest in opening up a dialog. McCone responded that he would be sending Donovan back to Cuba at the end of April; following that visit McCone characterized Castro's tone as mild, frank and conciliatory. He also commented that in asides, Vallejo had told Donovan that Castro realized a viable Cuba (and Cuban economy) required a rapprochement with the U.S.; Castro simply did not know how to go about that so it had been impossible to discuss the subject in any detail with Donovan.

However, at the end of April, Castro had recorded a personal interview with ABC news reporter Lisa Howard. The interview did not air until May 10, 1963 but Howard had been debriefed by the CIA and on May 1, Richard Helms wrote Director McCone a three-page memorandum on the debriefing, covering the economic problems faced by Castro and his recognition of the need for improving relations with the U.S. The memorandum was copied to a number of Agency and Administration chiefs including the Defense Intelligence Agency, National Intelligence Board, State Department Intelligence, Presidential National Security advisor McGeorge Bundy, Attorney General Robert Kennedy and others. A note on the memorandum indicates that it had been read by the President.[128]

Helms also took the opportunity to comment on Lisa Howard's offer to serve as an intermediary; it appears that over time a number of officials seem to have become either defensive or jealous of Howard's connection to Castro. That list included not only Helms but later McGeorge Bundy who aggressively intervened to stop Howard from presenting Castro's ongoing offers to President Lyndon Johnson.

In May, for apparently the first time, discussion at a Special Group Augmented meeting included remarks by McGeorge Bundy to the effect that they were facing the prospect that it might be impossible to get rid of Castro. Defense Secretary McNamara then remarked that it might be necessary to "buy off

Castro," ending the American embargo in exchange for Castro breaking his ties to the Soviet Union.[129]

FRUSTRATION IN MIAMI – SUMMER, 1963:

Task Force W and the multi-agency effort to topple the Castro regime had stalled out after the Missile crisis of October 1962. Its military component, OPPLANS and contingency plans, remained but with the no invasion pledge in place and still a diplomatic issue (regardless of Castro's stonewalling of U.N. inspections) there seemed little chance that any element of that would come into play, unless there was an internal coup within Cuba. The search for such a coup was being pursued, with a new project designated AMTRUNK, essentially an effort to find civil or military figures in Cuba who would work at overthrowing Castro. There was little enthusiasm for that initiative at JMWAVE, both Shackley and Morales felt that it would be fruitless and some two years later they would be proved correct. A final review of the project determined that virtually all the internal Cuban contacts (AMWHIP) had been compromised by Cuban intelligence and, in some instances, by Castro himself.

The Special Group and RFK had been pushing a new Cuban action initiative for some six months. Desmond Fitzgerald had taken over the CIA portion of the Cuba project, but as of summer, no list of sabotage operations had been agreed to, much less finalized. Only routine intelligence and supply missions (with the exception of TILT) were being run into Cuba. The build up of covert vessels and assets that had occurred during Mongoose was being used in support of those missions, but during 1963 both specially equipped CIA "mother ships" (LEDA and REX) were compromised and received media attention. It would be October before a list of some 13 sabotage missions would even be approved.

Operations officers at CIA headquarters were becoming increasingly frustrated with the Kennedy administration, feeling it was not really serious and that they were involved in nothing more than "busy-ness, busy-ness." In Florida, off Cuban shores and inside Cuba, their men and their exile surrogates were risking their lives while the White House was unable to face up to what it would really take to bring down Castro. Officers such as Nestor Sanchez and Sam Halpern would express themselves forcefully in later years – "I tell you one thing, I didn't know the word busy-ness...Helms never mentioned that (relating to remarks made by RFK during a June SGA meeting), *and it was a good thing he didn't because you might have had a Seven Days in May at that point. If that word had gotten out ...there might have been a revolt of some kind.... I might have led it!"[130]*

The "fallout" from the new Administration crackdown on raids by U.S. based exile groups, the orders to conduct only politically constrained and "deniable" covert operations (something that would also hamstring both the CIA in

Cuba and the Amy Special Operations Group/SOG in Vietnam) were extreme among the exile community in Florida. With the FBI, the INS and even local police agencies cracking down on the exiles throughout the country – and especially in Florida and New Orleans – some of the most militant and aggressive exile military leaders considered themselves not only to have been abandoned but literally betrayed. In Miami, the Cuban Revolutionary Council (the successor to the Bay of Pigs era FRENTE) disintegrated, with extremely harsh words towards the new Kennedy policies. The Student Directorate, increasingly losing CIA support, began to frantically seek other sources. Its members would travel to both the Midwest (Chicago and Detroit) and Dallas, seeking weapons from right wing arms dealers. In Dallas they would make contact with a gun shop owner who would seek his own sources to fill their orders, one of which involved a National Guard armory theft in Terrell, Texas. That theft very likely involved a Dallas middle man named Jack Ruby. Ruby himself had a long history of Cuban interests, including an effort to sell supplies to Castro and close friends from the days of the Havana casinos (friends who had worked in the casino overseen by John Roselli and whom Ruby began to connect with again in 1963).[131]

Fitzgerald himself seemed to be obsessed with the use of Rolando Cubela, a covert asset who had been high in the Castro leadership, but who had become relegated to a minor role by 1963. Castro did allow him to travel as a representative of the regime and that at least gave the CIA the opportunity to connect with him. Fitzgerald was repeatedly advised that Cubela was a security risk but given the lack of alternatives, he continued to court Cubela aggressively. Little was to come of it and eventually Castro did have Cubela arrested; he was given a very mild sentence prompting speculation as to whether or not he might have been at least passively performing as a double agent.

The only really new Cuban initiatives launched by the summer of 1963 would be with the "autonomous" Cuban groups, under the leadership of Manolo Ray and Manuel Artime. Both men were supported by Robert Kennedy, and the CIA was actively funding both their groups. The plan was to ensure that they were able to set up operations outside the U.S. and establish political deniability from U.S. support. Ray had been consistently looked on with skepticism by the old Cuba project hands; he was viewed as too leftist (even though he maintained what was the largest group of supporters within Cuba). The JMWAVE personnel were less than enthusiastic about the autonomous projects in general and especially so in regard to Ray. Shackley is quoted as saying that he was asked for his opinion on the autonomous groups and responded that they were a lousy idea. In regard to Ray, Shackley was of the opinion that Ray was attractive to the Kennedy's because he was a "leftist" but as far as Shackley was concerned any support for Ray was "a waste of time."[132]

Artime was viewed as perhaps more politically correct but the old CIA hands also had little enthusiasm for him and their support for a new Artime off shore initiative, AMWORLD. AMWORLD was supported by a specially compartmentalized group within JMWAVE (LORKE) and led by long time Cuba project officers Henry Hecksher and Carl Jenkins. Shackley was also outspoken on Artime, describing the AMWORLD project as strictly "an RFK operation" and an "exercise in futility." Artime's second in command, Rafael Quintero described the half-hearted participation of the CIA officers he was personally working with, "Henry (Hecksher) was reluctant to work with us because somebody dropped it in his lap and he didn't want it...but he was a very professional man and he felt we were wasting our time with what he was doing and it would only work if we could have some professional advice..."[133]

This dysfunctional situation with the autonomous groups in general, and CIA officer distrust of JURE in particular, escalated dramatically as AMWORLD proceeded. Ray and JURE had good reason to feel that their support was less than enthusiastic and were certainly interested in what JMWAVE was doing with the other groups. DRE had not been designated as an autonomous group – largely because it was so hard to control – but it was still receiving funding and its military wing was still active, although increasingly independent of CIA control.

The personal animosity between Artime and Ray was long standing; the sponsorship of both their groups had not minimized that hostility. As of July, 1963, Artime was emphasizing "the irreparability of his break with Ray" and citing events even prior to the Bay of Pigs.[134]

For CIA Operations and JMWAVE, matters came to the head when Morales and Shackley concluded that JURE was actually running an infiltration and spy operation against JMWAVE itself. They began active counter-intelligence activities against JURE, using their covert Cuban intelligence assets (the AMOTs) and even preparing a list of JMWAVE officers and assets, which they felt had been compromised by JURE. Things at AMWORLD went ever further, with Hecksher issuing a directive authorizing AMWORLD boat groups to fire on JURE boats if encountered at sea or near Cuba (again, there is no evidence that the directive was reviewed or sanctioned by the Special Group or RFK).

James Angleton

Tracy Barnes

Richard Bissell

Allen Dulles

Edwards

Desmond Fitzgerald

William Harvey

Henry Hecksher

Richard Helms

John Martino

David Morales

David A. Phillips

Rip Robertson

Ted Shackely

John Roselli

Allen Dulles, Richard Bissell, President Kennedy, John McCone.
April 1962

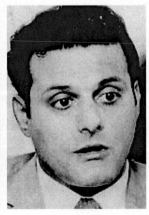

Frank Sturgis

13 END RUN

As of May 1963, senior CIA, State, and Administration officials were aware of what seemed a credible and serious outreach by Fidel Castro towards normalization of relations with the U.S. Associated memoranda indicate that there was also a high sensitivity to the political danger associated with such a dialog. Senate subcommittee inquiries were seen as a particular risk.

To a large extent, any Presidential response to Castro seems to have been stymied by a combination of political concerns by the President, Bundy and Robert Kennedy as well as security concerns expressed by Helms and McCone. In a response to Helm's May 1 memo, McCone responded that the "Lisa Howard report be handled in the most limited and sensitive manner" and "that no active steps be taken on the rapprochement matter. One could interpret that to mean that Helms was to ensure that Howard didn't pursue the matter on her own initiative (as she would later that fall).

Faced with a political backlash and CIA opposition, the President (who clearly did want to pursue a dialog) seems to have tabled the matter, although records of a June 6 Special Group meeting show that the group discussed "various possibilities of establishing channels of communication to Castro" – although it was characterized as a "useful endeavor", no actions were taken.

This impasse began to change dramatically and rapidly in September 1963, when Lisa Howard's friend William Attwood (an advisor with the U.S. delegation at the UN) read an article on Cuban relations by Howard. He called her and after their telephone conversation, he volunteered his services to establish a Castro back channel through the Cuban UN delegation. That approach was endorsed by Averill Harriman, Undersecretary of State for Political Affairs. Attwood proposed to begin a dialog based on the premise that, short of regime change, the U.S. priorities would be the departure from Cuba of Soviet military personnel, a cessation of subversive Latin American activities by Cuba and a general Cuban policy of non-alignment. Contact would be made with an acquaintance of Attwood, Carlos Lechuga, a Cuban U.N. delegate. The contact would be socially initiated through Lisa Howard.

In a dramatic contrast to such dialog, during the fall of 1963, Rolando Quintero, Artime's second in command, proposed the idea of kidnapping Cuban U.N. Ambassador Lechuga as an act of reprisal, possibly holding him hostage for certain demands. Quintero was told that such an act was out of question due to the political consequences; however, Hecksher ended the CIA response by stating that "As regards AMWORLD activities of the aforementioned type in other countries, each case would have to be weighed on its own merits and in the context of how an abortive or compromised abduction could affect AMWORLD equities in those countries."[135]

Attwood's memo was endorsed by the chief U.S. representative at the U.N., Adlai Stevenson and by Harriman. Clearly senior State Department officers were in favor of the Cuban back channel approach and offered to pursue it with the President. And without doubt, they anticipated opposition from the Agency. In his endorsement, Harriman commented that "....unfortunately, the CIA is still in charge of Cuba."[136]

By September 24, Attwood had met with President Kennedy and received his approval to proceed with the initiative; he had also met socially with Lechuga at a cocktail party at Lisa Howard's apartment. Lechuga had been quite encouraging, suggesting that Attwood come to Havana for talks. When informed of the invitation, Robert Kennedy responded that it would be too risky for Attwood to go to Cuba; it would leak and Republicans would call it appeasement and demand a Congressional investigation.[137]

On November 11, Vallejo called Lisa Howard and stressed the need for absolute security about the private communications. As reported by Attwood, he also said that "Castro would go along with any arrangements we might want to make...He emphasized that only Castro and himself would be present at the talks and that no one else – he specifically mentioned Guevara – would be involved. Vallejo also reiterated Castro's desire for this talk and hoped to hear our answer soon." There was obviously political risk on both sides, but clearly both President Kennedy and Fidel Castro were interested in some sort of accommodation.

Attwood and Bundy talked again the next day, November 12, and Attwood visited Howard's apartment on November 13, but when they called Vallejo at home in Cuba, there was no answer, so they sent a telegram. The following day Vallejo called Howard, and set up a phone call for November 18 when, as Attwood reported. "Miss Howard reached Vallejo at home and passed the phone to me. I told him...of our interests in hearing what Castro had in mind...Vallejo...reiterated the invitation to come to Cuba, stressing the fact that security could be guaranteed. I replied that a preliminary meeting was essential to make sure there was something useful to talk about, and asked if he was able to come to New York..." Attwood and Vallejo then talked about setting "an agenda" for a later meeting with Castro.

During this period Howard's home effectively served as a communications center and a series of telephone calls were made between Attwood and Vallejo as well as Howard and Vallejo. Vallejo told Lisa Howard that they would like to have a U.S. official meet directly with Castro. In consideration of security, they would pick up the delegate in Mexico, using a private plane. The individual would be flown to Castro's private retreat near Veradero Beach, where Castro would speak to him personally. Even if such a Cuban visit could not be made immediately, Vallejo did not reject continuing the dialog at the U.N.

These offers caused quite a stir. Kennedy was obviously interested but wanted to establish an agenda before an actual official dialog. And on November 5, the Special Group endorsed a Castro contact working through Attwood at the U.N. However, Helms advised it would be better to delay and study "all possible angles" before any further contacts. Caution was also expressed by Bundy who suggested a Vallejo meeting in the U.S., but noted that Cuba would have to make some policy changes if anything meaningful were to result.

The telephone contacts continued, and on November 16, at 2 am, Vallejo again extended Castro's invitation to Attwood. Attwood took the position that a preliminary meeting (most probably to rough out an agenda) would be necessary before a trip to Cuba and Vallejo replied that he and Castro "would send instructions to Lechuga to propose and discuss an agenda for a later meeting with Castro."[138]

Attwood passed this on through Bundy and was told that Kennedy would want to meet with him after an agenda was roughed out and decide the next step, possibly proceeding to a Cuba meeting with Fidel. Kennedy was obviously serious because an archived tape of his discussions with Bundy revealed a conversation about how that could be done, with the probability that Attwood would have to give up his current position to serve as a personal intermediary.[139]

For the record, we now have further strong evidence that Castro was quite serious and enthusiastic about conducting a negotiation with the United States. Unfortunately the proof came after President's Kennedy's assassination, with an offer to his successor, and it was a most dramatic offer. In early February 1964, Howard had gone to Havana to do another TV news special on Cuba. While with Castro, Howard was given an extraordinary verbal message, addressed personally to the new President. The points in the message were as follows:

1. Please tell President Johnson that I earnestly desire his election to the Presidency in November...though that appears assured. But if there is anything I can do to add to his majority (aside from retiring from politics), I shall be happy to cooperate... *If the President wishes to pass word to me he can do so through you [Lisa Howard]. He must know that he can trust you; and I know that I can trust you...*

2. If the President feels it necessary during the campaign to make bellicose statements about Cuba or even to take some hostile action – if he will inform me, unofficially, that a specific action is required because of domestic political considerations, I shall understand and not take any serious retaliatory action.

3. Tell the President that I understand quite well how much political courage it took for President Kennedy to instruct you [Lisa Howard] and Ambassador Attwood to phone my aide in Havana for the purpose of commencing a dialogue toward a settlement of our differences...

I hope that we can soon continue where Ambassador Attwood's phone conversation to Havana left off...though *I'm aware that pre-electoral political considerations may delay this approach until after November.*

4. *Tell the President (and I cannot stress this too strongly) that I seriously hope that Cuba and the United States can eventually sit down in an atmosphere of good will and of mutual respect and negotiate our differences. I believe that there are no areas of contention between us that cannot be discussed and settled in a climate of mutual understanding.* But first, of course, it is necessary to discuss our differences. I now believe that this hostility between Cuba and the United States is both unnatural and unnecessary – and it can be eliminated.

5. Tell the President he should not interpret my conciliatory attitude, my desire for discussions, as a sign of weakness. Such an interpretation would be a serious miscalculation....

6. Tell the President I realize fully the need for absolute secrecy, if he should decide to continue the Kennedy approach. I revealed nothing at that time....I have revealed nothing since....I would reveal nothing now.

There is no reason to believe that Castro would not have given the same message to President Kenney if that had been possible. The lack of any response from Johnson or his administration is discussed in depth in the referenced articles and is beyond our current subject. Still, it must be noted that despite Castro's instructions that this was a personal message and the only person he would trust to personally deliver it to Johnson, and bridge the contact was Howard. In that respect, McGeorge Bundy's aggressive effort to block her from delivering the message seems highly questionable. Bundy went so far as to distribute an internal memorandum to White House aides she might contact, describing her as a "self important creature" that would be extremely persistent. He stated that she had been offered every opportunity to deliver her message through appropriate channels, but that under no circumstances would she be allowed to do as Castro had requested.

On November 18, 1963, President Kennedy delivered an address on Cuba. It contained language suggesting that if Cuba were to drop its Soviet relationship and stop Latin American subversion "everything is possible." His speechwriter has stated the wording was specifically intended to signal Kennedy's interest in normalizing the relationship.

But Kennedy went further than that, utilizing yet another back channel – a French journalist who had been introduced to him by Attwood in late October prior to his planned trip to Cuba. Reportedly, the President's understanding of Castro's situation and his acknowledgement of certain American "sins" in pre-revolutionary Cuba had impressed Jean Daniel. Kennedy had told him that the Cuban embargo could be lifted if Castro would stop his support for leftist subversion in Latin America and had invited Daniel back to talk after his return from Cuba.

On November 22, Daniel was in Cuba, talking with Castro. Both Daniel and Castro later commented that they felt that Kennedy was in the process of building bridges to Cuba. Daniel had told Castro that Kennedy sincerely believed in the idea of coexistence, but that was on November 22 and after 12:30 Dallas time, there would be no more Kennedy initiatives for coexistence with anyone.

"THE NEED FOR ABSOLUTE SECURITY ABOUT THE PRIVATE COMMUNICATIONS"

The CIA had been well aware of the initial contacts between Castro and Kennedy, facilitated by Lisa Howard. Howard had been debriefed by the CIA, and Helms had even written a memorandum to McCone about her. She continued to make trips to Cuba and maintain personal contacts with representatives of Castro. While CIA had been involved in some of the initial discussions of a U.S. response, they had definitely been moved out of the loop by September, when the dialogs became increasingly serious. At that point, the dialog had evolved into one strictly between the President and unofficial intermediaries such as Howard, Attwood, Lechuga and Vallejo. The CIA, clearly not a fan of rapprochement, was not an active participant, not privy to the private conversations from Howard's apartment, from the United Nations building, or of the calls to Cuba. Or, were they?

THE NATIONAL SECURITY AGENCY AT WORK:

Details of NSA call monitoring are extremely difficult to obtain. A November 26, 1963 FBI memorandum notes that production Group B (Cuban) of the National Security Agency maintained copies of radio messages between the U.S. and Cuba numbering some 1,000 a day and that it had the capability of computer scanning the messages against search criteria including names. We know this only because at that time the NSA was soliciting input from the FBI on a list of names related to Lee Oswald, names which could be used in searching the message base. The NSA was planning a full three-month search of its message data. Given NSA security restrictions, we know little directly of its operational activities. The data we do have is from a handful of scattered documents and information from former employees. Given that talking about a former NSA job might well be prosecutable, most of our detail comes from the former employees who actually chose to defect. Duncan Campbell performed a study of what information is available and readers are referred to his article "Inside Echelon." Basically, in addition to military signals intelligence, the NSA monitored traffic from a great number of countries, including its own allies. This included both commercial and diplomatic traffic, including all traffic on international leased carrier circuits. Intercept operators and analysts worked against a "Watch List" of names, companies and even commodities. The watch lists were compiled from is customer agencies, including the CIA, FBI and DIA.[140]

Other sources relate that, as NSA employees, they routinely participated in monitoring messages between United Nations staff and their home countries as well traffic going to and from Embassies within the United States. *That monitoring paid special attention to telephone conversations not only between the embassies themselves but from taps placed on the diplomatic staff's residential telephones.*[141]

Beyond that, we have at least some indication that one of the parties in the Kennedy/Castro contact had suddenly become a subject of interest to the CIA in the fall of 1963. Of course the Agency had been aware of Vallejo's personal relationship with Castro as early as 1960, however, aside from one 1960 document summarizing that relationship, there seems to have been no special intelligence interest in him.

Yet, in October 1963, (with no precursor documents) we find a message indicating that Vallejo had indeed become a subject of intelligence interest at the highest level of the Agency. The message shows the Mexico City station providing background information on Vallejo to the CIA Chief of Western Hemisphere. Then in a follow up communication from CIA headquarters (Directors Office) to the Mexico City, more background on Vallejo is discussed. In addition, that message indicates a possible contact point for Vallejo via one of the Miami Stations' AMOT Cuban intelligence assets.[142]

While Attwood, Howard and even the President may have thought that Howard's apartment and the U.N. provided a secure channel for a dialog with Castro's representatives, they simply did not appreciate the reality of the situation. Only following the disclosures of the 1970's did Kennedy White House aide Arthur Schlesinger and William Attwood came to understand the full risks of the dialog in which they had been engaged - and the possibility of what it might have triggered.

Following interviews with both men, Anthony Summers reported that both Schlesinger and William Atwood had come to feel it likely that "the exchanges between Washington and Havana had leaked. Atwood had been instructed to maintain extreme secrecy over the whole matter...*with hindsight, there were two glaring security loopholes... The National Security Agency intercepted calls to Havana, and U.S. intelligence agencies reaped the harvest of information...*Arthur Schlesinger says now, *'I think the CIA must have known about this initiative... They had all the wires tapped at the Cuban delegation to the United Nations.'*"[143]

Attwood himself went further in addressing the possible consequences of information being leaked through and within the CIA:

> *"If the CIA did find out what we were doing, this would have trickled down to the lower echelon of activists, and the Cuban exiles more gung-ho CIA people who had been involved in the Bay of Pigs ... I can understand why they would have reacted violently...this was the end of their dreams of returning to Cuba and they might have been impelled to take violent action."*

Given the personal hatreds arising from the Bay of Pigs, the sense of betrayal resulting from the Cuban missile confrontation and the anger produced as the Kennedy administration aggressively moved against Cuban exile missions staging out of the United States beginning in the spring of 1963 – it's hard not to accept Attwood's view that word of negotiations and an impending agreement between President Kennedy and Fidel Castro could indeed have been the trigger for a violent response. And certainly the personal dialogs in process were far from secure given the aggressive NSA monitoring of all communications to and from Cuba. Unfortunately, some four decades of effort have shown that NSA files are virtually impenetrable, they have been held more secure than virtually any other agency documents and finding an official record confirming NSA monitoring of Vallejo, Lechuga, Howard or Attwood is simply not in the cards.[144]

14   OTHER OPTIONS, OTHER "EARS"

Beyond NSA activities, there is a strong possibility that senior CIA officers acted directly to monitor the backchannel Cuban contacts; it is almost inconceivable that the Agency would allow itself to be isolated from such information, especially when the contacts were being made by private individuals representing the President.

It is well documented that first Dulles and later Helms personally turned to Counter Intelligence head James Angleton to produce domestic intelligence, regardless of any laws or the Agency charter that specifically forbids such activities. In fact, it was Angleton's post office mail intercept programs and his aggressive domestic intelligence activities against the anti-Vietnam war effort that eventually resulted in his being fired from the Agency after Dulles' and Helms' eras.

Angleton's sources for such intelligence collection were legendary, he had direct access to the CIA Office of Security; we have reviewed earlier how one of that offices "cut-outs" (former FBI agent Maheu) testified to his relationship with the CIA and his use of "wires" and "bugs" to collect information from foreign diplomats.

Reportedly, Angleton's own personal orientation was towards electronic eavesdropping, His CIA career was not that of a typical clandestine officer, in fact people in the Soviet Division commented that he had never run an agent, never put together a recruitment; had never broken in an agent, never caught a spy. What he had done, starting in Italy during WWII, was to make connections and pay for information. While stationed in Rome during the war he ran a network that burgled codes, cipher books and sensitive documents. They also targeted the mistresses of Ambassadors and Vatican representatives. He had also been obsessed with "bugs" and electronic spying. Angleton would repeat that WWII for decades, becoming the master of collecting rumor and gossip, much of it social. He would share that information very selectively, with the Directors of the Agency and to gain new foreign intelligence sources.[145]

At least some of Angleton's influence over Directors Dulles and Helms came from the sharing of the private information that Angleton provided – social, political, and sexual gossip from around Washington DC (including that obtained from both domestic sources and electronics). For example, Angleton bugged the house of a senior Treasury Department officer who did a great deal of entertaining for foreign guests and the diplomatic corps. Director Dulles knew and approved the action. It also appears that much of the work that Maheu did for the Office of Security may have actually delivered information to Angleton.[146]

In effect, Angleton served as Dulles' and later Helms' personal, domestic intelligence source. The CIA Directors had Angleton and his "sources," allowing them to leverage the same sort of political power more often associated with FBI Director Hoover's infamous special file collection.

Readers only generally familiar with Angleton's legend should definitely read Tom Mangold's ground breaking study of Angleton's true career (*Cold Warrior: James Jesus Angleton: The Cia's Master Spy Hunter*); the differences between his actual accomplishments and his "legend" are amazing. When William Colby took over as CIA Director, he had teams study Angleton's Counter Intelligence efforts and they could not confirm a single spy or mole ever caught by Angleton. Beyond that they could not identify a single specific proactive operation against Russian intelligence. Angleton failed to engage in what counter intelligence normally addresses, penetrating the opponent's intelligence services. Worse than that, Angleton displayed a personal obsession with Soviet defectors and following the defection of Oleg Golitsyn (a mid level KGB Soviet officer) Angleton came to believe every further defection was actually part of a grand KGB plan. He conceived the master plan to have been constructed by the KGB, working with Angleton's long time personal nemesis Kim Philby (Philby had been a major a British double agent for the Soviets, whom Angleton had failed to detect but whom William Harvey had). Angleton boasted of "knocking back" some 22 Soviet defectors – but later the CIA and FBI verified that all 22 were legitimate. Mangold presents a variety of information demonstrating that Angleton had been responsible for a massive loss of potential intelligence from the heart of the KGB and GRU (Soviet military intelligence).[147]

When Angleton's safes and vaults were opened after his departure (drilled open as none of his staff had the combinations), the CIA investigative team came across some that had not been opened for 10 years. In total, there were more than 40 safes with tapes, photographs and bizarre things, which his successor, George Kalaris, refused to even describe. It is unclear that the tapes were played or inventoried but their existence seems to corroborate Angleton's own remarks and the rumors about his domestic bugs and taps. What was clear was that none of the documents or files had been logged into the CIA filing system and it took a special team three full years to accomplish that. Angleton had essentially built his own alternate agency with its own communications networks, its own files, its own rules, and beyond any review or supervision.[148]

Angleton had been officially designated by the Agency as its liaison with the FBI. The Bureau viewed the relationship a bit differently, designating Angleton as a "confidential informant" with the designation T-100. This relationship gave him the ability to repeatedly ask for FBI wire taps and burglaries ("black bag" jobs), which they did perform for him on occasion (it seems to have been largely dependent towards the changing views of Director Hoover as to when such requests were accepted or denied). Apparently, on occasion, his FBI contact may also have given him access to underworld-connected assets as well; one document records his ongoing use of a "mob lawyer" in New York City over a period of some years.[149]

Angleton's biographers point out that Angleton was outside the normal chains of CIA organization structure and command and for that reason was often used for special projects requiring extreme digression. Such assignments apparently approved by Alan Dulles and Richard Helms. Examples include the collection and sanitization of certain documents associated with Frank Wisner (an early head of the agency who suffered a mental breakdown and committed suicide), the retrieval and sanitizing of the personal diary of Mary Meyer (an extremely close friend of President Kennedy, someone with personal access to the White House and the President during 1962 and 1963), and the retrieval and sanitizing of Mexico City Chief of Station Winston's Scott's personal papers (reportedly containing materials Scott had retained on Lee Harvey Oswald's 1963 visit to Mexico City). In the case of Mary Meyer, Angleton was actually observed breaking and entering both her home and work shop on separate occasions and Angleton remarked to a very close mutual friend that he had actually "bugged" her home and bedroom.[150]

It should be noted that as far as Helms, Angleton and the Agency were concerned, both men and women with close, high level connections to the national government – and women with intimate connections to the President – were legitimate national security targets due to their exposure to foreign agents or traitors. Angleton's interest in the Meyer/Kennedy relationship had been revealed in personal remarks by Angleton to her former husband, a CIA officer, a year before the personal relationship between she and Kennedy developed. After her death, Helms acknowledged the Agency interest in her and Angleton's recovery of her diary as well as its review and sanitation by Agency employees.[151]

Given McCone's and Helms' stated concerns about President Kennedy's Cuban contacts and Helms' efforts to delay any direct dialog, is seems quite possible that they would have taken steps to conduct their own direct monitoring of the contacts between Howard and Attwood with Lechuga and *Vallejo*. They could have turned to the NSA through Staff D; they could have turned to Angleton's resources, which would have gone beyond the NSA, directly into Howard's apartment. Most likely they turned to both. If they did call in Angleton, no doubt the backchannel contacts would have seriously worried him given that his oft presented view of the Soviet master plan viewed all such outreaches as part of their grand strategy. He certainly felt that way about "détente."

"Détente is a sham, a tactic; it is Soviet Communism's Potemkin village for waging the cold war." – James Jesus Angleton

Beyond that, any such conduct on President Kennedy's part might have made Angleton suspicious of Kennedy himself. Angleton's Special Intelligence Group actually investigated several major international and domestic political figures and Angleton believed that the following individuals were actual Soviet assets:[152]

Harold Wilson, the British prime minister

Olof Palme, the Swedish prime minister

Willy Brandt, the West German Chancellor

Averill Harriman, Gov of New York

Lester Pearson, Canadian Prime Minister

Henry Kissinger, Secretary of State and National Security Advisor

Angleton's total list of Soviet moles included some 30 world leaders, top politicians, foreign intelligence officers and CIA intelligence offices including William Colby (who became CIA Director following James Schlesinger). Schlesinger himself described Angleton this way – "Jim's mind was devious and allusive, and his conclusions were woven in a quite flimsy manner...his long briefings would wonder on...but it was always smoke, hints and bizarre allegations. He might have been a little cracked but he was always sincere.[153]

While speculative, there is even reason to wonder if President Kennedy himself may have been concerned about exposure of the back channel communications with Castro. In November, as the dialog through Lisa Howard's New York apartment and Lechuga's office at the United Nations escalated, President Kennedy made two quick trips to New York. On the second trip, for apparently the first time, a Secret Services Protective Service agent was dispatched to the President's hotel "to conduct a technical survey" of the facility and the President's rooms. Although Chief Rowley of the Secret Service admitted that it did employee electronics experts (capable of "sweeps" and countermeasures), he demanded that his Warren Commission testimony go off the record when the subject of such activities was brought up, declaring it a matter of "national security."

Beyond that, researcher Vincent Palamara has provided proof that the one known Secret Service electronics expert can be confirmed as participating in the President's trips to both Florida and Texas in November, 1963. It may also be significant that as recently as 1995, after having been advised by the ARRB not to destroy any JFK related records, the Secret Service destroyed three folders full of Protective Service Reports pertaining to President Kennedy's travel in the fall of 1963. The folders contained information on the President's Chicago and New York trips. In addition, an entire box of files relating to Presidential protection and a file pertaining to travel to "other places" during the period of July-November, 1963 were also destroyed.[154]

Attwood's concerns about the Cuban back channel communications which had become so active and promising in October and November seem quite reasonable, in fact it would have been rather incredible not to find CIA senior officers monitoring those contacts and in particular ensuring that they knew exactly what was being said during the talks at Howard's apartment and the calls to Cuba. It would be equally amazing to expect to find any written record of such activities, including where the information would have gone within the Agency. And as far as the NSA monitoring is concerned, again it would be incredible if Cuban's U.N. staff would not have been on the "watch list" and if Castro's personal confidant had not been as well.

TRICKLE DOWN:

Decades after 1963, William Attwood worried that if word of the Castro outreach had indeed circulated within the CIA it *"would have trickled down to the lower echelon of activists, and the Cuban exiles more gung-ho CIA people who had been involved in the Bay of Pigs."* The two obvious questions which arise are: a) how would that have happened and can we trace the probable flow of such an explosive message? and b) can we find any evidence that such a thing actually happened in the months prior to the President's trip to Texas?

The first question may well have had a very simple and very direct answer. If Richard Helms had indeed directed the parties involved in the Cuban negotiations to be monitored, either via the NSA or covertly by James Angleton or both, Angleton would have known about it. Michael Holzman describes Angleton's work day as almost singly devoted to reading; he had access to all the highest level daily reports from the Defense Intelligence Agency, the National Security Agency (its Daily Intelligence Summary concerning their electronic intercepts), and the National Indications Center at the Pentagon as well as the CIA's own daily reports and summaries. Beyond that, with his authority for vetting all personnel assignments, he was allowed access to every single Agency personnel, operations or communications file. With his rank and clearances (and Director-level-influence) Angleton was able to delve into virtually any intelligence matter and anything smacking of a sophisticated Soviet master plot would have drawn his immediate attention.

A Cuban outreach would have worried Angleton immensely. But whom would he share it with? Certainly with the Director, but we know Helms was already personally concerned and questioned the President's direction in the matter. Angleton's biographers emphasize that Angleton's routine was to share his worries, but only at the highest level and only with the long established senior Agency cadre. And in this case, the obvious person for him to approach would have been the former head of Task Force W, the former head of Counter Intelligence and the man that Angleton had personally been involved with early in the renewed effort to assassinate Fidel Castro – William Harvey.

Harvey would have been easily accessible to Angleton in the spring of 1963; he had no specific assignment and was simply marking time until his assignment to Rome developed. The one thing he seems to have continued was his contact with Roselli and with some of the assassination team personnel in Florida. Angleton had become involved with the subject of Cuba even before Harvey came into it, working with information from Morales' Cuban Intelligence team (the AMOTs) to prepare a summary of Cuban intelligence for the Director at the of 1962, just as Harvey was coming in to succeed Bissell on the Cuba project. How much personal contact Angleton may have had with Morales or the AMOTs remains unclear. We only have one report, which suggests that he was to be assigned to oversee institutionalization of the Cuban intelligence team, based largely in the individuals that Morales had prepared to go into Cuba. We also know that Angleton joined with Harvey in the early stages of Harvey's restart of the Castro assassination project and that Angleton even provided one of his own foreign sources inside Cuba to backstop Harvey with field intelligence. In addition, we have the note that simply stated that Antonio Verona, the head of the Cuban Revolutionary Council and Harvey and Roselli's long time contact in the Castro assassination effort, had been of "operational interest" to James Angleton.

Given that Angleton knew and was worried about the Kennedy/Castro initiative, it seems almost inevitable that Angleton would have taken the issue to William Harvey. And no doubt Harvey would have been profoundly disgusted. Harvey had just spent over a year trying to kill Castro (indeed the project was still in progress at the time the back channel contacts started, whether or not President Kennedy was aware of it), he had virtually sacrificed his own career in an effort to bring down the Castro regime and now the President of the United States was entering into a friendly dialog with Fidel. One can only imagine the emotion in such a conversation between Angleton and Harvey.

And then, by the end of April, Harvey was back in Florida, meeting with Roselli and most likely with Morales as well. The meetings were private, they were lengthy and without doubt they involved much drinking. It is impossible to read Stockton's biography of Harvey and not think that Harvey would have shared the word about Kennedy and Castro. If the Angleton and Harvey discussion had been profound, this set of conversations would have been mostly profane. And being alerted to the situation, Morales had his own channels to monitor the situation, using both WAVE's Cuban intelligence service (largely created by Morales himself) as well as WAVE sources in Mexico City.

If for some strange reason, Howard had not been on Angleton's radar before the Helms memo, she certainly would have been by the middle of May. And

Harvey remained available to Angleton in Washington, with nothing much to do, until he relocated to Rome at the end of June. Interestingly, Harvey went out of his way to have Roselli come back and meet with him only days before Harvey and his wife actually moved overseas. We have no idea what might have passed between Harvey and Roselli, and on down to Miami and Morales. Certainly by summer, Morales might have easily have had the message that would inflame his own operations officers, the cadre that had been with him since Guatemala, through the disaster of the Bay of Pigs, with the emotions of the Russian missile crisis and who were still risking their lives on a routine basis with missions into Cuba. Worse yet, what might it have done to the Cuban exiles?

Sam Halpern is on record as saying that CIA officers might have "revolted" if they had learned that their efforts were being characterized as "busy-ness" by RFK; what might they have done if they learned that they were engaged in "busy-ness" while negotiations with Castro were actually in progress? How much greater would have been the reaction of the men actually involved in planning and carrying out the ongoing missions into Cuba? Which leads us to the second part of our question – is there any evidence, even if anecdotal, that the Castro backchannel dialog did indeed make its way to the exiles in Miami?

HSCA investigator Gaeton Fonzi spent a great deal of time in Miami; he interviewed many violent anti-Castro Cuban exiles. He found one of the most fervent, and violent, of them to have been a former CIA employee, Rolando Otero. Otero hated Castro, Communists and Castro fellow travelers in Miami, but he also believed that President Kennedy had been killed by CIA officers and his fellow Cuban exiles. Otero believed that for two reasons, first because of information he had gotten second hand from one of the most connected Cubans in Miami, a former Brigade member who had participated in anti-Castro missions, even after release from Castro prisons (an individual who we will definitely return to later). And he believed it because of the word he heard being passed in select circles in Miami in the later summer and fall of 1963.[155]

"HE'S AGAINST US!"

In sealed HSCA testimony, Otero described a rumor passed to segments of the exile community. The message was, "*like Kennedy was a Communist, he's against us; he's messing up the whole cause!*" The rumor was being passed by exiles tied into certain CIA operations officers. Later a very select group (including Otero's associate, who he said had a more detailed knowledge of the attack in Dallas) was told, shortly before the assassination itself, that something big was going to happen. There would be a big change and they must be prepared to support it. No details, not when, not where, not precisely why but be prepared for it. Finding more sources like Otero is a challenge, and again likely to give us only second hand information. However, one corroborating statement has been reported.[156]

Felipe Vidal Santiago had commanded the Havana Maritime Police and later was appointed to the Cuban embassy staff in Caracas. He initially made contact with the CIA while in Caracas and was encouraged to work in place as an asset. Against the Agency's wishes, he managed to exfiltrate his brother Ivan out of Cuba and that led to a break between he and the CIA. Vidal then moved on to Miami and connected with a number of "operationally" active individuals but refused to join any particular group. Although he was respected for his maritime experience, he remained somewhat of a loner, even while organizing small missions into Cuba. Vidal had a reputation for independence and for activism but he was very much outside the circle of exiles directly associated with the Agency and JMWAVE. FBI informants described him as associated with a number of American anti-Communist paramilitary activists, including Roy Hargraves and Michael Collins. Informants also reported that he was felt to be impetuous and unpredictable. That view seems to be confirmed by CIA informant Frank Sturgis to his case officer Bernard Barker in August 1962. Sturgis reported that Vidal was seeking help in a project that would involve a provocation air attack on the U.S. Guantanamo base, using B-26 aircraft that could be identified as Castro air force planes.[157]

Early in 1964, Vidal embarked on what turned out to be his final mission into Cuba, this time the Cubans were waiting and he was captured, tortured, and later executed. While being interrogated, *Vidal reportedly wondered off on a tangent that surprised his captors; he talked at length about what he had been doing in the fall of 1963.* According to Fabian Escalante, a senior Cuban intelligence officer, Vidal spoke at length on his intense effort to communicate a very important message to other exiles. *The message was that Kennedy had opened up negotiations with Castro (something actually unknown at the time in Cuba, except to Castro's confidant Vallejo), and considered by those listening to Vidal's remarks to be outrageous. Kennedy was going to get the Russians out of Cuba and open up normal relations with Cuba; the exile cause would be doomed.* Such talk no doubt did seem incredible to his Cuban interrogators; they were only interested in more detail about exile missions against Cuba, Vidal's associates, and how he had been getting past their security on previous trips.

If Vidal did indeed make such remarks, he was certainly talking about something that he should not have known. But such remarks would have been very consistent with Otero's dialogs with Gaeton Fonzi. It is also worth noting that Escalante made no representation of any remarks by Vidal about the Kennedy assassination, only his story in regard to the explosive news of Kennedy/Castro negotiations and some sort of pending settlement between the two countries.

If Escalante is to be believed, Felipe Vidal Santiago knew something that the head of Cuban intelligence didn't; something that was known only to Fidel Castro, two of his most trusted aides and the most senior levels of the United States government. Even if the information had been passed to Morales via

Harvey and Roselli, how could such details possibly get to Vidal? There are a number of possibilities but we may find one channel in the known associates of John Martino.

JOHN MARTINO AND FRIENDS:

We came across Martino earlier; a former Cuban prisoner, an anti-Castro activist, highly visible in the Miami papers - deeply involved with Eddie Bayo and select Alpha 66 personnel in the TILT project. Martino remained active in anti-Castro activities during 1963, joining a John Birch sponsored speaking tour, bringing out and promoting his new book, *I Was Castro's Prisoner*. He became particularly vocal following the Kennedy assassination, coming forward with promises of detailed information implicating both Lee Oswald and Jack Ruby as agents of Fidel Castro. At first the FBI was responsive to his stories; Director Hoover was quite interested in possible Cuban sponsorship of Oswald and had even proposed to President Johnson that they leave that option open in the FBI's report on the assassination (Johnson responded negatively; no options for conspiracy were to be in the report). But Martino was unable to provide the promised details and lost favor with the Miami Bureau office. They had no knowledge of the TILT mission and seemed not to have appreciated Martino's exile connections. However, they were able to verify that one of Martino's closest friends among the exiles was Felipe Vidal Santiago.[158]

It was only after Martino's death that a much different story came to be known, and then only in confidential reports by two of his closest friends. Not long before his death (and after he himself had developed considerable doubts about his own actions in 1963), Martino had told them something much different. He didn't elaborate, or provide any great detail; his remarks were low key and more in the nature of getting something off his chest. What he had to say was explosive; he described his own limited and intermediary role as a courier in a conspiracy against President Kennedy. The conspiracy had involved Cuban exiles and the establishment of Lee Oswald as a patsy intended to place the blame on Fidel Castro and Cuba. Unfortunately, the HSCA's investigation of those reports was quite limited. Martino's family certainly wanted nothing to do with the story at that point in time. It would not be until 1995, not long before her own death, that his wife would verify it. Later other family members would add their own corroboration.

Martino's full story is told in *Someone Would Have Talked*, with reference to the related HSCA documents and elaboration from one of Martino's sons (Dr. Edward Martino, who as a young boy had been taken into custody in Cuba along with his father). Certain points in Martino's story, particularly those relating to the manipulation and role of Lee Oswald will be revisited later in this study. For the moment we need to focus on one particular area, one possibly lost in the book's details. The point which must be stressed is that there is very good reason to believe that Martino was personally connected with a pair of officers by now very well known to the reader. Agency figures whom we have followed from their initial involvement in Guatemala and PBSUCCESS through their reunion in Miami for the Cuba Project. These were men whose trainees (and friends) had died at the Bay of Pigs. Men both involved with John Martino in the 1963 TILT mission. David Morales was in charge of that mission and Rip Robertson was the actual mission operations officer, going with Martino, Bayo and Pawley on the boat mission.[159]

MARTINO AND MORALES:

In order to appreciate the significance of John Martino having an extended personal knowledge of David Morales, we need to briefly revisit Morales himself.

Morales was the archetypical "man of mystery," his CIA service was virtually all covert, whether in Latin America, in Cuba or in SE Asia, he worked under either under State Department Consular or U.S. AID covers. His covert activities were covered by aliases such as Delgado, Mensa, Mendoza, or Dr. Manuel Mendez in internal JMWAVE documents he was identified only with the crypt "Stanley Zamka." He was given a series of "backstopped" identities and addressees when working inside the United States. A great deal of CIA security effort went into ensuring that his affiliation with the Agency remained confidential. Gaeton Fonzi tells the fascinating story of how details on David Morales, also known as *El Indio* or "the big Indian" finally emerged, well after the HSCA had disbanded. Fonzi had come across his name from a "Highly Sensitive" document, naming key Agency operatives and that listed him for interview, but Morales was not a priority to him, as he appeared to be a very minor figure within the Agency.

Fonzi was stunned when years later he finally learned Morales' true history and position within the CIA – rising from being an Army Corporal in Germany to a paramilitary trainer in Guatemala, coming out of that assignment as one of the officers, along with David Phillips, taken to receive a personal commendation from both the Director of the CIA and the President. Following that, Morales had gone on to work as a counter intelligence officer for the Cuba project, selecting and training the exiles who eventually were used to form the Cuban Intelligence Service (AMOTs). His performance in the project eventually led to Morales being promoted to second in command of the entire JMWAVE station, as the Chief of Operations. After tours in SE Asia and work in Latin America, Morales concluded his career, serving in the 1970's as a special consultant to the Joint Chiefs on counter-insurgency operations, retiring from the CIA at the effective rank of Brigadier General.[160]

Fonzi simply could not believe that none of the JMWAVE station personnel he had interviewed had even mentioned their boss or that David Phillips, who he interviewed for several hours, had barely mentioned Morales when asked about him. Fonzi had received no response on his request to the CIA for documents on Morales; he was not even acknowledged as a CIA officer, nor does CIA service show in his final obituary. To the world, Morales had been an Army noncom, eventually serving in the State Department and with the U.S. Agency for Development.

Fonzi was further amazed when he realized that David Morales was the individual referred to as "El Indio," "Indio," or "the big Indian" – stunned because the HSCA had been looking for "El Indio," had questioned people about him because there were reports ranging back as far as the Garrison investigation, that El Indio had somehow been involved in the murder of President Kennedy. Garrison had received an anonymous letter from Miami that gave him the lead that one of the individuals involved in the conspiracy against Kennedy had been called "Indio."

But by the time Fonzi was able to put all the pieces together (with the help from private researchers such as Bob Dorff and Gordon Winslow and with investigative assistance from Bradley Ayers), the HSCA inquiry was long over. Fonzi's own book on the HSCA inquiry was not published until 1993. In the interim, Ayers played a key role in developing information on Morales; Ayers had worked as an Army trainer at JMWAVE and known Morales personally. He described Morales as running operations with a "heavy hand," famous for his temper and crossed by nobody at all. Even his JMWAVE boss Ted Shackley didn't ask Morales a lot of questions.[161]

By the time Fonzi began working on his book, he also realized to what extent David Phillips had failed to comment on his long time fellow officer, of over 20 years. Of course, Phillips has briefly mentioned Morales, but in typical Phillips fashion, in a very round about way. In 1978, Phillips had published a spy/assassination novel, *The Carlos Contract* and *one of its main characters was "El Indio."* Phillips characterized "El Indio" as "the best dark alley operator" around. The fictional "El Indio" had recently retired from the Pentagon and had disbanded the personal task force he had personally organized for the "really sensitive operations." In his normal fashion, Phillips also added a few details that would have served anyone looking for the real "El Indio" in entirely wrong directions.

Nobody in the Agency talked about David Morales and nobody outside the Agency was even supposed to know that name. Of course, Morales was known to people like William Harvey and John Roselli through his operational support of the highly compartmentalized Castro assassination missions. He was known to his boss, Ted Shackley (who locally in Miami was known only by his own crypt, "Andrew K. Reuteman" or alias Tad Brickham). Morales would have been known to Angleton, through his counter intelligence assignments and the formation of the AMOTs. But beyond that, he was truly a shadow warrior – with one exception.[162]

Amazingly, John Martino's 1963 book *I Was Castro's Prisoner* contains discussion and praise of 'David Morales," *not with any alias but with Morales'* *true name!* In Chapter 4, Martino goes on at some length about the officials at the U.S. Embassy in Havana, and how they had literally abandoned him in prison. In that dialog he actually names Earl Williamson as the CIA officer on the Embassy staff and describes Williamson "quietly" being withdrawn and replaced in that position by David Morales. But Martino didn't just identify Morales as CIA; he went on to praise Morales at some length, for having been the only individual with the insight to recognize Fidel Castro as a Communist from the very beginning. Martino describes Morales' efforts to warn his superiors, to warn Washington. He also complained that all Morales' warnings had been ignored.

One can imagine that the CIA Office of Security would have been stunned if they had realized that in 1963 Martino's book was naming their current Operations Chief. Generally security went ballistic over anyone naming a serving officer or even a former officer as being a CIA employee. The Agency never, ever formally acknowledged Morales as an employee. His retirement "resume" and even his tombstone and obituary make no acknowledgement of his CIA service. Morales himself was so sensitive to the subject that some time after his retirement, he actually reported David Phillips to the Agency on a probable security violation, because Morales felt that Phillips might have identified him as a CIA officer to a journalist. There was a serious investigation of the inquiry, which Phillips denied. Related memoranda suggest the CIA itself was not too sure, but Phillips remained in high esteem within the Agency and was not cited or reprimanded. He had resigned at the peak of his career during the Church Committee inquiries, to form an association of former intelligence officers, an association which could assist in aggressive legal action defense of its members. At some point, it appears that the two former career officers had drifted apart. There is no sign Morales made personal inquiries to Phillips on the press incident, he immediately reported it as a security violation.

Exactly how Martino came to have his inside information about Morales is unclear. A Cuban arrest order for Morales was issued in June 1959, and by July 30, Morales was back in the U.S. Martino himself had been just been arrested in Cuba on July 29, 1959. Is it possible that the two men had some sort of association in Cuba that we do not understand? If so, Morales would have to have known of Martino well before Martino's association with the Pawley/Bayo/TILT mission.

This remains an area for research as documents suggest that Morales was involved with a CIA team (led by "David Christ;" true name Daniel Carswell) which had placed bugs in the Chinese embassy in Havana, only to be picked up during a break-in/retrieval mission. That mission was clearly a Staff D project; Christ himself was head of the audio section of CIA Technical Services. Little is known about what cover the team might have used in its mission; however, Martino did operate an electronics firm in Miami, which did business in

Havana. The lawyer who eventually negotiated the team members release included Martino in the same group effort while being covertly sponsored by the Agency in his legal efforts. Martino and the Christ team were released by Cuba at the same time and traveled back to Miami in October, 1962.[163]

Martino's knowledge of Morales has no simple explanation, but it is a fact. Clearly the two men had either been personally involved or Martino had learned a good deal of highly confidential information about David Morales from someone close to him. It also is known that Martino had become personally associated with someone named "Rip" and that would most likely be Rip Robertson, a long time colleague of Morales, going back to their service in Guatemala. Martino's wife described "Rip's" ongoing visits to their house during 1963. She would have had no way to know that "Rip" himself was one of the senior WAVE special operations officers, dedicated to covert missions into Cuba. Robertson had become an operations team leader at JMWAVE following the Bay of Pigs. His acts at the Bay of Pigs and his ongoing personal dedication to eliminating Castro made him one of the few CIA officers truly trusted by the exiles. A *Harper's Magazine* article of 1975 contains remarks by Cuban commandos who had worked with Robertson in military missions through 1963, Ramon Orozco and Nestor "Tony" Izquierdo.

Izquierdo himself received little mention compared to other Cuban exiles of the period but his fight against Castro had begun in Cuba, where he fought with Artime's anti-Communist, anti-Castro rebel group. After coming into the United States via Mexico in 1960, he joined the CIA effort against Castro, participating in support of the Bay of Pigs landing. Upon his return to the United States he worked with Rip Robertson in JMWAVE operations. Later Izquierdo rejoined Artime and Quintero in their effort to fight Castro from outside the U.S. His anti-Castro and anti-Communist efforts continued for a number of years and he was actively involved in combat against the Sandinistas at the time he died in a 1979 plane crash in Nicaragua. A statue honoring him was erected in 1992 in the Martyr's Boulevard section of the "Little Havana" area in Miami.

Robertson was viewed as the epitome of a CIA "paramilitary" (in the slang of the time, a "cowboy"). He was also described as routinely disobeying orders and going into Cuba with his teams. Orozco also described a mission that Robertson led against Russian ships in Oriente province, although as far as is known, *neither the Kennedy administration or the CIA ever sanctioned missions directed against Russian targets.* Fellow officers were also highly impressed with Robertson, describing him (and themselves) as literally being engaged in "a crusade against evil" in their activities.[164]

Given his operational status and the secrecy of his missions, Robertson should certainly have had no ongoing contact of any sort with Martino. It would have been totally outside of mission regulations and a serious security violation. Frequent visits to the Martino household would have exposed Robertson to a variety of non-Agency Cuban exiles and that was a serious matter by that time in 1963. Still, it seems that Robertson/Martino contacts did continue well after the actual TILT mission and a TILT document shows Martino contacting the CIA via Robertson (crypt Irving Cadick) in regard to the missing Bayo team in September, 1963.[165]

Although we don't clearly understand the exact origin or extent of the Martino/ Morales/Robertson association, there are a number of indications that at least some connection between Martino and Morales continued well beyond 1963. For example we know that Martino eventually received some very high-level personal introductions in Guatemala. Those introductions allowed him a quick entry into the import/export business, sourcing a variety of military products and selling them in Guatemala. This occurred at the same time Morales was doing counterinsurgency consulting with Guatemala and other countries in the area. When Morales retired and went into the commodities import/ export business, Martino's sales shifted to commodities (some possibly illegal as his business, "Sud Import Export," was briefly investigated by the FBI).[166]

15 PASSING THE WORD IN MIAMI

Gaeton Fonzi's HSCA work gave us our first indication that word of some sort of Castro/Kennedy dialog was indeed passed to CIA officers and radical exiles. Word may have been passed via Martino but more likely he was only one of a trusted few. Fonzi's initial source on the message was Rolando Otero. Otero had heard rumors being passed within very select exile circles in the late summer and fall of 1963. Otero had heard more than just rumors though, he had heard of actual exile participation in a conspiracy against JFK. We then found similar information reportedly coming from Felipe Vidal Santiago, a close personal associate of John Martino. Vidal and his friends are of considerable interest in regard to events in Dallas. Vidal himself traveled to Dallas on repeated trips in the fall of 1963 and indeed was in Dallas on November 22. But before we return to Vidal, we need to pursue the ultimate source of Otero's information, a man whom Fonzi investigated in considerable detail. And as we learn more about that individual, we will learn that he was also close to friends and Cuban mission partners of none other than John Martino's good friend Felipe Vidal.

BERNARDO DE TORRES:

As part of his HSCA investigative work, Gaeton Fonzi did indeed identify Otero's source. In fact, he went beyond that, working Otero's source to identify an individual who had reportedly been in Dallas on November 22 and who might be the key to naming some of the actual participants in the attack on the President. Readers are referred to *The Last Investigation*, Chapter 28 for the details of Fonzi's complex investigative work and the frustration of that work leading to nothing other than the individuals identification and some meaningless, anonymous testimony to the HSCA.

The reason that it led to nothing more than that, given its explosive potential, was that *at the exact point in which Fonzi and his partner had set up a sting on the individual, one which might have revealed his operational associates (people who had been involved in the Dallas attack), they were ordered to call it off.* At that point they already knew the man in question had a variety of very deep government connections, and that he remained operationally active with one or more government agencies. In a last minute call from Washington, *Fonzi was told he "might be getting into something bigger than all of us" and that he was not authorized to do "that kind of stuff." It was at that point when Fonzi fully realized that he was not involved in a truly serious investigation.*[167]

But Fonzi had documented Otero's ultimate source and with the release of HSCA records we also know his true name – Bernardo De Torres. Fonzi could only cite the code name he had been assigned (a family name actually), "Carlos." But we know a good deal more than Fonzi did in the 1970's. Although "Carlos" testified to the HSCA that, "I never worked for the CIA, I never talked to anybody associated with the CIA," he had actually been a member of the CIA recruited and trained Cuban Brigade, seriously wounded and captured at the Bay of Pigs landing, imprisoned in Cuba and released only in December, 1962. At that time he returned to Miami, joining his brother Carlos who operated a detective firm in Miami. It would only be fair to say that via his brother and the private investigative firm, Bernardo De Torres became quite well connected within the Miami exile community. De Torres himself rejoined the reformed Brigade 2506 in Miami, becoming its head of intelligence. Beyond that, he quickly joined with one of the aggressive Alpha 66/Commandos "L" mission leaders.

"Tony" Cuesta had been the subject of a major *LIFE* magazine coverage, first leading a mission against a Russian construction site in Cuba in September of 1962 (at the very beginning of the Cuban missile crisis), then returning in October for yet another attack against the Russians, killing Soviet personnel at Isabela De Sangua. In March of 1963, he led a raid, which engaged in a firefight at a Soviet military camp and then sunk the Russian merchant ship Baku (a *LIFE* photographer had accompanied the mission). It was Cuesta's March 1963 raid that triggered the Kennedy administration crackdown on exile raids staging from the United States. *LIFE* photos of the Baku mission show an individual who appears to be identical in appearance with Bernardo De Torres.

Antonio Cuesta Del Valle a.k.a. Tony Cuesta had been a businessman before going into exile in the United States. He joined one of the first aggressive paramilitary organizations to form against Castro, Los Halcones Negros (the Black Falcons). Then he joined Alberto Fernandez as a crewman on the Tejana, the first CIA sponsored infiltration ship (with financing engineered by David Phillips). Upset over the Bay of Pigs, Cuesta (along with his fellow Tejuana crewman Eddie Bayo) turned away from the Agency, becoming one of the most visible members of Alpha 66 and a spin off named Commandos "L."

Eventually Cuesta's luck ran out, much as Bayo's appears to have, and he and his team, armed with submachine guns, hand grenades and plastic explosives, were surprised. Some were killed in the engagement, including Herminio Diaz Garcia, but Cuesta vowed Castro would never take him alive, and when it was clear they were trapped he triggered a hand grenade. Instead of killing himself, it blinded him and blew off his right hand. Cuesta spent considerable time in a hospital and apparently after giving it considerable thought, determined that he only way he could have been surprised as he had been, was that someone had leaked information, and had effectively set he and his team up.

In 1978, President Carter arranged for a group of imprisoned exiles to be released. Security Chief Fabian Escalante met with Cuesta before his journey back to the United States. The two had become somewhat close and Escalante had facilitated his extensive medical treatment. In 1995, a year after Cuesta's death, Escalante disclosed that Cuesta had shared something he thought Escalante might find of interest – that certain exiles, including one of his boat team (Herminio Diaz Garcia) had been involved in the assassination of President Kennedy.[168]

Bernardo De Torres is also known to have made friends with a close-knit circle of Americans who were supporting the exile cause, but doing so entirely outside CIA operations. These individuals were considered to be freelancers and mercenaries by U.S. Government agencies. However, they had established strong relationships with some of the more independent and aggressive of the Cuban exiles, individuals such as Felipe Vidal and Bernardo De Torres. In particular, De Torres was close to Michael Collins, Steve Wilson and Roy Hargraves; he can be found in photos with members of that group and appears to have assisted them with some of their independent missions against Cuba.

Hargraves had been involved in such efforts for years, having begun by conducting military training for some of the most conservative of the exile groups, such as the Authentico Party and AAA, groups associated with Sanchez Arango, Dr. Tony Varona (of the Roselli assassination project) and Manuel Artime. In 1963 Hargraves had led a successful mission into Cuba, capturing two fishing boats, winning a running gun battle with Castro patrol vessels and extracting his team and the Cuban boats to the Bahamas, causing immense political furor in doing so. Hargraves became quite close personally to Felipe Vidal, later, following Vidal's capture and execution, Hargraves would go on to organize an abortive effort to stimulate a false provocation attack on Guantanamo Naval base.

Vidal himself had tried his hand at organizing a provocation against Guantanamo in 1963, one using at least one B-26 bomber. His effort had been leaked to the CIA via their informant, Frank Fiorini/Sturgis. FBI and CIA documents confirm that Vidal was in Dallas in the fall of 1963 and that he was associated with anti-Castro Americans including a close association with Hargraves. Vidal was described as impetuous and unpredictable, a lone player not involved with other groups but known to all of them. The reports also discuss a mission organized around two boats owned by Hargraves and Vidal – the boats Rubio and Four Jays (one equipped with a 55 mm tank gun). The mission failed due to a suspicious fire on one of the boats; it was to be accompanied by photojournalist Dickey Chappell.[169]

TRIP-WIRE IN MIAMI:

Largely due to the constraints placed on Gaeton Fonzi during the HSCA inquiry and the difficulty of doing research among the exile community, it is unlikely that the leads originated by Fonzi will ever be further developed. We are unlikely to learn further detail about De Torres and his possible knowledge of events in Dallas.

Still, there is a bit more to the De Torres story that can be told. That story suggests that, if nothing else, he played a very active (and a very well connected) role in stalemating investigation of exile participation in the JFK conspiracy. He appears to have served almost as a "trip wire," being in a position to identify anyone who came to Miami with such interests. And the first person to seriously do so appears to have been New Orleans District Attorney Jim Garrison. Garrison's investigators were looking for Miami sources who might be able to help them identify certain mysterious Cubans who had been reported with Lee Oswald in New Orleans during the summer of 1963. Garrison needed some very low profile, yet well connected help, in that search. And after a number of referrals his investigators ended up with none other than Bernardo De Torres.

It appears that Garrison's people first contacted De Torres in December 1966, and he began actively working for them (on a paid basis) in January 1967. This meant that any very early knowledge of Garrison's JFK investigation (highly secret at that point in time) could well have come from De Torres himself. That becomes important in light of the fact that one of the first and most ambitious efforts to tilt Garrison towards a Cuban conspiracy came via information placed by John Roselli. That effort began in December 1966.

Roselli eventually met with Garrison in Las Vegas and tried to sway him to a Castro conspiracy. But well before that, Roselli had managed to place explosive conspiracy information in Washington. His story was provided to Earl Warren, the Secret Service, the FBI, President Johnson, and Drew Pearson. Roselli told them of a CIA sponsored Castro assassination team which had been turned on Kennedy by Castro. Roselli offered details and names and put himself as a key element of the real CIA Castro assassination project both before and after the Bay of Pigs. His credentials were impeccable in that regard.

When it eventually appeared in Pearson's column, the Roselli story was described as an "H Bomb" but *its circulation to Earl Warren and Federal law enforcement agencies had also served as a test of whether President Johnson and the Government would respond to new information on the Kennedy assassination.* The Roselli effort and its permutations are discussed at length in *Someone Would Have Talked.* As a test it established on thing quite consistently – nobody was going to bite. Nobody, not Warren, the FBI, the Secret Service nor the President was going to wade back into the issue of conspiracy, regardless of how dramatic the "evidence" or the credibility of its source (and Johnson knew all about Roselli, having ordered Richard Helms to brief him on that full Castro assassination project story; Helms had complied).

Roselli's preemptive effort certainly worked and when his story appeared in Pearson's widely read column, it pointed any conspiracy suspicions towards

Castro. From that point on, in private, Johnson would speak about Kennedy most likely being murdered by Castro, as a response to U.S. assassination attempts against him. Whether or not Johnson actually believed that, it made a very intuitive and credible sound byte whenever the subject of conspiracy might arise.[170]

As far as Garrison's investigation went, it's fair to say that his connection with De Torres provided him nothing except false leads and some much undesired publicity. First, De Torres was asked to identify an individual in a photo with Oswald and he responded with the name Roberto Verdeguer, an individual who in no way resembled the man. Roberto and his brother had been close to Fidel Castro; Roberto had been Chief of the Cuban Air Force until his defection just before the Bay of Pigs. His brother had been reported as smuggling weapons in for Castro before the revolution, associated with Eladio Del Valle. However, both brothers had defected and represented themselves as having become opposed to Castro. But word had circulated in Miami that given their history with Castro, they might well be undercover agents. The best that can be said, given the lack of any actual resemblance to the man Garrison was seeking, is that this might have been a quick effort to point Garrison towards Castro and secret agents, to snag Garrison in the "Castro did it" scenario. Garrison himself would tell the HSCA that he felt De Torres was one of his only sources of misinformation and that whatever he had provided never went anywhere.

De Torres had an even more significant impact on Garrison and his investigation, that of unwanted publicity. Invoices for payments to a Miami detective (De Torres) would surface in the Garrison investigation in New Orleans. In Miami, on February 17 and February 22 De Torres himself made highly public statements about the Garrison inquiry, about Garrison's interest in Cubans. De Torres was featured in a series of highly visible media statements in Miami papers, alerting the Cuban community to Garrison's investigation and expressing a belief in it – an investigation that he stated that he felt would be successful and would lead directly back to Fidel Castro.

BACK TO THE BASICS:
Attwood and Schlesinger came to worry that word of the Kennedy/Castro approach might have leaked down through the CIA, to certain officers and the Cuban exiles that they had been working with in anti-Castro activities. HSCA investigator Gaeton Fonzi has written about traces of just such a leak in Miami, evidence that word had indeed trickled down to Miami, to exiles who could indeed have received word from CIA Operations officers such as Rip Robertson and David Morales. It appears that independent exiles such as Felipe Vidal might have gotten that word, which they passed on, warning that the exiles might shortly have their feet cut out from under them with some sort of compromise between the Kennedy administration and Castro. Of course all this is something we are unlikely to find in any document; it would

have been hard enough to investigate even immediately after the assassination.

In that regard, it is interesting that the HSCA took the trouble to note the apparent failure of the CIA Miami Station to investigate the possible involvement of radical exiles in a conspiracy against President Kennedy. Station chief Ted Shackley refused to make any comment on the subject. Then again we have seen that Shackley seems to have suffered a great deal of "memory loss" and it seems we should not place too much faith in what he did and didn't say. Much more importantly we now know that at least one former station officer described orders from Station supervisor Warren Frank to work their exile contacts for any possible indications of exile involvement. In addition, the station's Cuban intelligence group (the former AMOTs), then in charge of David Morales' friend Tony Sforza were tasked with participating in the investigation and that the overall effort had been specifically ordered by Station chief Shackley.

The officers were given a comprehensive list of areas for their investigation – any exile that had disappeared or gone out of contact immediately before or after the assassination, any exiles who might have requested sizable funds, weapons or cars. Lists were to be prepared of radical exiles, of Cuban-Americans capable of funding or orchestrating an attack on the President or provoking an armed conflict with Cuba. Particular attention was to be given to listing individuals capable of funding such efforts. *It would seem that someone within the Agency, if not Shackley himself, had good reason to suspect that something might have indeed gone "terribly wrong" and that they had a very good grasp of where and what they should be concerned about.*

We have other examples of such internal investigations being ordered within the Agency, during the Garrison investigation, during the Congressional committee inquiry into political assassinations, but each and every time CIA staff recalls making the inquiries they also recall things that never seem to show up on actual reports or documents, at least ones placed in the files. And of course we have no written indication of what JMWAVE investigation described here actually produced, the officer stated that lists and reports were indeed compiled and submitted but whatever they contained remains a mystery.[171]

The reality of the situation is simple, anyone who wishes to trace a CIA incited or supported conspiracy beyond this point is moving into a "wilderness of mirrors," they will not find documents (although such might have once existed), they will not find investigative reports or even notes; it simply won't happen. Anyone naïve enough to expect such documents still exist should examine the documentation left by such CIA projects as MKULTRA or the various Castro assassination efforts discussed earlier in this work.

Beyond that, we also can't expect to find written confirmation from the actual participants or legal confessions. A culture of deniability had evolved within the CIA, a very dangerous culture. We offered the insight from the Church Committee report that communications was so convoluted, so intentionally vague and so circumlocutory (to ensure deniability) that even with documented executive actions, it was impossible to find an origin, an actual order or a directive. President Kennedy himself was stunned when he found that his remarks about getting rid of the Diem regime had led to the murder of the Diem brothers.

The various political assassinations/murders we have examined also reflect another facet of the culture of deniability that had become embedded within the Agency and within "Special Operations" – the use of surrogates. From Guatemala in 1954 to the Bay of Pigs in 1961 on to special operations against North Vietnam through the 1960's and finally in Nicaragua in the 1970's it would be exiles, rebels, even in some cases mercenaries who would "carry the ball" in paramilitary actions. And when it came to deadly covert acts, such as the assassination of Patrice Lumumba or Fidel Castro, the people carrying the poisons or the rifles would certainly not be U.S. citizens, not CIA officers. The CIA employees would be in the office, at the radio, on the sidelines. If possible, in the really serious actions, such as assassination, they would make sure that evidence was left, evidence pointing to someone else, if at all possible towards the Russians. We have seen the guideline for that in the few personal notes left us by William Harvey, on the ZRRIFLE project. Of course we would not have seen even that if Harvey had not kept his own notes and if they had not survived two apparent attempts to recover them via break-ins and burglaries at his residences after his retirement and his death.

Finally, if worst came to worst, as with Trujillo, Diem and even Lumumba, the Agency was able to rely on its final fall back position (one reflected in the CIA's position offered in response to Congressional committee inquiries on assassinations) – "well we might have been in contact with the people that did it but we didn't order them to do it, they acted on their own initiative" so "we" really didn't kill anyone.

In going beyond this point we venture into a "wilderness of mirrors," we have to either adjust our expectations and standards for proof or decide to play it safe and just buy the cover story. But that doesn't mean there won't be a trail of some sort. And we will find that there is such a trail in the JFK assassination. But that trail runs through people, not through a nice clean chain of forensics evidence. So let's get on with it.

16   ROOTS OF CONSPIRACY

One of the things that make it difficult to trace the "passing of the word" is that there had been considerable anger in the exile community for the better part of a year prior to the President's murder. The first solid report of any actual effort to attack Kennedy came after the release of the Cuban Brigade from Cuba, during a December, 1962 ceremony in Miami's Orange Bowl. The ceremony featured a welcome speech and presentation of the Brigade flag by the President. Police reports and newspaper articles of the time reveal that there was a report of a potential sniper at the Orange Bowl, a young Cuban exile armed with a rifle, in addition a dynamite bomb was found in the vicinity of the Presidents motorcade route to the stadium.

Beyond that, the Kennedy administration's decision to shut down exile groups operating from U.S. territory triggered great anger in the Miami Cuban community and among prominent leaders of the Cuban Revolutionary Council (CRC). That decision was triggered by the ongoing Alpha 66 and Comandos "L" raids into Cuba, raids focused on Russian ships and personnel. In particular, the March "Baku" attack by Tony Cuesta, (apparently accompanied by Bernardo De Torres) and his Comandos "L" team received major *LIFE* magazine coverage and put particular pressure on the President. The new administration policy also caused the Cuban Revolutionary Council to scrap plans for setting up a military training camp in the New Orleans area (that effort had begun in 1962), with the intention of moving it outside of the heavy media coverage of such training in south Florida. The plan for the New Orleans camp was scrapped when the Administration began cracking down on all independent exile military activities. As government funding and support began to be withdrawn from the Council, its head, Tony Varona, was particularly biting in his denunciation of the President. For all practical purposes, the CRC effectively disintegrated during the spring of 1963.

Another difficulty is presented by the fact that the idea of an attack on the President, one placing the blame on Fidel Castro, had begun to circulate almost immediately following the negotiated compromise of the Cuban missile crisis. As early as October 1962, documents show a CIA informant in Guatemala reported a conversation between purported Castro agents, which included discussion of a planned attack on Kennedy. Letters from Miami, addressed to an off shore, CIA supported anti-Castro radio station appeared to confirm the plot. An extensive FBI investigation failed to substantiate any element of the story and there was suspicion that the whole thing was a propaganda effort targeting Cuba (given David Phillips ongoing involvement in anti-Castro propaganda it is possible that this, as well as the Alpha 66 Russian attacks may simply represent another facet of Phillips/Bishop's personal effort to "put Kennedy's back against the wall"). Interestingly, a completely independent source also reports that talk of a "provocation" attack against Kennedy began among Alpha 66 members in late 1962 and that certain of its associates began searching for a potential "patsy" who could be linked to Castro as early as the spring of 1963.[172]

Separating strong talk and incidents from the "trickle down" of the Kennedy/Castro negotiation message is difficult, but if Escalante's information from Felipe Vidal is accepted, it does offer us a clue. Vidal reportedly stated that he spent much time in the summer and early fall of 1963 trying to get across the urgent message to certain of his fellow exiles, of trying to convince them that Kennedy was not just restraining them but involved in a dialog that would truly shut the door on all their efforts. This suggests that Vidal himself only got the word sometime after the TILT mission in June.

It may well be that the early indications of a Castro outreach were discussed in the April meeting, in Florida, between Harvey and Roselli (with Morales likely in attendance). It would have provoked strong emotions but at that point the whole thing was extremely tentative, just a warning sign. But in a June 6 Special Group meeting, there was discussion of "various possibilities of establishing channels of communication to Castro." The meeting notes show that the discussion was characterized as a "useful endeavor," indicating at least tacit support from the groups recognized head, Robert Kennedy. Given RFK's intense emotional antipathy towards Castro (Rafael Quintero relates a story in which Kennedy told him he was obsessed with getting even with the Cuban leader because Castro had humiliated him and his brother); such conversation would have certainly signaled a serious change in direction. And within two weeks of that meeting, Harvey asked Roselli to come back to Washington for a private meeting, immediately prior to Harvey's departure to Rome.

We have no real insight into the content of that meeting, even Harvey's biographer remarked that it seemed to be impromptu, that the Harveys were already staying at a neighbor's house (in preparation for their move) and Roselli also ended up staying the night at the neighbors. Interestingly, as a further indication of the actual closeness between Harvey and Angleton, the FBI observed Roselli arriving in Washington and being picked up by Harvey. The agent tailing Roselli immediately reported the sighting to the FBI's CIA liaison, Sam Papich. At the time, Papich happened to be visiting his CIA contact, James Angleton. Angleton determined that Harvey and Roselli would be dining at a restaurant in downtown Washington and called the restaurant to talk with Harvey. After their conversation, he told Sam Papich, his FBI long-time friend, it would be best to "go easy" on the contact between Harvey and Roselli.[173]

Also in June, the TILT project would have to have validated Martino's commitment and connections to both Robertson and Morales. While speculative, it's reasonable to think that the process of "trickle down" began with word passed through Martino by the end of June, at least with remarks to his closest personal exile friend Felipe Vidal.

But at that point in time there was no specific "conspiracy," only talk, only emotion. It may well be that the CIA officers involved in passing the word felt that would be enough; they knew the effect it would have on the people they had trained and supported over the previous three years. And indeed, all involved would have understood that any action against the President would have to be staged so as to point towards Castro, otherwise they would be dooming their own cause. Given that, it is logical to assume that as of July and August, the gating factor would be to find a suitable "patsy."

CONNECTING WITH LEE HARVEY OSWALD:

Oswald's personal story is long and complex, however, for our purpose we need to focus on his activities beginning in the summer 1963, when he became involved in a variety of activities that publicly established him as a Castro supporter, a Fair Play for Cuba Committee (FPCC) activist and as someone working against the anti-Castro exiles; having attempted to infiltrate at least one exile group in New Orleans. A strong case can be made that Oswald's activities were leveraged to support intelligence collection as well as a propaganda initiative against the Fair Play for Cuba Committee (FPCC), an initiative in support of the new AMWORLD/Artime autonomous group effort that was to be moved to Latin America.

The basic fact that Oswald became knowingly involved in intelligence activities is revealed in his willingness to change "personas" as needed. As an example, following his return from the Soviet Union, Oswald had drafted a lengthy manuscript on his experiences in Russia and his own fundamental beliefs. That manuscript contained the following:

> "The Communist Party of the United States has betrayed itself! It has turned itself into the traditional lever of a foreign power to overthrow the government of the United States., not in the name of freedom or high ideals, but in servile conformity to the wishes of the Soviet Union…The Soviets have committed crimes unsurpassed… imprisonment of their own peoples (sic)…mass extermination… The Communist movement in the United States of America has turned itself into a "valuable god coin" of the Kremlin. It has failed to denounce any actions of the Soviet Government when similar actions of the United States government bring pious protest. (I have) many personal reasons to know and therefore hate and mistrust Communism."

Yet by August 1963, Oswald was sending letters to the Communist Party of the United States (CPUSA) and the Socialist Workers Party. Those letters described his planned move to the Washington D.C. area and offered his services to both organizations. In a letter of August, 28 to the CPUSA he described being persecuted by the FBI and asked for advise on whether or not he should go "underground." More letters were written on September 1, asking for instructions on how to contact CPUSA and SWP representatives following his imminent relocation to the Baltimore/Washington area. Later, at the end of September, Oswald reportedly presented forged CPUSA identification on a visit to the Cuban embassy in Mexico City.

Oswald had become well known to the Cuban exiles in New Orleans that August, and had gotten media visibility as a Castro supporter in newspaper, radio and even television news coverage. His pro-Castro, FPCC leafleting was captured in several news photos, the leafleting was brief, as Carlos Bringuier (whose shop was a block or so away) and others arrived quickly to confront Oswald – reportedly calls were placed to the newspapers with tips about the incident. Although not often mentioned, Oswald was accompanied by two other young men who were also passing out leaflets. The men had been hired by Oswald to help, further creating the impression of an actual FPCC chapter (at the time Oswald had neither job nor income for that or for printing leaflets). The court appearance of Bringuier and Oswald was covered by local television stations, and it is of interest to note that one of the Cuban exiles attending the hearing was Augustin Guitart, Sylvia Odio's uncle and a close friend of Tony Varona, who reportedly visited and stayed with Guitart in November of 1963.

Oswald's pro-Cuba activities received extensive attention and promotion by the Information Council of the America (INCA), which circulated its materials throughout Latin America. INCA was experienced and active in anti-Castro and anti-Communist media activities. The CIA (and David Phillips) had utilized INCA publications in its pre-Bay of Pigs propaganda efforts. While not directly funded by the Agency, CIA officers had contacts with is members." INCA was heavily involved in orchestrating and using Oswald's media appearances during the summer of 1963; it had even prepared a record containing Oswald's remarks (using him as an example of how Americans could be duped by the Communists and Castro) and at the time of the Kennedy assassination, INCA was preparing to widely promote the record as a counter to Castro's growing influence on potential radicals.[174]

There is also considerable evidence suggesting that certain of the New Orleans exiles, including Carlos Bringuier and Carlos Quiroga, may well have suspected that Oswald was engaged in a "doubles" game, appearing as a fervent Castro supporter when in truth he was being monitored by American intelligence agencies. Bringuier (a long time associate of Tony Varona) and Quiroga (initially suspected by the CIA and FBI as a potential Cuban double agent) became extremely active following the assassination, promoting the idea that Oswald had been acting for Fidel Castro.

It should also be noted that David Phillips was reported to have been involved in developing anti-Castro propaganda in New Orleans before the Bay of Pigs and that he himself would likely have been very much aware of propaganda activities going on in New Orleans in 1963. At that time Bringuier was very involved with the Cuban Student Directorate (DRE) and DRE propaganda had been mentored by Phillips, just as its military operations had been under the review of David Morales. Even more interestingly, David Phillips admitted knowing and having contact with Warren DeBrueys, the FBI subversive's desk agent in New Orleans. And there is considerable circumstantial evidence indicating that DeBrueys himself was in contact with Lee Oswald in the summer of 1963, very possibly in an attempt to use him as an informant in the FBI's crackdown on the more militant local exiles, including associates of Bringuier's DRE group.[175]

During 1963 routine reports on DRE activities and contacts in New Orleans should have been going to their CIA case officer George Joannides (whose specialties were propaganda and psyops). Oswald's apparent attempt to infiltrate the group, the street confrontation, the televised court hearings and the radio debate would all have been major news for such reports. Yet, as Jefferson Morley has found, no mention of Oswald appears in any of the CIA's DRE records (while those same records are full of much more trivial matters). The absence of any mention of those New Orleans events is especially curious since the CIA's own mission for the DRE (AMSPELL) focused on "political action, propaganda, intelligence collection and hemisphere-wide" activities – a mission in conformance with the assignment given to David Phillips by SAS chief Desmond Fitzgerald. Fitzgerald put Phillips in charge of Cuban operations in the fall of 1963, responsible for just such activities.[176]

It is possible that Phillips might not have been initially involved in the New Orleans activities of Oswald, the DRE, and INCA. But Phillips himself admitted that, as a sort of CIA guru on psyops and propaganda, he had served as a consultant on such operations within the Agency. Specifically, Phillips ran anti-Castro propaganda operations in 1963; he admitted to that responsibly in a sworn deposition, although preferring to describe himself as "a consultant." Then again Phillips was a man famous within the Agency for not "leaving fingerprints" on his operations.[177]

It strains credulity to think that Phillips would not have been aware of what was happening with Oswald, the FPCC, and the DRE in New Orleans in the summer of 1963. It also strains credulity that none of the DRE records mention any of the New Orleans activities – but then again the ARRB was unable to locate any of the monthly DRE reports that were prepared from December 1962 through April 1964. And some 33 known files on the subject are still being fiercely withheld in the face of legal action to release them, as of 2011.[178]

Based on a good deal of New Orleans research, including work by first generation skeptic and Warren Commission critic, Harold Weisberg, as well as by DA Garrison's investigators, we do know that while in New Orleans, Oswald came into contact with certain unknown Cubans/Mexicans. These people were not locally known and were never successfully identified. Bringuier described them as "Mexican Communists" but in reality they were likely something very different. Our clues to exactly who they represented come from two sources, John Martino and Richard Case Nagell; neither man knew the other and information from each independently corroborates the other.[179]

Following the Kennedy murder (which he had spoken of in advance to his family), John Martino described having seen Lee Oswald while in New Orleans that August. He spoke as if he had merely observed him handing out leaflets, however, Oswald's two known leafleting outings occurred before Martino's scheduled speaking appearance in New Orleans (also of interest is the fact that Oswald wrote to the FPCC of his leafleting and his encounter with anti-Castro exiles before that event actually occurred, suggesting that Oswald was indeed cooperating in some type of propaganda operation against the FPCC). In his final remarks to his friends, acknowledging a conspiracy against Kennedy in which he had played a supporting role, Martino stated that the exiles had identified Oswald as a patsy and approached him as if they were Castro agents. At that point they were also quite aware that Oswald was engaged in an intelligence activity and essentially manipulated him with full knowledge of his double role.

Richard Case Nagell's story is much longer and more detailed, far too detailed to cover or support here but that is done in references cited. Nagell related that he had come to know Oswald in Japan when both men were assigned there; Nagell was in Army counter intelligence. He had been introduced to Oswald when Oswald had reported to his superiors having been approached by a bar girl probing for information; following that Oswald was used in a type of dangle to the Communist sponsored bar girls in a couple of Tokyo locations which catered to American servicemen. Nagell had also become associated with a senior CIA officer in Tokyo, a man whom he would later encounter in Mexico City in 1962. That individual, working under deep cover in Mexico City, had connected with Nagell and used him in a variety of assignments, as a completely cut out CIA asset. Such an arrangement would have been completely consistent with Mexico City operations as all covert activities had to be totally compartmentalized from the operation of the Mexico City station. Such procedures are described in the CIA's own history of the Mexico City station, previously referenced.

Nagell's activities involved various Cuban targets in both Mexico and the United States, among them were certain specific Cuban exiles and their associates and certain FPCC organizations, particularly the very active groups in New York and California. Nagell told author Dick Russell that in pursuit of various assignments he re-contacted Lee Oswald and that Oswald's initial FPCC contacts were actually in support of Nagell's own efforts. It appears highly possible that Oswald's FPCC activities may have been successful enough to bring him directly to the attention of CIA officers involved in their own propaganda operations against the FPCC.

What we also know from Nagell is that during the summer of 1963 he lost contact with his CIA connection and found himself on his own, and the subject of attention of a number of Cuban exiles who had become quite suspicious of him. Further research has led some researchers (Larry Hancock and Dick Russell) to conclude that Nagell's CIA contact may have been Henry Hecksher, an individual initially discussed for his participation in PBSUCCESS. We also know that Hecksher had been brought into the Cuba project from assignments in SE Asia (following a Tokyo assignment), but his actual detailed Cuba project activities are totally unknown, until the point at which he was assigned as head of the AMWORLD project in the summer of 1963. Among other aspects of that assignment, which involved exile leader Manuel Artime, it is known that AMWORLD personnel were concerned about Artime's contacts with certain old-line Prior-era Cuba politicians, such as Tony Varona and Rolando Masferrer. Interestingly, Nagell's remarks on the exiles he was assigned to investigate are a perfect match for those concerns and such an investigation would have to have been done with an outsider, someone totally unknown to the exile communities in New York, Miami and New Orleans – making Nagell a perfect fit for the assignment he describes.

For our immediate purpose, the most important revelation from Nagell was that he observed Oswald in New Orleans, in contact with two Cubans, at least one known to Nagell. Those Cubans were representing themselves as Castro agents and recruiting Oswald for a trip to the Washington area in September. We have independent corroboration of such activity in Oswald's own letters to the CPUSA and SWP about such a move; in particular, his letter to the Communist Party USA. That letter, mentioning "going underground," created an interesting change in image for Oswald, moving him from a political activist towards something much more radical. Nagell attempted to call Oswald off, telling him that the "Cubans" were actual anti-Castro exiles and they were manipulating him. Nagell could not understand why Oswald refused to break off contact with them but shortly afterwards Nagell became aware that the Cubans had determined he himself was a threat and he left New Orleans, essentially on the run.

What Nagell himself did not seem to suspect, was that Oswald might have been recruited into an intelligence dangle specifically designed to identify either radical exiles or actual Castro agents. By the summer of 1963 the FBI itself was just as concerned with exiles attempting to wage military action as they were with Cuban spies, both were considered as "subversives" and there is persuasive evidence that Oswald was in touch with the FBI while in New Orleans. Such a role would explain Oswald's decision not to break contact with the exiles described by Nagell. And as to something planned for Washington, we have further confirmation that Oswald was indeed planning that move and that it wasn't to go job hunting.

As Marina Oswald was packing for her move back to Dallas, to reside with Ruth Paine in the time before the birth of her second child, she received a visit from a Quaker mother and daughter (alerted by Ruth) who were helping her pack. Lee Oswald struck up a conversation with the younger woman and mentioned an upcoming trip to Washington D.C. The girl asked him the purpose of his trip. He seemed unprepared for that question and became flustered, making a remark about going there "to get a gun." What neither Marina or anyone else close to Oswald at that time knew was he had also, on September 17, applied for and received a 15 day tourist permit for travel to Mexico, valid for the next 90 days. One can only speculate on the combination of something being planned for Washington D.C. and Oswald's possession of a Mexican visa.[180]

Oswald's trip/move to Washington never happened, very possibly because the exiles felt that Nagell might have reported what was going on and called it off. They had no way of knowing that Nagell had lost contact with his CIA "handler" and that the only thing he could do at the time was send a written warning to FBI Director Hoover. The saga of that warning letter is a story in itself; of course it was never confirmed by the Bureau. But immediately after the assassination, an FBI headquarters officer from Washington, questioned Marina Oswald about Oswald's travel to Washington and Mexico, suggesting that there had indeed been something in Oswald's file about Washington.[181]

THE KENNEDY CONSPIRACY – EARLY SEPTEMBER 1963:
The best picture that we can draw is that during August and September, word was circulating there was a major problem between the exiles and JFK. Of course a limited number of individuals were on board with the new AMWORLD/Artime project but even that was being positioned as totally divorced from U.S. Government support, so it brought the administration no general good will. Even Artime's recruiting personal efforts, targeting exiles within the U.S. Army and Air Force, were disguised as totally unsupported by the U.S. government (although Artime was fully supported and heavily funded by the U.S.). Within the overall exile discontent, certain individuals had been given a much worse picture of the President, one not just of neglect but one of active and ongoing betrayal. In response, those individuals had decided that the President must be eliminated and that to do so the act would have to be laid at the feet of Fidel Castro and his agents.

Word had been passed and certain of the most radical and independent exiles appear to have begun to plan a move against President Kennedy during September and early October. We see evidence of that in reports of an attempt to patsy Lee Oswald and involve in some action in Washington D.C. There is also a suggestion that certain exiles traveling to Chicago posed a threat to the President during a planned motorcade and appearance there in October.

By the end of August, in New Orleans, Lee Harvey Oswald had just become one of the most visible and high profile pro-Cuba activists. Oswald not only promoted his own activities with the media but both local Cuban exiles such as Bringuier and the INCA media group made sure that Oswald got maximum news coverage. Even "spontaneous" events, such as Oswald's leafleting confrontation, received media coverage, apparently due to calls to local newspapers. Then again, it's likely that the incident was not all that spontaneous, since Oswald himself had written about it to the FPCC, before it occurred. Even the police were suspicious. New Orleans police Lt. Francis Martello stated that Oswald "seemed to have set them up, so to speak, to create an incident, but when the incident occurred he remained absolutely peaceful and gentle."[182]

The exiles in New Orleans were well connected to key people in Miami; Bringuier was in contact with the CIA, and the DRE (AMSPELL) was monitored in ongoing reports by their CIA case officer. Beyond that, Bringuier was a long time associate of Tony Varona and various exiles from Miami frequented his home during their travels. A number of anti-Castro Americans and exiles had been traveling to New Orleans beginning in the fall of 1962, first in an abortive attempt to set up a CRC training camp but later to put together missions against Cuba. By the summer of 1963, the FBI was actively involved in monitoring exile activities in New Orleans and confiscating weapons and explosives.[183]

Lee Oswald was identified to people in Miami, approached by exiles posing as Castro agents and even observed by John Martino. They knew he was being used by U.S. intelligence agencies and that was a risk. He had to be contacted by individuals not readily recognizable by the locals. Oswald himself was posing as being pro-Castro, anti-Castro, both making statements in support of Cuba for the media and talking about eliminating Fidel Castro in more private conversations. He was all over the map, but nobody was being picked up for talking to him; that would have ended his use as a "dangle." And that was certainly a fine background for using him as a "patsy" in a conspiracy. It indicated that Oswald would "cooperate" to maintain himself in circulation (something that greatly frustrated Nagell). Oswald's letters to the Communist Party USA (including his query about going underground) and the Socialist Workers Party illustrate some level of cooperation. But something happened (most likely Richard Case Nagell's appearance in New Orleans) and whatever was being discussed for Washington D.C. was aborted. Things had gotten too "hot" in New Orleans.

But the conspiracy itself seems to have evolved a great deal as September passed. One reason for that may be that the Kennedy/Castro negotiations literally "reignited" after several months of being in abeyance. Attwood called Howard, volunteering his services though the U.N. to connect with the Cubans. A number of memos were exchanged within the State Department and JFK again expressed his support. By September 24, Attwood himself had met with the President and received approval for a new initiative. He had also met socially with Cuban U.N. representative Lechuga at a private cocktail party at Lisa Howard's apartment; Lechuga had invited Attwood to Cuba for talks. Anyone monitoring the situation (and Howard's apartment and telephone) would have been privy to the new, fast paced developments. On September 13, the news of JFK's fall trip to Texas was announced. And during late September, John Martino's travels took him both to New Orleans and Dallas. Any leak of an actual pending meeting between JFK's personal representative and Fidel Castro would have taken matters to a new level, adding intense time pressure and very possibly bringing about full scale commitment for a plan to attack JFK in Texas.

In this same time frame, someone looking a great deal like Lee Oswald was reported as having been in Texas. In one incident a high profile, former arms buyer and smuggler for Castro was visited; "Oswald" tried to obtain guns from him and then specifically asked for a scope equipped high caliber rifle, offering several times the going price for one in any gun shop in Texas. In another incident "Oswald" (when not present), was described to a well connected woman exile as an ex-Marine, an expert marksman…except you never knew how to take him, he could do anything…kill Castro…he thinks we (the exiles) should have shot President Kennedy after the Bay of Pigs"…and that we still should. "Oswald" was traveling in company with some rather mysterious exiles, people who clearly were not exactly who they claimed to be.

Of the two incidents, the attempted gun incident is perhaps the more significant, not only because it would have positioned Oswald in a much more "militant" character (especially following his letter to CPUSA about going underground) but because the effort was directed towards a man closely associated with Castro, someone Fidel had even taken the trouble to visit on a trip to the United States, following the revolution. Oswald's true name was used in the incident and later the former gun smuggler, Robert McKewon, would tell Dick Russell that he had recognized the Cuban with "Oswald;" he had been someone from the days of the Castro revolution, he had seen him while smuggling guns into Fidel's forces. Beyond that, the incident associated Oswald with an individual who would later come to national prominence in Dallas, Jack Ruby (Rubenstein). Back in 1959, Jack Ruby had been very much interested in doing business in Cuba, in sales to Castro, and perhaps in doing favors for some of the Havana gambling figures who had come under intense pressure after the revolution. He had contacted McKewon repeatedly, trying to gain introductions to Castro and his people. If information, provided by Martino and his friends, after the assassination had been taken at face value, information painting both Oswald and Ruby as agents for Fidel Castro, the McKewon connections would have in themselves been explosive and Oswald might have been viewed as being sent to McKewon by Ruby. Certainly there would have been ample information to connect Ruby to smuggling, to weapons dealing and to a serious interest in Cuba.[184]

As for Oswald himself, things would get even more confusing as during the two months prior to the assassination. He appears to have been impersonated on different occasions and would be reported in multiple places at the same time in both October and November. That, along with the recruitment of Jack Ruby to support conspiracy operations in Dallas, suggests that the conspiracy had developed into something much more sophisticated, with more knowledgeable people involved. By the end of September, it appears that the Kennedy conspiracy had come under professional direction. CIA officers were moving from incitement to assistance "advisors", a change that became even more obvious in October.

Unfortunately, starting in New Orleans, we have to deal with tracing and separating the strands that were being woven around Lee Oswald. One thread involves his use as an intelligence dangle, quite possibly providing information to both the FBI on Cuban exiles by participating first in propaganda and then later even more complex intelligence games by the CIA. The second thread involves actions being taken by the conspiracy to position Oswald as increasingly radicalized, enough so that he would be accepted as a having been an active tool of Cuba and Fidel Castro. That thread also suggests that Oswald was intentionally associated with individuals suspected with having ties to Castro and to Cuban intelligence activities.[185]

17 HIGH STRANGENESS IN MEXICO CITY

Less than two months before the assassination, rather than immediately following his pregnant (and soon to deliver) wife to Dallas, "Oswald" did indeed make a trip to Mexico. A trip not announced to either his family or the woman Marina Oswald would be staying with in Dallas. In fact, at the time of his family's departure from New Orleans he was talking about a trip to Washington.

Superficially, "Oswald's" activities in Mexico City were straight forward, limited and basically fruitless. When all the reports are put together, they picture Oswald having become frustrated with his contacts with the Soviet embassy in New York. He had written several letters to the embassy during the spring broaching the return of Marina to Russia, with or without himself. But then with Marina soon to have a second child, he decided to go to Mexico City and appeal to the Cubans to grant him a travel visa to go through Cuba to Russia – although his wife and family don't seem to have been a major factor in that request. Oswald had traveled internationally previously and should have been well aware that his chances of getting a Cuban transit visa were slim at best; first of all it would have violated the U.S. law against their citizens travel to Cuba, second he had no "sponsor" for Cuban travel. It is known that the Cuban embassy was granted travel visas to very specific individuals, those endorsed by the FPCC and members of the Communist Party USA (CPUSA). However, those arrangements had to be made well in advance.

Oswald had no such endorsements, although he did present the Cubans with materials concerning his FPCC activities and reportedly also a CPUSA membership card. The card immediately brought him under suspicion since it was well known that CPUSA issued no such identification. Worse yet, Oswald, international traveler that he was, had not even thought to bring along a photo for his Cuban visa travel request. At that point Oswald went to get his photograph taken (the photograph exists; it shows a nice, neatly dressed Oswald) and it does not match the description of his clothing or appearance later given by Cuban embassy staff. At that point, he was told once again he simply could not be granted a visa, but if he already had Soviet travel papers it might be a different matter. Then, Oswald went to the Soviet embassy, made a plea for papers and returned to the Cubans saying that everything was fine.

The Cuban secretary (Sylvia Duran), obviously not trusting Oswald at that point, called the Soviets and was told that in no way were things fine. However, they offered to allow Oswald to make an application and mail it to New York for approval, but he had not even taken the form. Things became tense and Oswald left the Cuban embassy, only to visit the Russians the following day (Saturday), catching an embassy officer coming in to play volleyball and making another fruitless plea. At that point Oswald supposedly gave it all up as a bad deal, hung out in Mexico City for a couple more days and then headed on to Dallas.

At first blush, Oswald's behavior sounds both inconsistent and disjointed, but the above story was sufficient for the Warren Commission following the assassination. Upon closer examination the story gets far more complex. It takes us into the middle of intelligence activities continuing around Lee Oswald, some of which he may have been aware of and some he most definitely was not, demonstrated by the need to impersonate him in Mexico City. One conclusion that can be firmly drawn is that the CIA was very much involved with Oswald around the time of his trip to Mexico City and that several senior officers consistently lied about just that for decades afterwards.

Much of the following Mexico City analysis is based in primary research performed by Professors John Newman and Peter Dale Scott as well as that of investigative reporter Jefferson Morley. Readers are referred particularly to Chapters 18-20 and the "Epilogue" of Newman's 2008 edition of *Oswald and the CIA*, as well as Chapters 17 and 18 of *Our Man in Mexico City* by Jefferson Morley. Unless otherwise noted, the following is based in Newman's and Morley's most recent work as well as in early research by Peter Dale Scott and the most current work of Bill Simpich. However, the final analysis, interpretations and conclusions are strictly the authors'.[186]

When Lee Oswald appeared at the Cuban and Russian embassies in Mexico City in October of 1963, he was entering one of the most massive intelligence operations run by the United States. The CIA's Mexico City station was well respected, regarded as one of the largest and most active resources for foreign intelligence collection, political action and covert operations – the lynchpin in United States activities against Communism and Cuba throughout Latin America.[187]

The station was opened in 1950 when the CIA was assigned responsibility for intelligence in Latin America, taking over that role from the FBI. Howard Hunt initially opened the office (in a far less than graceful fashion, involving conflicts with the U.S. Ambassador, misunderstandings with CIA headquarters and continuing arguments over responsibilities), but in 1951, Chief of Station duties were taken over by a former FBI officer. One of the stations' first intelligence collection activities was to establish a telephone tap operation and that was soon extended to telex. Initial focus was on the Russian embassy but after the Castro revolution, extensive attention was focused on the Cuban embassy and personnel. Technical intelligence would become one of the primary activities of the station. In addition to phone taps, over time the station established six separate photo safe houses for ongoing surveillance of the Russian and Cuban embassies.

Winston Scott became station chief in 1956 and the station grew dramatically; in 1960 Cuba had become the stations' primary intelligence target, taking priority over the Russians. By January of 1963, four secretaries had been added to support the technical collections against both the Soviet and Cuban embassies. Station activities concentrated on recruitment of Cuban embassy staff, placing taps on all lines and assigning case officers to handle informants and penetration agents. Eventually the Mexico City station came to support some 200 indigenous agents. By 1964 the station had 50 agents working specifically on Cuba as a target.

Initially, the station had formed an extensive double agent network targeting the Soviets and Cubans. The doubles were especially useful in identification of individuals working in and visiting the embassies but produced little concrete foreign intelligence. Because of that the stations efforts eventually switched to recruiting "access" agents, who had social or business contacts with the embassies. These individuals produced much more substantive intelligence. By 1966 the double agent effort was totally terminated.

In 1963, when Lee Oswald appeared in Mexico City, CIA station activities included:

LIKAYAK – access to international passenger lists, air shipments, spot photography of travelers, a mobile photo truck, camera installations at the airport and apparently some access to Mexican government files and mail relating to international travel.

LIFIRE – a travel monitoring operation with focus on all travel to and from Cuba; the Cubans had been found to be shipping arms to Latin America through Mexico and also sending cash through Mexico City to support arms buys and transshipment to other Latin American countries.

LIFEAT and LIENVOV – extensive telephone taps of the Russian and Cuban embassies.

LIEMBRACE – a physical surveillance capability using multiple teams including photographic embassy surveillance; the Soviet and Cuban embassies were constantly monitored with photo surveillance from six different photo safehouses. The camera monitoring the door to the Cuban embassy was also equipped with a circuit that allowed audio monitoring of visitors. The camera and audio circuit was activated as people neared the door.

A fully detailed study of Oswald's visit to Mexico City is far beyond this work. For purposes of our Kennedy conspiracy inquiry we will focus on the contacts and telephone calls relating to the Russian and Cuban embassies. These contacts can be shown to have generated the "rumors" later described by President Johnson. Johnson cited those "rumors" as having the potential to incite an atomic exchange, leaving 40 million Americans dead. That argument was used frequently in the weeks following the Kennedy assassination, to force suppression of any detailed investigation of the President's murder. It was obviously a persuasive argument but it was more likely a cover story for the real issue at hand, something known only at the level of Johnson, McCone, Bundy, Hoover and possibly CIA Deputy Director Helms. Unfortunately, the minutes and memoranda of the meetings and calls that would have exposed that issue seem to have disappeared.

DANGEROUS DETAILS – NOT RUMORS:

As we will see, there were no such "rumors" as Johnson intimated. Instead, there were certain very concrete incidents, and those incidents appear to have been quickly determined "not" to have pointed at Oswald being an agent of either the Russians or Cubans. In fact, they suggested something entirely different than the Soviet/Cuban fear that Johnson continued to use as leverage.

Lee Oswald arrived in Mexico City at 10 am on September 27, 1963. By around 11 am he was at the Cuban embassy requesting a transit visa to the Soviet Union. He presented secretary Sylvia Duran with several documents including Fair Play for Cuba materials and reportedly a fake Communist Party USA card. But Oswald carried no personal endorsement from either the FPCC or CPUSA (which did have an arrangement with Cuba to allow members to immediately get visas). He also had no personal photo, required for all visa applications (a fact known to Oswald who had routinely obtained visas for international travel on prior occasions). Oswald was informed that he must present a photo but more importantly that he would need a Soviet endorsement for transit travel.

Oswald responded by going to the Russian embassy, where he met with both embassy officers Kostikov and Nechiporenko. Both men were known to U.S. Intelligence as being probable Soviet intelligence officers (as was true of virtually all male staff of the embassy) and at the time the FBI was running a double agent against Kostikov. The agent (code name "TUMBLEWEED") had been doubled in Europe, had moved to the United States and was providing information to the FBI in regard to his contacts with Kostikov. He had already made at least one trip to Mexico City to meet with Kostikov and discuss assignments, reportedly including the collection of information for potential sabotage activities in the United States.

At the Russian embassy, Oswald made an emotional plea for a transit visa, stating that he had come to Mexico because he was afraid the FBI would arrest him for further contacts with the Russian embassy in Washington. The Russians advised him that they could give him an application form for the visa but that it would still have to go to Washington and would take months for action. Oswald did not accept their offer and neither took nor completed a request form while at the embassy on that Friday afternoon.[188]

Oswald then returned to the Cuban embassy and lied to Sylvia Duran, telling her there was no issue with his Russian visa application. Duran was skeptical as she was well aware of both Russian and Cuban visa protocols. She immediately called the Russian embassy. The call was tapped and taped by the Mexico City CIA station system and the existing transcript reveals that the Russians asked Duran for her name and number and called back shortly to tell her they could not give the man an approval in anything less than four or five months. Duran mentioned that the applicant (Oswald was not named in the call by either party) had hoped to wait in Cuba for the Russian approval but since he knew nobody in Cuba they could not give him a transit visa. At that point, on the afternoon of his first day in Mexico City, it is clear that Oswald's luck had already run out. Indeed Oswald also apparently realized it; reportedly he became excited and quarreled with one of the senior Cuban embassy staff members.

Oswald never returned to the Cuban embassy after his first day in Mexico City. Professor Newman notes in his analysis that Oswald's name was not mentioned in the Friday telephone call, so at this point there was no information available to the CIA staff which would have triggered an intelligence response specifically to Oswald.[189] Of course that assessment assumes no prior knowledge of Oswald's visit.

What occurred next was a good deal more interesting. The following day, September 28, 1963, was a Saturday and both the Russian and Cuban embassies were routinely closed on the weekends. But when Russian counsel Nechiporenko arrived at the embassy to play a regular Saturday volleyball game, Oswald was outside waiting. Again he became highly emotional, reportedly stating that the FBI might kill him if the Russians would not help. This made no impression on the Russians and they simply offered him another chance to complete an application, which they would send to Washington for him. Again, he refused.

As of Saturday morning when he left the Russian embassy, defeated in his quest, there should have been several photos of Oswald entering and leaving the two embassies. Later, the CIA would go on record as claiming there were none. That claim has proven to be highly questionable. There were photos, the cameras were working, as David Phillips slipped and revealed that at a later date. When the FBI was checking rumors of a particular individual meeting with Oswald in the Cuban embassy, Phillips responded by stating that the individual in question had not entered the embassy during the period in which Oswald was there. As of February 1964, all surveillance photos were available and had been checked; the man had not entered the embassy. Of course, if that were true, Oswald should indeed have been photographed on his own separate visits to the Cuban embassy. Why no photos of Oswald at the embassies were ever made available remains a major part of the Mexico City mystery.[190]

Matters got even stranger within an hour of Oswald's departure from the Russian embassy. At that point the phone tap system recorded a call, apparently from the Cuban embassy to the Russian embassy.[191] The transcript of that call still exists and reveals a rambling dialog, in which both a female and male (who did not identify himself by name) spoke to the Russians, with the man asking about the status of his application (which we now know that Oswald did not actually make, not even accepting a form) and the woman clearly representing herself as a Cuban embassy staff member. During the call, the male mentioned Kostikov by name and remarked that he had not supplied his address while with the Russians because he did not know it. The Cubans had that information. Such a remark would seem meaningless, unless it was interpreted that Oswald was being housed by the Cubans, or they were, in some fashion, taking special care of him.

In *Oswald and the CIA*, Newman presents a strong case that both the male and the female callers in the dialog were impersonators. Duran denied making the call and indeed she would not have been at the Cuban embassy as it was closed. This is corroborated by the fact that the CIA station staff translators, both very familiar with Duran as the desk person at the Cuban embassy, were unable to identity the woman in this call. The translator report also notes that the male caller spoke very poor, broken Russian, yet very good Spanish. Of course, Oswald's Russian was good, far better than any minimal Spanish he might have picked up.

Newman also points out that this call shows little evidence of being made with knowledge of what either Duran or Oswald had discussed previously. The woman makes no reference to Duran's earlier conversation with the Russian embassy and puts the man on directly with the Russians. The man stated that when he was at the Russian embassy he could not give them an address, because he had to get it from the Cubans. He told them he now had it and agreed to go to the Russian embassy and give it to them (which did not happen). The primary purpose of the call seems to have been to either try and connect with Kostikov, who indeed had just met with Oswald at the Russian embassy, or to at least put his name on tape. In addition, the call could be interpreted to mean that Oswald had some special relationship with the Cubans. Newman posits the call was made by someone who had Oswald under surveillance, but who was not in direct contact with him.

Sylvia Duran denied both a Saturday Embassy visit by Oswald or making a telephone call with him; Nechiporenko denied that the call could have even been received at the Russian embassy since their switchboard closed on Saturday. Newman suggests that may well be true since the supposed purported Russian on the call could easily have just asked "Oswald" for his address while on the telephone call. It is indeed possible that the entire call was made by unknown parties. Jefferson Morley points out that David Phillips actually appears to have Duran's statement altered in translation – she had firmly stated that Oswald had not visited the Cuban embassy after Friday, while the translation of her statement simply indicated that she did not recall whether a Saturday call had been made.[192]

A second call, which appears to have been another impersonation, was made on October 1 (Tuesday). *In that call, Oswald's name was mentioned and recorded.* That was the key that the translators had been advised to watch for and indicates the point at which "Oswald" was identified as the person visiting both the Russian and Cuban embassies.[193]

It would be several days, until October 9, until Mexico City officially transmitted a cable to CIA headquarters on the Oswald/Russian contact, and even then the cable only described Oswald's contact with the Russian embassy and specifically with Kostikov. The cable mentioned telephone calls and intercepts but provided no further information; at the same time a photograph of an individual who had visited the Russian embassy was sent to headquarters (the individual in the photograph was not identified as Oswald in the message and in fact was not Oswald). Mexico City requested a current photograph of Oswald but Headquarters did not actually send one until after November 22.

On October 10, CIA headquarters sent a cable to FBI, State and Navy describing the Kostikov contact and incorrectly described the individual (Oswald) as the man pictured in the photo. It identified the man as "Lee Henry Oswald" Newman points out that headquarters was very much aware that information in that cable was incorrect and incomplete and he goes into extensive detail in evaluating this as suggestive of another intelligence operation going on around Lee Oswald.

In addition to the mystery of the Saturday and Tuesday "impersonation" calls, there is also the question of at least one other likely Oswald "impersonation" call to the Russian embassy. One of the Mexico City staff translators, Mrs. Tarasof, specifically described another lengthy call, stating that the caller specifically identified himself as Lee Oswald; spoke only English and that "Oswald" asked for financial aid from the Soviets. He stated he had already asked the Cubans for financial aid. *It appears that requests for financial aid and offers of information in exchange may have been made only in the recorded telephone calls, not by Oswald in person.* Years after the assassination, both David Phillips and Thomas Kelly of the FBI (which apparently had its own access to the phone taps in Mexico City) both commented that Oswald had offered money and requested assistance in return from both the Cubans and Russians.

Mr. Tarasof, the other CIA translator, also stated that the translators had been superficially asked to try and identify the man who was contacting the Russians; it was a "hot" topic at the Mexico City station, as it had to do with a known defector. He also commented that the "missing" conversation/tape was designated as "Urgent" for priority handling – suggesting the call was an immediate operational priority within the Mexico City station and that Oswald had definitely been a person of interest to the CIA while he was in Mexico City.

CHECK THE FILES!

We have a number of anecdotes from different agencies and offices that immediately upon hearing the name of the suspected assassin broadcast from Dallas, the common reaction was to rush to the files and see if the name Oswald showed up. And of course it did, in numerous places, including a series of FBI files that contained references to a recent appearance in Mexico City and contact with a suspected KGB agent. Beyond that, somewhere at FBI headquarters were the additional files on Kostikov and "TUMBLEWEED," revealing that Kostikov was known to be running at least one double agent inside the United States. The immediate question must have been whether or not he had been running others, including the Presidential assassin? Surely that question would have been communicated to Director Hoover.

Strangely, we have no record that Hoover, or anyone else for that matter, talked to the President about Oswald having met a suspected KGB officer only weeks before the assassination. But we do have a record of the FBI Director warning the new President that Oswald had been impersonated in Mexico City!

Based on the FBI Kostikov files, an immediate suspicion that the Russians or Cubans might have been somehow involved with Oswald would have been reasonable. And that might explain a great number of things that occurred on Friday night immediately following the assassination – including calls from Washington ordering law enforcement officers in Dallas to make sure that Oswald was charged as the lone participant in the assassination and that discussion and investigation of conspiracy was to cease. It would also explain the fact that Johnson's first call from his office the next morning was to Hoover, inquiring about the situation relating to Oswald, Mexico City and the Russian Embassy.

That Hoover was talking with Johnson about Mexico City is clear, they seem to have been all over it. In contrast the CIA seems to have been totally lost, with major disconnects in understanding between the Mexico City station and CIA Headquarters. What remains of their communications shows no immediate concern specifically about an Oswald/Kostikov connection. On the other hand it is entirely possible that the Kostikov information may not even have been circulated within the Agency. The available FBI documents on Kostikov indicate only James Angleton (the FBI's liaison with the CIA) had been informed of Kostikov; there are no documents showing that such information was communicated within the Agency, even within the Counter Intelligence division. Given what is now known of Angleton's own practices, this is not as surprising as it once might have seemed. In *Cold Warrior*, Tom

Mangold, writes that circa 1962, Angleton had begun to consider all Soviet defectors as fakes, simply pawns in the grand game the KGB was playing against the CIA. Mangold describes the fact that even the defectors in place, in the U.S., were being handled by the FBI and not the CIA counter intelligence staff. The FBI was interested in the security/subversive behavior of such individuals but nobody was using them for active counter-intelligence against the Soviets. And it would be years before a series of new senior CIA officers realized how much Angleton's prejudices and sequestering of information Agency had cost them.[194]

What we see in the CIA communications is totally a matter of low-level communications, none involving the CIA Director nor indicating his personal involvement. The communications reflect considerable confusion and total disconnects about what information (tapes, transcripts, photos) were actually still available. Whether this reflects actual confusion or a developing obfuscation within segments of the Agency is a key question. Another is to what extent any of the information was being shared with President Johnson or even with Director McCone.

Good News and Bad News

What little we do know about communications with the President relates to contacts between Director Hoover and Johnson. Hoover and one other senior FBI officer went on record stating that actual tapes of at least some of the Mexico City telephone calls were reviewed by FBI agents and compared with Oswald's voice. Hoover stated that had occurred early on Saturday morning and Hoover had the information for his early morning talk with Johnson. At that point Hoover told Johnson that *the early morning FBI voice comparisons had revealed that it was not Lee Oswald on the telephone calls to the Russians, rather it was some unknown party – in fact Hoover told Johnson explicitly that Oswald had been impersonated in Mexico City.*

The reaction to such news should have been explosive. Clearly, neither the Russians nor Cubans were going to impersonate Oswald talking to their people, asking for money, making offers and implying that the Cubans knew where he would be staying in Mexico City so the Russians could get that information from them. *The good news would be that if Oswald had been impersonated then it would not be a Communist conspiracy. The bad news would be that it just might be a domestic one.* One thing would have been certain, if Oswald had really been impersonated in Mexico City, clearly Oswald was not just a "lone nut."

It would be complex enough to involve not only an impersonation of Oswald but of the Cuban embassy secretary. And it would seem to involve some inside knowledge of exactly how the Mexico City CIA station taps and electronic intercepts on phone lines worked within both the Russian and Cuban embassies. Worse yet, the mention of both Oswald and Kostikov's name would imply that the "parties unknown" had working and current intelligence knowledge relating to Oswald's visits to the embassies. As Newman notes, the conversations suggest that the impersonators had Oswald under some level of surveillance.

If Oswald had not been manipulated by the Russians or Cubans, (as might well have been initially suspected Friday evening), the impersonations suggested something perhaps even more sinister. Fear of a Communist conspiracy would be replaced by fear of something very different, something "domestic." *What seems most amazing, given the implication, is that according to the existing transcript, President Johnson seems to have made no comment at all in regard to the news about Oswald being impersonated!* Or did he?

REWIND, ERASE, RE-GROUP – WHAT IMPERSONATION?

As it turns out, it may be that we were never intended to know of the impersonation at all, that it had been described by Hoover to Johnson and that Johnson had apparently shown no interest. Researcher Rex Bradford has given detailed study to both the existing transcript of the Hoover/Johnson call and the tape which still exists. *In studying the tapes as compared to the transcript, it became apparent to Bradford that the tape that should have contained the conversation is now blank.* After considerable further research and dialog with the Johnson Library, *Bradford received confirmation that the tape had been intentionally erased by parties unknown.* Apparently either those parties were unaware of the transcript or were unable to destroy it as well?[195]

Two other examples of tape censorship related to the President's assassination are known and may be related. The airborne communications from Air Force One, during its flight back from Dallas, was tape recorded. William Manchester learned of that and requested the tape for historical reference in his book on the events of the assassination. That request was initially denied by President Johnson, but after considerable time Manchester was provided with an "edited" version of the recordings. Studies by the Assassination Records Review Board, comparing open Air Force One communications channels (as described by the actual communications personnel on the plane) versus the Air Force One transcript now available, suggests that the tape was indeed heavily edited and that possibly hours of transmissions may not be in the existing transcript.

The third instance involves the CIA telephone tap tapes from Mexico City. A close study of CIA communications between Mexico City and Headquarters during the 48 hours after the assassination suggests that initially there was no doubt that Oswald related tapes and transcripts were still available in Mexico City. However, by the end of the weekend, the memoranda suggest (apparently by some unspoken agreement), both locations were speaking of the tape recordings as if they no longer existed. Eventually the FBI would also take the same position, totally repudiating multiple FBI statements about the tapes and voice comparisons.

Yet, at least two Warren Commission staff members not only knew that the tapes had not been erased but they had actually listened to at least portions of them months after the CIA and FBI had both moved to the official position that the tapes had been erased prior to the assassination. David Slawson and William Coleman have described listening to such tapes during their trip to Mexico City in April of 1964. Slawson and Coleman confirmed that to both authors Peter Dale Scott and Anthony Summers.[196]

The existence of the tapes was also reportedly acknowledged "off the record" to the Assassinations Records Review Board and noted in the testimony of Anne Goodpasture of the Mexico City staff and author of the official CIA Mexico City station history. The following is an excerpt of the relevant portion of Goodpasture's ARRB testimony, the remarks that did go "on the record:"

> **Gunn.** I have spoken with two Warren Commission staff members who went to Mexico City and who both told me that they heard the tape, after the assassination obviously. Do you have any knowledge of information regarding tapes that may have been played to those Warren Commission staff members?
>
> **Goodpasture.** No. It may have been a tape that Win Scott had squirreled away in his safe.[197]

Yet, although the Warren Commission staff members knew of the tapes' existence, there is no indication that they performed the same voice comparison that the FBI had the evening of the assassination – or that the knowledge of the tapes was conveyed other than to Chief Counsel J. Lee Rankin. In fact there is no indication that the Warren Commission was aware of the Hoover/ Johnson call or the FBI's initial finding that Oswald had been impersonated in Mexico City, obviously a matter that would have been a vital concern in any comprehensive investigation.

Respected researchers have long suggested that the impersonation calls and their suggestive association of Oswald with a known KGB agent served as a "poison pill" which almost immediately triggered fears of a Communist conspiracy and suppression of an open investigation. In terms of Friday night, after a quick review of transcripts and memos, concerns over a Cuban or Communist conspiracy may well have been a driving force in suppressing investigation and resulting in charges of conspiracy against Lee Oswald being rewritten.

But as soon as all the related transcripts were collected and studied and as soon as voice comparisons were made, it would have become clear (certainly within 24 hours) that Oswald had been impersonated and that something much more complex was going on in Mexico City. The conversation in the second call, and especially in the now missing third call, would have clearly shown that some third party was involved, that the Russians and Cubans were not actually associated in a suspicious fashion with Oswald. The FBI did the voice comparisons, advising Johnson of the impersonations (and likely much more) on Saturday morning following the assassination. Their conversation was so explosive, the presidential tape of the conversation actually had to be erased — a "true smoking gun" indicating a cover up of some sort. Beyond that both the FBI and CIA were forced into a position of stating that all the Mexico City tapes had been erased, an untruth known even to Warren Commission staff members. *Hoover himself must have been infuriated by being forced to back off his original statements to the President — he later expressed his feelings in a note placed on an internal memo regarding cooperation with the CIA, clearly warning that it was dangerous to trust them, as illustrated by their lies about Oswald in Mexico City.*

Given all the official lies over the tapes (which certainly seem to support Professor's Newman's analysis that there were indeed impersonations) we are left with many questions, several of which are fundamental to our study of the Dallas conspiracy.

1. Were the impersonations an artifact created by routine, legitimate intelligence activities during Oswald's visit — leveraging his appearance at the two embassies to probe for reactions to an apparently desperate former defector?

2. Were the impersonations an indication of a much more complex, and covert intelligence project, one being shielded from even the Mexico City Station?

3. Was the issue seriously investigated and resolved or simply dropped?

It is known that the Mexico City station had conducted previous "pretext" operations against Americans contacting the Cuban embassy. Such activities fell under David Phillips, although they were something he never discussed.

In July, 1963 a caller to the Cuban embassy had offered information in exchange for money; his call had been picked up on the LIENVOY tap and his identity determined, using CIA assets inside the Cuban embassy. Phillips had authorized one of his agents, a Cuban exile, to follow up with a pretext call, representing himself as a Cuban embassy official and suggesting a meeting — of course he told the man he was never to contact the Embassy directly again. The affair was handled masterfully and when the man returned to the U.S., he was arrested by the FBI and successfully prosecuted.[198]

Yet in the case of the Oswald, it is difficult to see how without prior knowledge of his visit, how the pretext calls could have been made as recorded. In addition, that would imply that Oswald himself was not fully involved or aware of what was going on around him. Finally, there is certainly the possibility of a much more sophisticated operation going on around Oswald's visit, one planned in advance and with more ambitious goals of laying the background for some sort of Cuban "provocation," perhaps building a false record of actual Cuban sponsorship of a plot against the U.S. President. Such an operation would have been very consistent with Fitzgerald and Phillips, both known within the Agency for being "forward leaning" and with Phillips apparent compulsion to put JFK's "back to the wall."

Certainly that idea is quite speculative, yet there is some evidence for it. Professor Newman presents a substantial case that that someone inside Cuban Special Affairs Staff (SAS) in Washington had a very special interest in Oswald's files throughout the fall of 1963. Beyond that, actions were certainly being taken to control information, to ensure that Mexico City station did not become aware of Oswald's recent activities in New Orleans, especially his Cuba related activities. Jane Roman helped prepare some of the cables going from CIA headquarters to Mexico City station, cables responding to requests for information on Oswald. She has stated that she signed off on information in those cables that was not fully accurate, on information she knew was incomplete. But the most she would ever admit was that the information management exercise *reflected an active, operational interest in Oswald, as of October, 1963, that "is indicative of a keen interest in Oswald held very closely on a need-to-know basis."*[199]

Definitely, the most obvious person to have had such an interest would have been David Phillips, who was actually in Washington D.C. when the misleading cables to Mexico City were being drafted. The same David Phillips who would write in his autobiography that Oswald was "not even on the CIA's radar screen" while in Mexico City. Phillips had been in Mexico City when Oswald arrived; he was there when the first impersonation call was recorded. But on that same day, Phillips left for CIA headquarters in Washington (with travel authorized by Special Affairs Staff) and went on to JMWAVE in Miami before returning to Mexico City.

Not only the timing of Phillips' travel of interest in regard to what was going on with Oswald in Mexico City (we know that contrary to Phillips disassembling, things were indeed "hot" in regard to Oswald's appearance there) but in regard to a rather mysterious diplomatic pouch sent from the station in conjunction with Phillips' departure. On October 1, Mexico City station sent a cable directing that a diplomatic pouch sent on that date should be held in the registry until picked up by "Michael Choaden" a.k.a. Phillips, who would be at headquarters on temporary duty. Just what material was so sensitive that it could not be hand carried by Phillips but rather had to be sent separately via diplomatic pouch for Phillips personal pick up?[200]

Several of the "Oswald/Cuban plot" stories that came out of Mexico City following the assassination did have credible elements; they described actual individuals working in the Cuban embassies and gave details that would have only been available only through prior Mexico City intelligence operations.

In particular, the claim by a man named Alvarado, who described seeing and hearing Oswald take money to kill JFK while inside the Cuban embassy, was heavily endorsed by David Phillips; others seem to track back to Phillips' intelligence assets.

Did Phillips rush to put such stories together after the assassination, to provoke an American response against Castro? Or were they the remnants of a project that started during Oswald's visit to Mexico City, perhaps something that either aborted at the time or never reached fruition? The post assassination Oswald/Cuban sponsorship reports out of Mexico City didn't hold together all that well. There was no corroboration and they had internal inconsistencies – suggesting they were impromptu, an effort to take advantage of the situation.

Another post assassination anomaly is the intense effort by the Mexico City station to have Sylvia Duran not only picked up and interrogated by the Mexican Police but also actually tortured to reveal information about her personal contact with Lee Oswald. This was done over the adamant objections of CIA headquarters. We can only wonder what would prompt Station Chief Winston Scott to actually have a Mexican national, working as nothing more than a Cuban Embassy receptionist picked up and tortured by Mexican Police. Did he really think Fidel Castro would be using the young woman as a key contact in recruiting Lee Oswald to kill the President of the United States? Did he really think such arrangements would be made within the Cuban Embassy, visible to casual visitors (as Gilberto Alvarado reported)?

Undoubtedly, by November 23, any sort of intelligence activities going on around Oswald in Mexico City, including one that might have begun as early as summer in New Orleans, would have raised huge questions if revealed to the American public. Matters would only have been worse if unknown parties had been involved in the equation; parties with knowledge of Mexico City station surveillance and phone tap capabilities, parties actually able to penetrate those taps and impersonate Oswald in calls to both Russian and Cuban embassies. Very difficult questions would have been raised, not about the Cubans or Russians, but about the CIA itself. Someone on the "inside" was obviously involved with the Oswald visit to Mexico City – but who and with what motives?

In summary, the overriding issue seems to be that the Oswald/Kostikov association could have served to prompt a short term, knee jerk reaction to suppress investigation of a conspiracy. But once it was known to have involved an impersonation (actually multiple impersonations containing far more detail than just associating Oswald to Kostikov by name), one most probably conducted by parties very familiar with Mexico City station counter intelligence resources and with a special knowledge of the potential impact of a Kostikov/Oswald connection[16], it should have led in a very different direction. That direction could have been quite dangerous to the CIA itself (suggesting a poison pill incriminating the CIA, not the Russians or Cubans). The alternative is a conspiracy using Lee Oswald and knowing that Oswald was himself intelligence connected, either knowingly or even unknowingly, simply profited from the confusion created by a real CIA/Oswald intelligence operation in Mexico City.

It is even possible that the mysteries of Mexico City had nothing directly to do with the Dallas conspiracy, at least beforehand. Perhaps they had much more to do with the CIA and Oswald than with Dallas and a conspiracy to kill a President. As far as Mexico City and Oswald, it seems that even he accepted, after less than 48 hours, that he was going no place other than back to the United States (he had no money for international travel anyway). Also his wife, daughter, and a brand new baby ensured that his return would be to Dallas.

18   MOVING THE CONSPIRACY TO TEXAS

One reason for that view of Mexico City is that a conspiracy targeting JFK in Dallas seems to have already been in full swing, irrespective of Oswald's short stay in Mexico.

John Martino had been in Dallas at the end of September, on a paid, scheduled speaking tour, but he was back in Dallas again on October 1, on his own for the second time. During locally scheduled speeches, well attended by Dallas area Cuban exiles, he mentioned being aware of the fact that the daughters of Amador Odio, were living in Dallas, indicating that he had known Amador while in prison in Cuba. That was most likely a slip because Martino was not in the same prison as Odio, nor does he mention him in his book as he did much more minor figures.

Amador Odio had been a very prominent Cuban businessman, owning a trucking firm, which had made him one of the wealthiest men in Cuba. His daughter had married well, to the son of cultured, socially prominent Havana family. Despite his wealth, Amador Odio had crusaded against corruption in the Cuban government, being exiled twice by the Batista regime. At first he had welcomed the Castro revolution, and then abandoned Castro when his Marxist tendencies became known. Amador had become involved in support of anti-Castro activities and was eventually arrested and imprisoned when an individual (Renol Gonzalez) involved with an aborted attack on Fidel Castro, had been taken into custody at an Odio country estate outside Havana. That was the same abortive attack which led Antonio Veciana to flee Cuba, as Veciana's mother had rented the apartment from which Castro was to be attacked, an attack very possibly instigated and abetted by David Phillips during his clandestine activities in Cuba.

And in the same period of time as Martino's visit, an American introduced as "Leon Oswald," in company with two travelers from New Orleans, had visited Armador Odio's daughter Sylvia in Dallas. Sylvia was a socially connected young woman, being close friends with the owner of Texas Industries and his family and reportedly having dated Lawrence Marcus, one of the owners of the prestigious Neiman-Marcus department store. —who, instruments?

But Sylvia was also personally associated with Manolo Ray and with the leaders of his JURE movement. She had traveled to Puerto Rico in June, meeting with Ray and Ray's lieutenant Rogelio Cisneros. In turn, Cisneros had later traveled to Dallas to explore weapons contacts Sylvia had developed, holding meetings in her apartment.

Readers will recall that it was in this same period that JMWAVE and AMWORLD chief Henry Hecksher developed a major antipathy towards JURE. In addition Shackley and Morales had launched an investigation of JURE, taking the position that the WAVE station itself had been infiltrated and compromised by Ray. Hecksher later went as far as directing Artime's crews to fire on JURE vessels encountered during operations. We can only assume that Ray and all of his contacts were under heavy surveillance by JMWAVE's Cuban intelligence service, the former AMOTs.

Following the visit to Sylvia Odio, one of the young men called her back the following day, chatting with her but also going into considerable detail on the American who had been with them the evening before. "Leon Oswald" was described to Sylvia as an ex-Marine who was a crack shot and loose cannon, someone who could kill Castro but felt that the exiles should have already killed JFK over his betrayal at the Bay of Pigs. Sylvia had been suspicious at the time of the visit, refusing to prepare letters for the men and thinking her visitors might be spies or even Castro agents. She would write her father in prison and he wrote back (prior to the assassination); warning her that nobody he knew should be visiting her. It is important to note that Sylvia's visitors had actually used her father's secret "war names," names that could only have been known by individuals working with him in Cuba prior to his arrest.

John Martino appears to have slipped in Dallas, talking about personally knowing Amador Odio; he slipped again after the assassination when he stated that Oswald had tried to infiltrate both DRE and JURE – at that point in time the visit of "Leon Oswald" to Sylvia Odio, and the effort to get her to prepare and sign letters for JURE were known to no one, no one other than the people who had orchestrated the Odio visit.

The Odio visit represents one of the most complex of the "Oswald" pre-assassination incidents, possibly even being an actual intelligence probe, with an attempt to seed stories of a "radical" and dangerous Oswald covertly overlaid. It illustrates the potential danger of having approved intelligence activities "hijacked" by CIA assets with hidden agendas.

This incident portrayed Oswald as an "ex-Marine who was a crack shot and loose cannon, someone who could kill Castro but felt that the exiles should have already killed JFK over his betrayal at the Bay of Pigs." Despite any confusion about those involved or their complete agenda, that much is clear. But an even more dramatic visit occurred in the same time frame, one that moved "Oswald" a good deal closer to actually being a "shooter" and, at the same time, associated him with possible Castro sponsorship and even with his future nemesis – Jack Ruby.

That incident has been previously mentioned. It occurred near Houston, and it appears to have been very precisely targeted, associating Lee Oswald by name with a former Castro weapons dealer. Oswald and his Cuban associate tried to buy lots of rifles from the gun smuggler (McKeown) and when that failed "Oswald" made a separate pitch to buy just one specific rifle – a rifle which could be thought of as a much more legitimate weapon to shoot a President, than the one which eventually turned up in the Texas School Book Depository. It would have been a weapon that might have been traced back to McKeown, even implicating Cuba in the assassination. "Oswald" offered several times the going rate for the gun.

The former gun dealer, still on probation, figured the whole thing was some sort of a sting, particularly as he recognized the man with "Oswald" as someone from his earlier days of smuggling weapons into Cuba, at that time a Castro supporter. The weapons dealer also had a proven history with none other than Jack Ruby of Dallas, dating back from Ruby's own history with Cuba and travels to Havana. After the assassination, an FBI investigation of Robert McKeown would turn up the names of both Oswald and Ruby. Regardless of the mysteries in Mexico City or even of the Odio visit in Dallas, the McKeown incident suggests a conspiracy was well in play to frame Lee Oswald and Cuban sponsors. *– See John Armstrong*

TARGETING JFK IN DALLAS:
Both Mexico City and the Odio visit bring us back to the difficulty of separating the two Oswald "threads" – intelligence vs. conspiracy. The McKeown incident is much more definitive, exactly what we would expect to see as corroboration for the sort of conspiracy described by both John Martino and Richard Case Nagell. And that is a very useful distinction, raising the issue of what we would expect to see in a JFK conspiracy, incited and directed by CIA professionals acting in their well established role as "advisers." What would we expect to see in a conspiracy involving CIA operations professionals working with their exile surrogates?

The CIA had drafted its own "assassinations manual" as far back as Guatemala in 1954, when Morales and Robertson were training and mentoring the Guatemalan exiles/rebels. William Harvey had taken executive assassination to a new level of planning, laying out a series of guidelines for "the resort beyond the last resort," guidelines and cautions for total deniability. Those guidelines involved using individuals with no prior history of such acts, not known criminals. People with any sort of significant record were also out of the question. The individuals would have to be totally deniable and if at all possible someone whose act could be associated with the opposition, the Russians. Harvey's notes also mentioned the possibility that the individuals might have to be terminated after the action.

There had been several attempts to assassinate Fidel Castro, some using poison but others with very sophisticated plans for rifle attack teams. On at least two and possibly more occasions, three man rifle teams had been sent into Cuba for attacks on Castro, those attempts seem to have been defeated by the lack of reliable on-island support or simply failures to insert the teams. Those same resources were certainly available for a domestic shooting attack, the teams had been totally compartmentalized from JMWAVE, with only Morales and most likely Robertson having any idea of their existence, or the men involved. Of course, what was lacking for a domestic attack in Dallas was support "on the ground" from someone with detailed knowledge of how things operated in the city, especially within law enforcement. Lack of reliable support on the ground had led to the failure of a number of the Castro assassination attempts. Also, people would have to go ahead, for reconnaissance and to handle the "patsy" aspect of the plot. Those people would have to be completely independent of the shooting teams, and have credible reasons for appearing in Dallas and spending time there. Of course the good news for the conspirators was that Dallas, Texas would have been an extremely "soft" venue, when compared to Castro's Cuba.

We also know from "surrogates" such as Antonio Veciana, that the Cuban exiles themselves organized relatively complex assassination attempts on Castro. Veciana described a plan that had been prepared to kill Castro in Chile (during a period in which both David Phillips and David Morales were involved in the Latin American operations). The plot included multiple shooters with concealed weapons, an attempt to slow Castro's car during the attack (using a stalled vehicle), and the use of a car bomb as a back up. Beyond that, there was to be a designated patsy, associated with Moscow, a Castro supporter who had been turned against Castro. The project had even developed faked documents and photographs associating the patsy with the Russians; the patsy was to be killed after the attack as insurance. *Veciana described the plot as "very similar to the assassination of Kennedy."* One has to wonder if it were in fact not patterned off events in Dallas – which involved a stalled vehicle on Elm street, a fake ambulance call to the intersection at Houston and Elm in front of the TSBD, multiple concealed shooters (likely with silenced weapons), a back up car bomb and a patsy who was to be killed.[202]

However, for this study, our task is not to look at the attack itself but to search for indications of the conspiracy that was building up to it during the months of October and November. To do that we must explore two major areas: a) what preparations were required to put personnel into Dallas for the attack, and b) what was done to further establish Lee Oswald as a patsy, given the fact that he would not be a willing or conscious participant in the attack. Hopefully those indications will help us determine at what level the operation was being controlled.

It is also necessary to note, that by October, the conspiracy must have taken on a greatly increased urgency. At the end of September Attwood had met with

Lechuga socially at Howard's apartment and received a very positive response, being invited to Havana for talks. And early in October we find the first documents indicating that Castro's intermediary Vallejo are of sudden interest both to the CIA Chief of Western Hemisphere and the CIA Directors Office. Mexico City was being queried on him and an AMOT asset is mentioned as having possible access to him.[203]

By November, anyone monitoring Howard or Vallejo would have picked up the telephone call in which he mentioned the need for absolute secrecy and stated that "Castro would go along with any arrangements we might want to make for talks. Only Castro would be involved and specifically that Che Guevara would not be. He emphasized Castro's desire for the meeting and pressed for a quick response." The Kennedy/Castro contacts were clearly becoming very real and moving quickly. Howard's home continued to serve as a focal point in the communications and a number of calls were made between Attwood and Vallejo as well as Howard and Vallejo.

During the first week of October, the newspapers announced that JFK would be visiting Dallas on his planned trip to Texas. Martino had returned to Dallas on October 1 and by October 3, Jack Ruby began calling to try and locate former Havana casino manager R.D. Matthews. Matthews had been a manager at the Havana Deauville casino, where Ruby's good friend McWillie worked (later McWillie had moved on to the Sans Souci, the casino which John Roselli was brought in to clean up); Ruby had visited McWillie in Havana in 1959, following his abortive attempt to get an introduction to Castro from Robert McKewon.

John Martino had also worked at the Deauville, invited by the Roth brothers who had leased the casino; Martino performed a variety of jobs during the construction and opening of the facility. Matthews had been associated with Ruby in Dallas before going to the Havana casino. There have also been reports, denied by Matthews, that he had been approached for assistance in a pre-Bay of Pigs attempt on Castro.[204]

During the middle of October, Ruby left Dallas, traveling to New Orleans to recruit "talent" for his club. One report, places him in Florida, meeting with Roselli during this period and the Warren Commission could not account for all of Jack's time away from Dallas. During this period Roselli had gone missing from the heavy FBI surveillance of him in LA and Los Vegas; when he was next observed in LA he was heard remarking that he had "just been on the east coast." Unfortunately, although we know that the Miami FBI office was copied on Roselli surveillance and carried him as a subject of interest, no Miami office files on Roselli have ever been discovered.[205]

The circumstantial evidence for Ruby having been recruited into the JFK conspiracy is extensive, readers are referred to Seth Kantor's *The Ruby Cover-Up* and *Someone Would Have Talked* discusses Ruby's history with Cuban interests, his trips to Cuba, his activities in support of the conspiracy, his likely set up as a Castro agent (a second patsy to Lee Oswald) and his forced recruitment into the murder (termination) of Lee Oswald. Anecdotal corroboration of a Ruby-Roselli connection includes the report that Melvin Belli was recruited to defend Ruby by a call from Los Vegas (from a former Havana casino figure) as well as Robert Maheu's acknowledgement that Roselli knew Ruby and the report that Roselli himself remarked to Jack Anderson that Ruby was "our guy."

The recruitment of Jack Ruby to provide local introductions and intelligence in Dallas would also be a significant indication that the Cuban exiles were not carrying out the conspiracy against the President without advice and assistance. Only an endorsement from William Harvey and contact with David Morales could have brought Roselli into the conspiracy.[206]

And only Roselli's reputation and endorsement would have sustained an approach to Ruby, even if initially made by Martino. Ruby would have wanted reassurance for any such commitment, even if his role was described in a very circumscribed fashion – as it appears to have been. There was no need to talk to Jack about an actual attack on the President. Most likely, he was given some story about a mysterious intelligence operation, perhaps something provocative, and something being done to put pressure on Castro. Jack would have loved to do a favor for someone like John Roselli, especially if he was only playing a low risk role, providing information and making introductions. And that view of Ruby's planned role seems to be reflected in the fact that Jack actually invited a friend down to come down for the President's motorcade and "watch the fireworks."[207]

Ruby's dramatically changing role is also reflected in a detailed study of his changing emotions on the afternoon of the assassination, the urgent mystery calls to his club, his call to Al Gruber in LA and the fact that he actually began "stalking" Lee Oswald only hours after Oswald's arrest.[208]

At the end of October, Felipe Vidal traveled to Dallas and spent several days there in early November. Shortly afterwards Jack Ruby was visited by Al Gruber, from Los Angeles. Gruber had not seen Ruby for at least ten years and even when pressed, Gruber offered no real explanation for his trip to Dallas nor the nature of his visit with Ruby (Gruber said that he had been traveling on business, had car trouble in Missouri and since Dallas was right next door he thought he would drop in on Jack). Outside of his own family, Ruby's only call on the afternoon of the assassination would be to Al Gruber, in Los Angeles.

Ruby's recruitment and his role are both vital clues to the origin of the Dallas conspiracy. Of course a huge amount has been written about Jack Ruby, with perhaps the most meaningless being that recorded in conjunction with the Warren Commission report. There was a grave danger in probing too far into the Ruby connection, both to certain people in Dallas who knew too much about the real Jack Ruby and to the Warren Report, which needed to avoid an expanded vision of Ruby at all cost. Perhaps one of the best examples of that is the Commission's use of FBI interviews with known underworld figures as proof that Ruby had no underworld associations. Of course Ruby had criminal connections, not at the syndicate level but with gamblers, minor drug figures, smugglers, prostitution, all the street level crime found associated with the club and casino businesses that had become his world. Ruby operated on the fringes of the criminal world, he was no killer, no enforcer, and no major drug dealer. What he wanted to be was a success in the club and casino world; his friends and the men who he admired had succeeded there, had become gambling circuit figures who went on to work in the big name clubs and casinos in Havana, Miami, Las Vegas, and even at the Cal Neva at Lake Tahoe.

Those were men like Louis McWillie and R.D. Matthews, men who had made it out of Dallas, to Havana and then Las Vegas. McWillie had worked at the Deauville in Havana under Mike McClaney (John Martino was also an alumnus of the Deauville), then at the Sans Souci, while it was being cleaned up by John Roselli. Roselli had been called in by Meyer Lansky, the dean of the Havana casino crew; Batista had gone to Lansky for help in improving some public relations problems with Havana's casinos.[209]

Ruby had gone to Cuba in 1959, ostensibly to visit his friend McWillie but more probably to serve as a courier, with the possibility of doing some business on the side, selling jeeps and other items to the Castro government. It was at that point where Ruby had repeatedly tried to obtain the right introductions from Castro's former arms supplier, Robert McKewon.

By 1963 McWillie was working in Las Vegas and would also spend some time at the Cal Neva Lodge in Lake Tahoe. That spring Ruby renewed his connection to McWillie, but then Ruby would call a lot of people in 1963; he had serious tax problems, owed money he could not possibly pay and was running into serious club competition in Dallas. Ruby's attorney, Graham Koch, was trying to negotiate a payment of 8 cents on the dollar for Ruby's back taxes and his business account held a total of $246. Of course Ruby did club business in cash but he was clearly running on a day to day basis with no way to pay his debt and no obvious sources of new income. Ruby was not bashful about talking about his problems including money problems. His former friends quickly learned that Jack was struggling and there is good reason that by fall, Ruby had begun to turn back to some of his former activities, serving as the middleman in the sale of stolen weapons.[210]

Ruby's possible further contacts with McWillie are difficult to trace. The Warren Commission was informed that, following a call to Al Gruber in Los Angeles, Ruby had traveled to Las Vegas shortly before the assassination. There was considerable corroboration for that trip, including a report that Ruby used McWillie's name when registering at the Stardust, (but the registration has disappeared) and in the end, the Warren Commission chose not to list the Las Vegas visit along with Ruby's other recorded travel.

Some years after the assassination, McWillie would be found working for Mike McClaney again, at an offshore resort/casino in the Caribbean. McClaney had gotten into the Havana casino business with the support of Meyer Lansky and was reported to be close to both Lansky and John Roselli. Although there is no record of direct contact between Ruby and McClaney, McClaney himself had quite a history of involvement in anti-Castro activities, supporting Cuban exiles and admitting to an association with Antonio Varona. During 1962 and 1963 he worked though an associate named Sam Benton and recruited independent exiles for attacks on Cuba. One bombing mission was to be staged out of New Orleans and the FBI confiscated a store of explosives and bomb materials at a property owned by his brother, a New Orleans resident. Benton was also involved in anti-Castro activities with Roy Hargraves, a close friend of Felipe Vidal.

McClaney had befriended a variety of Cubans he had known while in Havana, helping them to enter the United States, allowing some to live on his estate and helping them get jobs. Interestingly on November 1, one of those Cuban exiles, Jorge Soto Martinez, made some fascinating remarks to Mrs. Lillian Spengler, an employee at the Parrot Jungle in Miami. Martinez was "chatting up" Mrs. Spengler, apparently trying to impress her and started talking about his friend "Lee" who was either in Mexico or Texas, was an American who spoke Russian and was a crack marksman. Mrs. Spengler remarked on the incident to fellow employees before the assassination. There is little doubt her report is accurate but she was discouraged from saying more about it by a local FBI agent. Certainly it leads to speculation about what sort of rumors were circulating among people that Soto Martinez was in contact with some weeks before events in Dallas.

Calls to McWillie and Gruber, rumors of meetings with Roselli and mysterious trips to Las Vegas are especially interesting in light of the fact that as of November 22, Jack Ruby had apparently come into a good deal of money.[211]

A bank manager (Bill Cox at the Merchant National Bank) reported seeing Ruby with cash he estimated at $7,000. His observation is corroborated by the fact that, when arrested after shooting Oswald, Ruby had over $3,000 on his person and in his car trunk. Beyond that, researcher Ian Griggs obtained an exclusive 2005 interview with Ruby's bartender and club manager Andy Armstrong. Armstrong described retrieving a quantity of cash from hiding in an air conditioner room at the club and then delivering it to Ruby in jail, an amount Armstrong estimated to be in four figures. Ruby instructed Armstrong to turn it over to his business partner, Ron Paul. Armstrong was well trusted by Ruby and had worked for him for almost two years; formerly Armstrong had worked at the Marilyn Belt Company in the Dal-Tex building, adjacent to the Texas School Book Depository. Other "new money" reports described the fact that Ruby had also just begun talking to a realtor about moving into a new location for his club, telling a friend that he planned to move into a new apartment in the exclusive Turtle Creek area of Dallas and making inquires about a Caribbean cruise.[212]

The case for Jack Ruby's use in the Dallas conspiracy is circumstantial, but convincing. His recruitment most likely came through people he had been associated with for some years; the same people who had been in Havana and involved with a variety of Cuba related activities. They were all members of the casino fraternity, not syndicate class criminals but successes in the high end of the club and gambling industry, the sort of success Ruby had not found. All of them had crossed paths with John Roselli, in Cuba, in Las Vegas. When the CIA had initially thought of assassinating Castro, they turned to just Vegas/ex-Havana players, ending up with John Roselli. And Roselli had in turn relied on Tony Varona to provide him support contacts on the island.

It is also significant that once Ruby came on board, all the key contacts with him appear to have come from either Los Angeles or Las Vegas, Roselli's home grounds. The cut-out seems to have been Al Gruber, whose explanations for many of Ruby's calls were almost humorous – he went to visit Ruby in Dallas because he had been in Missouri and Dallas was right next door or Ruby had called him after the assassination to discuss sending one of his pet dogs to Gruber. Gruber didn't say much about Ruby's call to him in LA the Sunday before the assassination. Unfortunately, there seems to have been no true, in depth investigation of Gruber or his associates. He was simply questioned and his remarks accepted. That leaves us little to work with, although the author has verified with long time Los Angeles private investigator Peter Noyes, that Gruber was certainly part of the "old school" LA network operating under Mickey Cohen. Roselli had "matriculated" within that same network. Gruber had lots of connections in LA, including ties to the local gambling circuit (primarily high stakes card games). John Roselli's final legal downfall actually came over nothing more than a rigged, high stakes Hollywood card game. It seems that Gruber's repeated contacts with Ruby in the weeks before the attack in Dallas are extremely significant, as was Ruby's call to Gruber following the assassination.[213]

When it became clear that Oswald would be returning to Dallas, and that JFK would be traveling there, Dallas was selected as the target city and Ruby was selected as just the sort of individual who could provide the needed field support. He had a prior history with Cuban interests, had tried to do business with the Castro regime and was in financial difficulties. Ruby provided deniability (no history at all with the CIA, or in any serious crimes; he had even been an FBI informant back in 1959) but perhaps as importantly, his history left open the possibility of setting him up as a type of patsy as well, someone who could have been hired to do minor activities without asking any serious questions.

RUBY'S CHANGING ROLE:

A study of Ruby's probable role and its dramatic change on the afternoon of November 22 is vital to understanding the operation of the Dallas conspiracy.[214] As previously mentioned, there is no evidence to suggest that Jack Ruby knew the President would actually be killed during the motorcade. Not only would that not have been necessary, it probably would have scared Jack to death. He became extremely nervous over even the minor role he was given.

Ruby knew something was going to happen, he may well have been told it was some sort of provocative act that would point towards Fidel Castro, all part of the ongoing anti-Castro activities. Whatever happened would be laid at the feet of Fidel and his supporters. There would be "fireworks" but at no risk to Ruby, was why he was secure enough to start talking freely about his suddenly positive spending plans rather than continuing to bemoan his tax and club problems.

What Ruby would have been asked to do was to provide Dallas intelligence, ranging from simple information about the motorcade route, buildings along the route, police security plans; there is no question Ruby had access to a great amount of police information. He was quite familiar with local law enforcement and had been for years. He was in the District Attorney's office routinely, at the police stations. His connections were good enough that Seth Kantor discovered Ruby was one of the few who knew of the initial Police plans to transfer Oswald on Saturday. A week or so prior to the assassination, Ruby had reportedly been out skating with police officer Harry Olsen and one of his entertainers. The detective had reported in with an ankle injury and was off duty on November 22, doing private security work (reportedly somewhere in Oak Cliff), but when questioned he could not provide the location or employer. He and the entertainer left Dallas for California not long after the assassination.[215]

Given the lack of a serious investigation of Ruby (when only two actual field investigators in Dallas began to get truly suspicious of Ruby and started pushing to find the real extent of his connections within the police department, protests were made and the Warren Commission dismissed them) we are left with anecdotes and suspicions. Ruby certainly was in a position to obtain advance information about the President's visit and related security; he was also in a position to identify police officers who might be induced to take some minor roles. There is strong evidence that at least one officer performed watch duty for individuals behind the picket fence on the north side of the plaza; police rushing to the scene were turned back by a known officer who said he had been stationed there all morning and nothing suspicious had occurred; police assignments show nothing of that sort.[216]

Ruby could also have assisted in providing information on buildings of interest in the downtown area, potential sniper locations. We have no idea what he might have done to locate individuals who could leave a door unlocked at the right time, let someone in a building, provide a description of who was working where, building sketches, etc. Jack knew a great number of people in Dallas, honest people and dishonest people. People could be bought with money or women. People could be blackmailed – nobody big of course, little people. But that's the sort of assistance the tactical team would need on the ground, it's the same sort of assistance they needed inside Cuba when Roselli went to Tony Varona for help. But then security was a good deal tighter in Cuba.

And…speaking of Varona, it may have been that the plotters figured it would be much safer to remain in contact with Lee Oswald from outside Dallas itself, or at least go through a cut-out well outside of the city. Following the assassination, an Abilene resident named Harold Reynolds repeatedly tried to bring the FBI's attention to the fact that he had seen a note left at his neighbors residence, a note signed "Lee Oswald" and reading "Call me immediately – Urgent." Reynolds neighbor was named Pedro Valeriano Gonzalez; he had come to Abilene from Miami. Reynolds went into considerable detail on Gonzalez suspicious activities immediately after the President's murder in Dallas.

Gonzalez had gone around asking about and collecting any and all photos of himself and his Cuban friends and after that he immediately left Abilene. Reynolds himself had observed several instances of meetings at Gonzalez' place, attended by visitors with cars whose license tags were from Florida and Louisiana. He also recalled two Anglos visiting Gonzalez before the assassination, one looking a good deal like Lee Oswald and one "a little dried up Anglo about 5'8" in height, in his 50's and with a weathered complexion," a reasonably good description of John Martino. What makes the report even more interesting is that Gonzalez had often talked about his friendship with Tony Varona.[217]

Given the fact that many of the more active Cuban exiles in Dallas, especially those engaged in looking for weapons, were under FBI observation, it would have made good sense to conduct tactical planning sessions elsewhere.

The view that Ruby's role was one of field support, not at all directly involving him with the actual events of November 22, seems to be corroborated by his invitation to a friend to "watch the fireworks" and his lack of concern about letting people know that his financial situation had dramatically improved. Certainly Ruby never anticipated that his role might suddenly became something more than he had ever dreamed – and that was definitely not something the plotters had themselves conceived.

A detailed study of Ruby's changing behavior over the afternoon and evening of the assassination is extremely revealing. As word of the attack began to circulate, Ruby, by that time back at the *Dallas Morning News* office, was observed to be "subdued, pale and numb," not even talking – he left the office around 1:10 pm and was next seen by Seth Kantor at Parkland Hospital. Ruby and Kantor knew each other and Ruby approached and spoke to the reporter, clearly trying to get a grip on what had really happened to the President, later Ruby would adamantly deny that he had been at Parkland. In his book *The Ruby Cover-up*, Kantor asks the basic question, "Why would Jack Ruby seek out a reporter at the hospital on Friday and then, after Sunday, deny having been there?" Part of the answer is that Ruby was distraught and not thinking clearly, desperate to understand what had really happened. Kantor himself summarizes Ruby's role very explicitly – Ruby was not involved in a plot to kill anyone on Friday, but by Sunday he was, having been ordered to kill Lee Oswald. Readers can find the evolution of Ruby's assignment, the rash of calls coming into the club shortly after Oswald's capture (from someone who would not leave his name), Ruby's call to Al Gruber in Los Angeles and Ruby's stalking of Oswald over the weekend in Kantor's book and in Chapter 18 of *Someone Would Have Talked.*[218]

BEYOND JACK RUBY:

The Dallas conspiracy had jelled with Kennedy's commitment to visit Dallas, with the certainty that Lee Oswald would return to his wife and new baby in Dallas and with the recruitment of Jack Ruby for field support. But beyond Ruby there were other critical elements. Of course the actual shooting teams were critical, but they were also readily available and totally reliable. Morales and Robertson were in direct contact with the teams that had been intensely trained for the Castro assassination missions into Cuba. Some of the men were likely Brigade veterans, others recruited for Operation 40 and well known to Morales. Some had actually been inserted on assassination missions into Cuba, only to abort in the face of the intense Cuban security measures.

Additional information, suggesting that the tactical team in Dallas included Cuban exiles, who had received special training during the preparation for the Cuba project, was submitted to the Assassinations Records Review Board in the late 1990's. That information pointed directly to the participation of individuals trained by CIA paramilitary specialists, very possibly individuals associated with the AMOTs and Operation 40. That story is tangential to this study but readers who have a copy of *Someone Would Have Talked* can find the details in the appendix titled "Echoes from Dallas."

As of summer 1963, the Castro assassination project had been officially terminated but the teams were still in camp, totally isolated and totally focused. Bradley Ayers, a newly assigned military trainer to JMWAVE in the summer of 1963, had seen the camp, had observed tremendously accurate snipers practicing. He probably shouldn't have been taken to that particular camp and Robertson quickly showed up to move him on to other locations. But Ayers had been told it was the "Roselli" camp, operating under very special directions, with its missions extremely secret; it was definitely not part of standard JMWAVE activities.[219]

The use of such shooting teams in Dallas would guarantee a covert, disciplined and military style attack; it also provided a key cover for the entire conspiracy. If any of the tactical team were killed or taken into custody, any investigation would quickly reveal a secret of immense national security, the multi year U.S. government effort to kill the leader of another country. Investigation of that would lead to William Harvey, to ZRRIFLE and to the entire history of the CIA, and U.S. President's acceptance of foreign political assassinations.[220]

The effectiveness of such a "backstop" had previously been discussed but its significance cannot be stressed enough. In 1967, at the very beginning of the Garrison investigation, John Roselli personally took the story of CIA assassination teams to Washington D.C. It was offered to Earl Warren, to the FBI, the Secret Service and directly to President Johnson. Roselli did spin his story, stating that a team had been captured and somehow turned on the President by Castro. But Roselli's own involvement with the assassination project was well known to Director Hoover, and following circulation of Roselli's story President Johnson demanded and was given a CIA briefing on the Castro projects. Even with Roselli's obvious credibility, it's clear that nobody wanted to inquire into the details of CIA Cuban exile sniper teams being turned on President Kennedy.

Although the assassination projects had been strictly kept from the Warren Commission, Warren still showed no interest, passing the Roselli story off to the FBI who showed no interest (in what Director Hoover had always declared would remain an open case), passing it on to the Secret Service who in turned showed no interest. President Johnson took no action, other than beginning to respond in private that he felt that JFK had been killed by Castro in retaliation for the attempts on his life. Roselli's story received major media attention through Drew Pearson's column and ultimately he would even be named as the source, yet there is no indication that a single major newspaper, TV network or investigative reporter ever approached Roselli to follow up the story. That would remain the case even after his name was tied to it through unauthorized statements by his lawyer, in an appeal to a judge based on his prior services to the government and his obvious patriotism The appeal occurred during his sentencing on a gambling conviction in Los Angeles; it apparently made no impression on the judge but certainly was not appreciated by either Roselli or his former CIA associates.[221]

The assassination of President Kennedy by individuals involved in clandestine, authorized U.S. foreign political assassinations was simply a show stopper; it seems to have been perfect insurance against any serious criminal investigation even when the secret was revealed by a credible source as early as 1967.

A point deserving further note is that although Roselli was known to have been involved in the Castro assassination projects by the time of the Church Committee and the HSCA, and was extensively questioned on the subject, there seems to have been no specific attention given to his 1967 story of sniper teams turned on the President. That seems to be an immense oversight – unless that was to be the subject of his third scheduled appearance, which never occurred, due to his murder?

WORKING IN DALLAS:
Beyond the sniper teams, beyond field support by Jack Ruby, it was also necessary to do "advance work" in Dallas. That advance work required reconnaissance, probably some contact with Ruby and certain actions to patsy Lee Oswald, associating him with the upcoming attack and positioning him as an impulsive Castro supporter who could have been manipulated by Cuban agents. There was some risk in the trips to Dallas, simply because there was some monitoring of the Cuban community. The FBI was actively involved in trying to block weapons purchases by the exiles and collecting intelligence on possible missions being prepared (under the Administration directive to stop missions from the United States) and of course the Bureau was constantly investigating reports of Castro intelligence agents being planted among the exiles.[222]

We do know that certain persons previously associated with the JFK conspiracy traveled to Dallas in October and November, specifically John Martino and Felipe Vidal. Martino's self admitted role was as a courier and liaison for the conspiracy. Vidal's role may have been far more operational, especially given the fact that he was in Dallas on November 22. Unfortunately we have nothing from Vidal himself. He was killed just months after the assassination, captured and executed on an independent mission into Cuba. Word of his participation in the conspiracy comes from Cuban intelligence officer Fabian Escalante (perhaps a questionable source to some readers) but also from an individual easily proved to have been personally close to Vidal and operationally involved with him in independent anti-Castro missions into Cuba – Roy Hargraves.

Hargraves was briefly mentioned earlier, as a close friend of Vidal and active in independent anti-Castro efforts, including a complex scheme to steal boats and collect insurance on them to fund missions (a scheme involving Mike McClaney's agent, private investigator Sam Benton). *But Hargraves deserves considerably more of our attention, having first been reported to the FBI as a suspect in the JFK assassination shortly after the President's murder.* The FBI report on Hargraves, released only in 1993, is simply titled "JFK Suspect." Much of what we know about Roy Hargraves is through the efforts of author Noel Twyman and his research assistant Anna Marie Kuhns-Walko. The following synopsis is largely derived from Twyman's book *Bloody Treason*; the 2010 eBook edition of *Bloody Treason* also contains a summary of Twyman's extensive personal interviews with Hargraves.

In 1963, a man named William Acker had worked in a restaurant on Flagler Street in Miami, becoming acquainted with Art Silva and his girlfriend; they had recently moved into a tourist court and had become acquainted with their neighbors, a man named Roy and his girlfriend. Roy was an ex-marine who was very involved in anti-Castro activities and associated with a number of Cuban exiles. According to Silva, Roy had several telescopic equipped rifles, grenades, dynamite and similar materials in his rooms.

Acker came to know Roy, meeting him on occasions and almost getting into a fight with Hargraves at a Christmas party in December of 1963. Hargraves had been cursing JFK, blaming him for the death of one of his close friends who had died at the Bay of Pigs and Acker had taken exception to that. More importantly, following the assassination, Silva had told Acker that *"Roy" had traveled to Dallas in late 1963 and had Secret Service credentials in his possession at the time. Before the trip, Silva had apparently heard Roy remark that he was into* "something big, the biggest thing this country has ever seen."[223]

The FBI made a minimal investigation of Acker's report, accepting the statement from an unidentified source that Roy Hargraves had been in Miami from November through March and also stating that it could not explicitly prove that Roy Hargraves was the "Roy" in question. The FBI also cast some doubt on Acker because he had spent time in a veteran's hospital after serving in North Africa, Italy, France and Germany during WWII. The FBI then sealed the report and there is no indication that it was considered by the HSCA inquiry.

Noel Twyman conducted research demonstrating that the "Roy" in question was almost certainly Roy Hargraves. The author located independent information confirming that Roy Hargraves did indeed live at the location cited by Acker and his friend Silva and in comparing Acker's report to the FBI's own records on Roy Hargraves, we find that they contain Hargraves' address, at the location cited by Acker.

There is good reason to take Acker's report very seriously, especially when it is considered along with the statement of a Dallas Police officer who had challenged a suspect behind the north fence line in Dealey Plaza, only to be shown Secret Service credentials (at a time when no Secret Service agent has ever been shown to have been on foot behind the fence). Even more importantly, in an extended series of interviews with Noel Twyman, Hargraves went on record as having traveled to Dallas, with his friend Vidal. Hargraves' story was that they went there as part of an "unknown operation," which turned out to be the attack on President Kennedy.

Certainly Hargraves' remarks to Twyman have to be carefully evaluated and of course even at the late date of the interview, Hargraves was careful not to put himself in the position of knowing in advance about a conspiracy. Still, he did describe his own construction of a car bomb (Hargraves was known as being an explosives specialist), which was placed on the far side of the overpass on Elm Street, apparently in the area of the access ramp to the freeway. We do know from photographs that a number of vehicles were parked on the access lane going onto the Stemmons freeway. The car bomb was a backup in the event that the rifle attack in the plaza had to be aborted. *[handwritten: ?, ? my Res m while he is all B.S.]*

In his first interview with Twyman, Hargraves stated that Vidal was present on Elm Street as the "signal man." In his second interview, he recanted a bit, stating, "That is not for me to say." During the interview Hargraves mentioned John Martino several times, stating that he felt Martino had been a "top level connection" to those organizing the conspiracy. Apparently, the fact that Martino had actually revealed certain details about the conspiracy were not known to Hargraves, when that was mentioned to Hargraves, he reacted sharply and left the room for a time. *[handwritten: B.S.]*

In a synopsis of that interview, in the second, eBook edition, of Twyman's *Bloody Treason*, Hargraves was adamant in not having personally done anything that resulted in the President's death. He did also speak at some length about Bernardo De Torres involving himself with the Garrison investigation – "burning money, doing damage control." Hargraves and his friend Gerry Hemming had volunteered to Garrison as well, however one of Garrison's investigators noted that they had contributed no real information and seemed to be primarily interested in whether or not Garrison had information to place a shooter in the Dal-Tex building. *[handwritten: Crapuganda]*

Finally, in his interview with Twyman, Hargraves did his best to continue the "Castro did it" scenario, claiming that Castro's intelligence apparatus was so effective that they had actually infiltrated segments of the anti-Castro activists and utilized them against the President. As with certain other of Hargraves' remarks, Twyman considered that to be a smoke screen.

"SETTING UP" OSWALD:

It's unlikely we will ever know the full details of the tactical operations in Dallas, the exact activities for the advance men, the management of the shooting teams, their location, and the shooting details. But it is clear that there was one other element in play, final activities to position Lee Oswald as the tool of Cuban intelligence. There is ample evidence that Oswald himself did not participate in that effort. Clearly, there are a great many things he could have done to implicate himself or to glorify his involvement – he did none of those.[224]

Someone else did though, possibly in Miami and most certainly in Dallas. In Dallas there were numerous reports, both before and after his employment at the Texas School Book Depository, of someone looking like Oswald, and occasionally using his name, applying for work at various locations at hotels and parking garages along the upcoming Presidential motorcade route. In one instance an Oswald look-alike, reportedly using his name, test drove a car, driving wildly and making remarks about having been in Russia and about coming into lots of money. Another incident involved a rifle left at a gun shop, for attachment of a telescopic sight. After the assassination two different anonymous phone calls drew attention to the rifle. In that instance a tag apparently carried Oswald's name, just as had a sales note at the car place had recorded Oswald's visit. During the course of investigation, both pieces of documentation were found to have disappeared.

But much more important is one very key incident, one that received no press coverage at all. If it had, things might have been considerably different immediately after the President's murder.

Ralph Yates was a refrigeration serviceman for the Texas Butcher Supply Company. His work took him all around the Dallas area. The week of the assassination, at around 10:30 in the morning, he happened to pick up a young hitchhiker near the Beckley Street entrance to the R.L. Thornton Expressway. The young man walked up to Yates' pick-up, carrying a package wrapped in brown paper, some four feet long. He told Yates the package contained curtain rods but that he would like to bring it into the cab with him. The young man was talkative, bringing up the name of someone Yates might know, but didn't, and then asking if Yates had ever been to the Carousel Club. Then the young man started talking about the upcoming Presidential visit, in a very memorable manner. He asked Yates if he thought someone might assassinate the President, perhaps shooting from the top of a building or possibly a floor high up in one. He pulled out a picture that showed a man with a rifle, asking if he thought the President could be killed with a gun like that. Then he asked Yates if he thought the motorcade route might change (a description had been published in the newspaper) and Yates said that he doubted it would be. The man said that he needed to get off on Houston Street and Yates actually exited the expressway, dropping him off at the corner of Elm and Houston (the location of the Texas School Book Depository). He observed the young man cross Elm Street.

Yates was struck by the conversation; he mentioned the incident to another employee, Dempsey Jones, on either Wednesday or Thursday. And on Friday evening, he was shocked to realize that the young man had strongly resembled Lee Oswald! CRAY

The following week, Yates went to the FBI, gave a detailed report, and asked for total confidentiality. Dempsey Jones was questioned, confirming he had heard Yates relate the incident before the assassination. Yates was given a polygraph examination, which the FBI recorded as "inconclusive," most likely because it could not be used to contradict his story. He told his wife that the FBI men themselves had told him the examination confirmed his remarks as being truthful, but since they could not be (Lee Oswald had been at work at the time) then the incident could not actually have occurred and he needed medical treatment. He was directed to report to a psychiatric hospital, and ended up receiving years of shock treatments and medication. He still stood by his story until his early death in 1975.[225]

One can only imagine the headlines if Ralph Yates, Sylvia Odio, and Robert McKeown had immediately gone to the newspapers with their "Oswald" encounters – Lee Oswald would have been confirmed not only of having committed premeditated murder but of having been associated with mysterious Cubans, very likely Castro agents of some sort. hmm̃⌇

Even without that, Oswald's purported affiliations were established quickly and effectively based on his activities in New Orleans, his media visibility and the almost immediate positioning of him as a Castro incited radical – solidified by the emotionally charged *LIFE* Magazine publication of a cover photograph with Oswald holding a rifle and copies of both Communist and Socialist newspapers. This positioning of Oswald was quickly supplemented by Cuban exile media outreach in both New Orleans and Miami. Carlos Bringuier and the DRE, assisted by INCA, were quick to position Oswald as a Castro activist and possible agent. John Martino, Frank Sturgis and others in Miami went to the media with similar stories, claiming inside information on Oswald's contacts with Cuban agents and that Oswald had made one or more trips to Miami and even into Cuba. Seth Kantor wrote of immediately contacting the Scripps Howard news agency headquarters and being referred to Hal Hendrix in Miami, a specialist on Cuban affairs.

Hendrix quickly provided extensive background on Oswald, his time in Russia and all the details of his activities in New Orleans. Indeed, Hendrix seems almost to have had at hand all the information on Oswald that the CIA in Washington had refused to provide to its Mexico City station in October of 1963. Of course, Hendrix can also be shown to have been a long time CIA asset and in particular a key element of David Phillips anti-Castro media network. How much of this follow-on media effort was simply opportunistic is impossible to determine, however, the quantity and availability of Hendrix's information on Oswald suggests, at a minimum, there had been some preparation to take advantage of Oswald in a yet to be disclosed CIA propaganda or psychological operation.[226]

As the media's treatment of Oswald has been proposed by some authors, they have been complicit in a cover-up of a conspiracy (a point which may well be true, especially in regard to certain actions of *LIFE* Magazine), an alternative can be found in the basic truth that media content is influenced by those with power in society (referred to in sociological studies as media "Hegemony"). Simply put, mass media present an ideology consistent with the centers of economic power and act to preserve the interest of those power centers. For a detailed study of media mechanisms and their reaction to the Kennedy assassination, readers are referred to *The Media and the Social Construction of the Kennedy Assassination*, Ross Franklin Ralston, Ross's overall treatment of the subject is excellent and he also devotes considerable detail to *LIFE's* questionable practices in its assassination coverage as well as issues with CBS news, including its various documentaries.[227]

For our purposes, it is interesting to note that the "framing" of Oswald did not involve any truly sophisticated artifacts. His media visibility in New Orleans was key, and his mysterious trip to Mexico City supported that. His apparent flight from the Texas School Book Depository and the recovery of "his" rifle were more than enough for press purposes in the first 48 hours. Newspapers all over the country carried headlines associating Oswald with Cuba and Castro, based on nothing more than the same background information Hal Hendrix had provided to Seth Kantor. But no viable evidence of that emerged later, nothing to connect Oswald to specific and known Castro agents, no documents, not photographs, no surveillance reports – in fact the lack of surveillance was more of a media question than anything else, especially after certain remarks about his meeting with subversives or being under observation by the FBI.

Over time a significant number of third party and anecdotal rumors connecting him with Castro and Castro agents would surface but none of which were terribly credible and many of which seem to have been planted, again in an opportunistic fashion. Other than having some knowledge of Oswald and his activities, the conspirators did seemingly nothing more than impersonate Oswald at various times and places, and much of that had little impact during the first 72 hours as it never made it to the press.

As to impersonations, there is little likelihood that we will ever know the identity of those involved. It is true that an associate of both Hargraves and Vidal, an ex-marine named Steve Wilson, bears an intriguing resemblance to Lee Oswald. Interested readers are referred to the photo comparisons on http://www.larry-hancock.com and can reach their own opinions. Individuals involved with Wilson have talked about his impersonating Oswald, just as individual parties involved with Rip Robertson in Africa later described his reminisces of having been in Dallas, actually in Dealey Plaza during the assassination of President Kennedy.[228]

David Morales' lawyer and best friend have described his hatred of JFK, and his diatribes against the former President, as well as one remark (while drinking and very possibly not even aware of what he was saying) following one such outburst, a simple statement that, "We took care of that SOB."

Such passing remarks are easily dismissed, although the coincidence of quite similar anecdotes (from family or close friends), all relating to a JFK conspiracy and all coming from individuals demonstrably connected with each other and clearly with the same attitudes, anti-Communist and anti-Castro obsession/history – William Harvey, John Roselli, David Morales, Rip Robertson, John Martino, Felipe Vidal, Roy Hargraves – seem especially noteworthy.

19 THE CULTURE OF THE "CADRE"

Over the years, especially during the Rockefeller and Church Committee inquiries, a great number of CIA officers and employees expressed skepticism and then amazement that their Agency could have been involved in political assassinations. Of course, for many divisions of the Agency, that was perfectly understandable. It was only within certain special areas such as Technical Services and Clandestine Operations that activities relating to deadly force were conducted, and even there, knowledge of such activities was restricted to certain officers and even certain projects. Yet by the end of the 20th Century, it was well established that such activities had occurred and that senior CIA officers had not only repeatedly suppressed knowledge of them but had felt compelled to commit perjury to protect the Agencies' secrets and its capability for further actions as might be required.

What is often not fully appreciated is the deep-seated world view held by those officers, and the personnel carrying out covert operations. These people were WWII era military, most with combat experience and all holding extremely anti-Communist views. The organization they had joined and committed their lives to had been formed on the premise that it was necessary for the United States to aggressively confront the Communists. It was their sworn duty to counter the "vicious covert activities of the USSR." As clandestine officers, they expected to use any and all necessary tactics, both law and morality simply had to be sacrificed to the needs of self defense. They were engaged in a war of beliefs, of faith. The language contained in the 1948 National Security Council document #68 (the document which generated the Agency) was "strident," declaring, "the Soviet Union is animated by a new, fanatic faith, antithetical to our own and seeks to impose its absolute authority over the rest of the world." A common belief within the clandestine division of the CIA was that that the United States was fully engaged in a war, albeit an undeclared war and that ordinary morality simply did not apply during a war; to think so was naïve, childish and possibly treasonous.

Generally speaking, that world view and the intense emotion behind it was shielded from the public, at least by senior Agency officers. Occasionally it surfaced, in shocking form.

In January of 1975, President Gerald Ford held a luncheon in the White House for the publisher of the *New York Times* and afterwards, Ford was asked if the

Rockefeller Commission investigation into the CIA would reveal any important information. Ford replied that the Commissions' mandate was very limited and there was to be no general inquiry into the Agency's secret history. To do so might blacken the name of the country and even past Presidents. When asked for an example, Ford stated "like assassinations"... and then quickly noted that remark to be "off the record." *The New York Times* chose to honor Ford's caveat, however word of the exchange passed on to CBS news correspondent Daniel Schorr and in a February interview Schorr asked the current CIA Director William Colby if the CIA had ever been involved in the murder of political leaders ... Colby's reply was succinct – "not in this country."

Schorr went public with the story, stating on CBS Evening News that President Ford had warned associates that if the current investigations go too far they could uncover assassinations of foreign officials in which the CIA was involved (something the investigations did indeed later confirm). In April, Schorr happened to encounter Richard Helms outside the Vice President's office. He reported Helms was furious and uncontrolled, his remarks shown one of the few windows into both Helms' true views and the beliefs of the hard-line, "old school" cadre of first generation CIA clandestine officers – during the encounter Helms literally screamed at Schorr:

> "You sonofabitch!," he shouted at Schoor. "You killer! You cocksucker! 'Killer Schoor' – that's what they ought to call you."

Strong language indeed from the man whose own biographer Thomas Powers described as "the gentlemanly planner of assassinations." Richard Helms was charged and convicted of perjury before a committee of Congress, clearly his beliefs were such that he was willing to cover up virtually any illegal act in order to protect the CIA, and the same can be said of many of he "cadre." It may seem shocking decades later, but even the investigation of CIA activities was considered unpatriotic, extremely naïve and bordering on treason by not only Helms, but as previously related, by the core of the CIA clandestine activity officers including Harvey, Angleton, and Phillips.[229]

In his November 2002 online article for *Slate*, *The Nasty Career of CIA Director Richard Helms*, Jefferson Morley gives us further insight into Richard Helms, including a key tactic in the CIA's practice of "deniable" assassinations. Morley noted that even loyal CIA officers felt that Helms' actions encouraged suspicion. The first CIA officer assigned to the CIA assassination (reviewing Agency files on Lee Oswald) had been quickly replaced by James Angleton. Later the officer, James Whitten, would state that he had been "appalled" that Helms had not disclosed certain relevant information to the Warren Commission, including its attempts to assassinate Fidel Castro. Whitten described Helms' actions as "morally highly reprehensible."

In other remarks, Whitten made it clear that he felt that he had been replaced by Angleton in order for Angleton to control the course of the investigation –

"Angleton then sandbagged me as quickly as he could." Whitten complained to Helms about Angleton's obstruction and was immediately relieved. "Helms wanted someone to conduct the investigation who was in bed with the FBI." And in classic fashion, Angleton proceeded to stonewall the Warren Commission. In one incident relating to a Commission request for Mexico City cables (in the words of his Deputy Roy Rocca to Richard Helms), "unless you feel otherwise, Jim would prefer to wait out the commission on the matter." And, as Morley notes, the cables were never handed over.[230]

Equally revealing is Helms' response to the murder of Chilean General Rene Schneider in 1970 (an affair reportedly orchestrated by David Morales, while David Phillips was in charge of the Western Hemisphere and Henry Hecksher was CIA station chief in Chile).

To quote Jefferson Morley's Helms article,

"In 1970, President Nixon and Secretary of State Henry Kissinger were disturbed by the emergence of a leftist democracy in Chile led by Salvador Allende. As the Senate Intelligence Committee later determined, the CIA reported that Chilean General Rene Schneider was seen as a lynchpin of the fledgling government, a respected military leader whose fidelity to constitutional principles was blocking a right-wing military coup. *Helms, while skeptical, dispatched his top operatives to Chile, where they provided money and encouragement to two groups of officers who spoke of their intention to kidnap Schneider. A few days later, the general was mortally wounded during a kidnapping attempt by one of the groups.* The next day, Helms commented that, "*the Chileans have been guided to a point where a military solution is at least open to them.*"

The coup did not materialize at that time. But Chile's leftist democracy had been badly wounded.

Over the years, Helms stoutly denied that the CIA intended Schneider to die, but a congressionally mandated investigation in September 2000 revealed a telling epilogue. A few weeks after Schneider's death, one of his assailants made contact with the CIA. The agency responded by sending him $35,000 "to maintain the good will of the group." In September 2001, Schneider's two sons filed a wrongful-death lawsuit against Helms and Kissinger in Washington court. Helms' passing excused him from the indignity of having to defend his actions in court."[231]

Yet Helms was far from alone in his knowledge of lethal CIA activities. Several senior CIA offices were privy to work done to develop both lethal chemicals (drugs, poisons and diseases) and non-lethal drugs (including a number of LSD derivatives) for use in interrogation and temporary incapacitation. Those individuals included Sheffield Edwards (Office of Security and conduit to the Roselli/Castro assassinations efforts), James Angleton (Counter Intelligence but also involved with William Harvey in his Castro assassination project), and Richard Bissell (Operations/Plans and one of the cut-outs for Agency eliminations activities). All three men were members of a group reportedly (and likely unofficially) referred to as the "Health Alteration Committee." The Church Committee obtained testimony that in 1960 this group had endorsed a proposal for a special operation to "incapacitate" an Iraqi Colonel suspected of promoting Soviet interests; the device to be used was a monogrammed, poisoned handkerchief. In the Colonel's case, the handkerchief did not reach him prior to a coup, which resulted in his execution. The request for the special action was apparently routed through CIA Counter Intelligence (Staff C / James Angleton). The Committee had endorsed the action and recommended to Deputy Director of Plans (Richard Bissell); the operational approval was signed off for Bissell by Tracy Barnes.

While the "Health Alteration Committee" may have served to screen and approve lethal and incapacitating actions of a tactical nature, as in the instance of the Iraqi Colonel, the process of bringing about executive level elimination of political leaders was apparently far more nebulous. The instances of approved Executive Actions recorded by the Church Committee reveal no paperwork nor do they suggest that there was a definite process and a final point of operational approval.

The obsession with "deniability," even in private conversations had created a very dangerous environment. Words used loosely (perhaps intentionally) could take on a whole new meaning when translated at different levels within the Agency. Apparently senior officers at the level of Dulles, Helms, Angleton, and Bissell routinely discussed a great many subjects in such abstract terms, so much so that certain decisions became subject to personal interpretations. The Church Committee report concluded:

> "...the system of executive command and control was so ambiguous that it is difficult to be certain at what levels assassination activity was known and authorized. This situation creates the disturbing prospect that Government officials might have undertaken assassination plots without having it uncontrovertibly clear that there was an explicit authorization from Presidents."[232]

Evan Thomas, in his 1995 book on the CIA, *The Very Best Men: The Early Years of the CIA*, provided a striking example of such "interpretative communications," demonstrating how actions could be initiated not only with no official sanction but also with not even a head shake. In one instance, Bissell reportedly "informed" his superior, Allen Dulles, of a plan to kill not only Castro but also other senior regime members including Castro's brother. Bissell simply used alphabetical designations rather than names and Dulles simply listened – he asked no questions and gave no approval, with Bissell later claiming that Dulles fully understood that he was approving the murder of the leaders of the Cuban government.

In such a culture, there was high risk of events taking on a life of their own. Especially in the field (as with the murder of President Diem in Vietnam) when dialogs were occurring with CIA surrogates – whether they were exiles, rebels, coup leaders, anyone involved in the Agencies ongoing "regime change" activities.

"GUIDED TO A POINT"[233]

This study has traced the origins and evolution of political assassinations, as pursued by the CIA over some three decades, from PBSUCCESS of the 1950's in Guatemala, through the various Cuba Projects of the 1960's and the Chilean activities of the 1970's. Initially, in Guatemala, there was little concern about discussing assassinations, even recording proposals, plans and training in meetings. A historical study of the early weeks of the Guatemala project, in its first PBFORTUNE incarnation, revealed that one tactic was discussed frequently and seriously in project planning sessions – *proposals for political assassinations*. In fact, months before its approval, Director of Plans (Operations) officers had compiled a "hit list." They worked from an existing Guatemalan Army list of Communists and with information from the CIA Directorate of Intelligence. Even the CIA's own historical study of the Guatemala project, while noting that *"assassination was not mentioned specifically in the overall plan,"* went on to say that the project chief *"requested a special paper on the liquidation of personnel on 5 January 1954."* That paper, according to the [ ] chief, was to be utilized to brief the training chief for PBSUCCESS before he left to begin training Castillo Armas' forces in Honduras on 10 January 1954. The day later, another cable requested 20 silencers for .22 caliber rifles – strongly suggesting that Armas' people were indeed going to be prepared for assassinations actions.

The senior officers responsible for that project (Dulles, Bissell, and Barnes) would move into high positions within clandestine operations by the time they became responsible for the Cuba project to remove Fidel Castro from power. Their attitudes and their conduct of the Cuba project, in which assassination plots against Castro became a constant over some three years, had set a pattern for their field operations officers. And two of the senior offices responsible for PBSUCCESS (Bissell and Barnes) became the key "approvals" personnel for the more radical operations proposals, including assassinations (referred to as sensitive or special projects). Indeed, Bissell seems to have become so reliant on the assassination of Fidel Castro that he allowed the Bay of Pigs landing to proceed, over strenuous objections of his own senior field officers.

By 1963, assassination had clearly become an accepted tactic, absolute deniability was the only guideline and the ultimate sin would be to talk about such things in group meetings or worse yet to record such discussions. The tactics had not changed since Guatemala, only the willingness to admit them. "Black lists" would be developed for the Cuba landing; they would be passed to specially trained exiles. Numerous attacks on Castro would be planned, ranging from the use of highly specialized poisons from Technical Services to highly trained rifle teams in a Florida camp, but of course no paperwork would record any of that.

And by 1963, the operations officers who had started out in Guatemala were still together, all working to eliminate Fidel Castro and a regime that was viewed as being at the forefront of Communist expansion, a government dedicated to bringing about revolution across Latin America. It was also a regime that had only recently worked at successfully emplacing long-range atomic missiles only 90 miles off the coast of America.

This study suggests that beginning in the spring of 1963, Richard Helms and James Angleton both became extremely concerned over President Kennedy's response to an approach initiated by Fidel Castro. Given the world view of both men, and especially that of James Angleton, that outreach had to have been perceived as a trap, part of the ongoing Soviet master plan to outwit the United States. After all, Angleton himself believed that the very real Sino/Soviet political split had only been a device in that cunning master plan. And clearly, Angleton had Richard Helms' ear, just as he had always had that of Allen Dulles. From that point on, Angleton ensured that in the coming months, the entire highly secret dialog that President Kennedy and his "backchannel" representatives were conducting was fully known to him and Helms. By October that dialog had become supercharged and it appeared official meetings were about to begin and that both parties had found grounds for a relatively quick agreement.

What Helms and Angleton said to each other on the subject will remain a mystery, what either might have discussed with Allen Dulles will remain unknown as well. There is no reason that Dulles would have taken the news any more positively than Helms. What words were exchanged, what was said about acting to stop such an agreement, about Kennedy being criminally naïve – all is sheer speculation. But circumstantial evidence suggests that in one fashion or another, quite possibly via James Angleton and William Harvey, word was passed down to the people who had been involved in the Castro assassination projects. Given what we know of the views of people like David Morales, such information could only have been explosive. But at that point, anything further had become totally deniable. Indeed James Angleton might well have been telling the literal truth when he remarked that he had no idea exactly "who struck John."[234]

Also at that particular point, we begin to see a very familiar pattern repeated. The field officers turned to their surrogates, to the people they had been working with, to those they knew were fiercely anti-Communist and fiercely opposed to Castro. Although huge numbers of adventure novels and conspiracy works have been written about the CIA's use of professional assassins, of mafia gunmen, to date all the real assassination activities of the Agency can be laid at the feet of surrogates – exiles, rebels, revolutionaries. Over and over again, from Guatemala to Trujillo to Lumumba, to Diem, to Schneider, what we find is the Agency being "associated" with the people that did the killing, always able to deny that it had itself performed any actual murders. There was always the final deniability – we didn't order it, our employees didn't do it, it was all voluntary, they took it further than we had intended, and it was beyond our control. Yet investigations would again and again determine that there were CIA field officers in contact with the parties involved. Sometimes they had served as military advisers, supplied weapons, sometimes money, sometimes just helped with logistics; but always with the fine line of deniability, guiding, but only to a point. You could never literally say the CIA itself had killed anyone.

Undoubtedly if anyone on the shooting team in Dallas had been captured or killed, the story would have been the same. They would simply have been fanatic Cuban exiles, acting on their own out of sheer revenge for the Bay of Pigs and the President's weakness on the Russian missiles. A CIA internal investigation might even have missed the fact that they were members of the Castro assassination team, after all, no one but Rip Robertson, Morales and possibly John Roselli would have known them. Other people involved such as John Martino, Felipe Vidal and Roy Hargraves could have been painted with the same "fanatic" brush. Even then, both Martino and Vidal were extremely unlikely to have been associated with the actual shooting. And of course after they had been suspected, as Martino and Hargraves each were at some point, there was little proof and a number of people willing to alibi them.

Only Lee Oswald posed any sort of risk, and of course, according to Martino, if the plan had worked he would have been taken out of Dallas and quickly eliminated, no doubt in an incriminating fashion. What Oswald was actually doing or expecting on November 22 is beyond this author's ability to resolve. However, Oswald's own actions do corroborate Martino's information that he was planning to leave Dallas. Beyond that Oswald himself remains largely a mystery, as do any intelligence operations that were in progress with or around him. Jack Ruby took care of that and a call from Las Vegas recruited a very skilled lawyer to take care of Jack.

But then, all that really didn't matter; John Roselli proved that. When he took the real story (with the "Castro did it" twist) to Earl Warren, the FBI, the Secret Service and the President nobody was willing to deal with it. And when it ended up in Pearson's syndicated column, nothing changed.

In the end, and in conclusion, we would be well advised to take seriously the words of David Phillips, spoken shortly before his own death. After vigorously denying anything at all relating to a conspiracy against the President for years and even taking early retirement from the Agency, at the peak of his career, to help organize an association that would defend career intelligence officers from legal action. His final words on the Kennedy assassination were:

> "My private opinion is that JFK was done in by a conspiracy, likely including American intelligence officers."

> –David Phillips, July, 1986 to Kevin Walsh, former HSCA staff member.[235]

EPILOGUE

The first known person to suspect that the CIA had been involved with the assassination of President Kennedy was – his brother Robert. Robert F. Kennedy not only expressed that specific suspicion, he also discussed it with CIA Director John McCone at length in the hours immediately following the attack in Dallas. In fact, rather than going to CIA headquarters to lead an immediate CIA inquiry into possible international sponsorship of the attack, McCone went to RFK's home. We have no idea what prompted Robert Kennedy to his first suspicion; although, it may well be that the warning from the Chicago cancelled trip and the exile security issues on the last Presidential trip to Miami were a factor. There is also anecdotal information from one of RFK's Cuban friends, who had been warned that certain exiles were a danger to the President.[236] It is also unclear what McCone could have said to reassure him. Certainly, RFK must have realized that McCone was not an Agency "old boy," not part of the "cadre," and hardly in a position to give RFK a definitive assurance. But RFK's suspicions were even more specific. Not only did he suspect elements of the CIA, he also specifically suspected individuals, Cuban exiles, who had been involved in the secret war against Castro. We know that because one of the first calls he made that afternoon was to Harry Williams who was in Washington with Manuel Artime for a series of strategy sessions with RFK himself. His first words to Williams were an accusation – "One of your guys did it."

Years later, anonymous informants to the HSCA would suggest that Artime did have some knowledge of a conspiracy against the President, and years after that, following the JFK Records Act passage and the establishment of the Assassinations Records Review Board (AARB), the ARRB was approached by an individual who provided information in support of his claim that he had heard Artime's second in command, Rafael Quintero, talking about the assassination and that Quintero and CIA paramilitary trainer Carl Jenkins were aware not only that exiles had been involved but also that some of them had been initially trained by the CIA.

In a similar vein, some years later, Wayne January would expand on an incident that he had first reported to the FBI back in 1963. His story involved the sale of a DC-3 aircraft that were going to a CIA cover company for use in the Artime/AMWORLD project.[237] A Cuban pilot was in Dallas the week of the assassination, inspecting and preparing the aircraft for transfer. The two men became good friends, and the pilot had told him it was a shame that his people were going to kill Wayne's President in revenge for the Bay of Pigs (he would never be allowed to betray them again). January had thought of it as just a type of "war story" at the time, scoffing at the Cuban who simply responded, "You will see." The Cuban pilot had flown out of Dallas the afternoon of November 22.[238]

We now know that some senior officer within the Agency must have had similar suspicions because JMWAVE chief Shackley ordered a highly secret investigation, using all his Cuban intelligence group assets, into the possible involvement of Cuban exiles and CIA associated assets. Who ordered that investigation and what happened to the reports are totally unknown. What we know of Richard Helms' rush to appoint James Angleton as CIA liaison to the Warren Commission is no great surprise. The Agency was quite successful and probably lied (with its own officers committing perjury) on a number of occasions to suppress information relating to Lee Harvey Oswald.

The FBI received a number of leads pointing to exile involvement, but perhaps the most striking were the specifics relating to the involvement of Roy Hargraves, including information that he had traveled to Dallas and was in the possession of fake Secret Service identification. The FBI investigation was exceptionally superficial and Hargraves continued his anti-Castro activities in Florida for a time. He continued to be frustrated in his missions, including having his boats confiscated by Customs in 1964 and being arrested for gun smuggling in 1965. In 1967, Roy Hargraves and Gerry Hemming were working on construction jobs in Baton Rouge and just happened to drop by New Orleans to offer their services to District Attorney Garrison.

Later in 1967, Hargraves moved his family to Los Angeles. In 1968, he was arrested and charged with bombing the Students for Democratic Society (SDS) center in Long Beach, California. Hargraves also spoke of attacking a Black militant center and implied he might have been involved in bombing the Free Press office in Los Angeles.[239] But by 1970, he was back in Miami "involved in a plan to cause military hostilities between the United States and Cuba." That plan also included Felipe Vidal's nephew and called for staging an attack on the U.S. Base at Guantanamo, implicating the Cuban regime. In another 1970 activity, Hargraves was suspected of planning to sabotage, or otherwise use, Southern Bell Telephone cables going into Cuba.[240]

Felipe Vidal wasn't reported to anyone, at least not immediately, but within months he almost died (along with Hargraves and an investigative reporter, Dickey Chappel) in a boat explosion – which all involved felt it to be either a warning or an outright effort to eliminate them. Rumors still circulate that Vidal, upset by promises that had not been kept, had or was about to share certain information with Chappel. Whatever he might have said died with him inside Cuba within a few months, and Chappel was killed during an assignment to Vietnam.

Rip Robertson took an exile team to Africa the year following the assassination. More second and third hand information circulates that while there (using the alias "Carlos") he spoke about having been in Dallas with a couple of Cuban friends on November 22. Robertson later served in SE Asia; his obituary states that he died in Dallas, Texas, in December 1970 at his mother's home. The obituary, much like that of David Morales, contains a considerable amount of misinformation. He is cited as being an Engineer, and mention is made of his service in Vietnam, in positions with the Department of the Army and with the Agency for International Development (AID) – the same covers used by Morales in his SE Asian service. His home of residence was given as McClean, Texas.

What the Dallas Police might have learned and kept to themselves is also a mystery. We do have statements that they were ordered not to bring charges against anyone other than Lee Oswald, regardless of what proof they might have had. And there is a tantalizing lead relating to that, courtesy of an HSCA staff member. During the 1978 HSCA interview of Starvis Ellis (an ex-Army military intelligence officer and friend of Dallas Police Captain Will Fritz. Chief of the Homicide and Robbery Division), the interview notes record Ellis' statement of seeing a bullet hit the street and his description of a shooting sequence quite foreign to the official Warren Commission Report. But what is most tantalizing is a note on the margin of the interview sheet, in the interviewer's handwriting. The note states simply:

"Martino (Marino) hired the shooter. Ask Captain Fritz."[241]

Whatever that handwritten annotation suggests, there is no sign that the HSCA pursued it or that it was associated with the two different sources who brought John Martino to the attention of the HSCA. Both sources passed on identical remarks made by Martino, remarks about being involved in a conspiracy against the President. Of course, by that time, Martino himself was deceased.

The HSCA also received leads suggesting that they investigate "El Indio" – but the same lead had been given to District Attorney Jim Garrison during his investigation. Somebody in Miami was trying to point investigators towards David Morales. But Garrison had no luck in his venture to Miami, encountering both Bernardo De Torres and receiving additional volunteer help from none other than Roy Hargraves. HSCA investigator Gaeton Fonzi went to great lengths to try and pursue the "El Indio" lead, but was totally stonewalled by the CIA in regard to David Morales. Fonzi even interviewed Phillips, who coyly held back only to later use "El Indio" as a character in his own novel, *The Carlos Contract*.[242]

David Morales continued work at JMWAVE in Miami until 1966, although there is evidence, including remarks to his friends, that he was involved in both the Dominican Republic and elsewhere in Latin America during that period. Morales spoke at length of being personally involved with the capture of Che Guevara. After 1966, he was assigned to Laos under an International Development Agency (AID) cover. From Laos, he went to South Vietnam, serving as a military advisor under a Department of Defense cover. In 1971, he rotated back to the United States and officially went to work for the Joint Chiefs as a Latin American counter-insurgency advisor (in Argentina, Panama, Paraguay and Uruguay). It was during this period that he also played a covert role in CIA Chilean activities.[243]

In 1975, Morales retired (his paperwork suggest that the retirement was "involuntary") and eventually moved his family into a highly secure and remote ranch in southern Arizona. In 1978, he fell ill and died suddenly of a heart attack following a trip to Washington D.C. His lawyer and friend, Bob Walton, had asked him why he spent so much money on alarm systems and other home security – was it because his remote home was only 30 miles from the Mexican border? Morales replied, "I'm not worried about those people. I'm worried about my own."[244] Morales' old colleague and former head of the AMOTs, (who reportedly ordered to head a post assassination inquiry into possible involvement of Cuban exiles) Tony Sforza, also died of a sudden heart attack some six months after Morales.[245]

William Harvey was recalled from Rome in 1966, largely due to his escalating drinking problem. While undergoing counseling for alcoholism, he received small, special assignments from Helms, but was often with nothing to do through 1967. One thing Harvey refused to break off was his ongoing relationship with John Roselli. Roselli continued to visit the Harvey's, and Harvey defiantly refused directions to break it off, effectively raising a serious trust issue at the top levels of the Agency. The FBI, still focused on Roselli, also let Harvey know that the relationship could spell legal trouble for him.[246]

Harvey stubbornly continued to meet with Roselli during the period of maximum potential media exposure, when Roselli was bringing his JFK assassination story to Washington – and eventually to Jack Anderson and Drew Pearson. The Agency was highly sensitive to this and apparently had its own doubts in regard to the full nature of the Harvey/Roselli relationship. One memoranda states, "It is difficult to assess Harvey's role in this affair...I cannot help but feel that there is something in his relationship with Johnny that he is concealing."[247]

Harvey officially left the CIA in 1968 and practiced law in D.C. for a period before moving his family back home to Indianapolis in 1970. In his biography of Harvey, Stockton writes that Harvey's lasting friends included not only John Roselli but also Ted Shackley and James Angleton (whom he was in contact with right up to Harvey's own death).

Harvey had very little good to say about other CIA officers such as Bissell and Helms, especially after the Church Committee hearings. And in 1976, some three months after Harvey's death and a month after Roselli's murder, the Harvey's Indianapolis house was broken into and his wife interrupted the burglary in progress – someone had been going through Harvey's office files.[248]

As for Johnny Roselli and Tony Varona, the veterans of many Castro assassination attempts, Roselli was killed in dramatic fashion in August 1976, shortly before his scheduled third appearance before a Congressional investigation committee. Roselli's long-time friend, William Harvey, had passed away only months before in June 1976. Their asset in the Castro project and veteran of many, many years of Cuban political struggle had dropped out of politics entirely in 1964, moved from Miami to New York City, and became a used car salesman.

For reference, the House Select Committee on Assassinations was formed in 1976 and continued its investigations through 1978. During this period, Harvey, Roselli, and Morales all died of various causes.

The individuals mentioned throughout this study certainly were on and off the "person of interest" lists of various law enforcement and Congressional investigative bodies. Their names were floated as suspects on many occasions. But as we have noted, Roselli's trail balloon in 1967/1968 was a clear indicator that nobody in power or authority really wanted to wade back into the subject of a JFK conspiracy, especially one involving CIA assets.

Oh – and as for David Phillips, after years of being suspected by his own family and refusing to reassure his brother, even on his own death bed, we can only repeat his final words on the subject – JFK was done in by a conspiracy, likely including American intelligence officers.

And Phillips was the man who would know.

ENDNOTES

---

1. The *Dulles Report*, a 193 page study submitted to the National Security Council in 1949, recommended that both covert and clandestine activities be consolidated into a single CIA office - that office would become designated at different points in time as either the Directorate of Operations or the Directorate of Plans

2. *The U.S. Intelligence Community*, Jeffrey T. Richelson, fourth edition, Westview Press, 1999, p. 17

3. IBID, pp. 20-23

4. *Dark Sun: The Making of the Hydrogen Bomb*, Richard Rhodes, 1995, pp. 23-24

5. IBID, pp. 224-226. It should be noted that the only known "offensive" recommendation to be presented to the NSC by the Net Evaluation Subcommittee occurred on July 20, 1961. President Kennedy was a participant in the presentation which concluded that the United States would be in a position to launch an overwhelming attack on the Soviets during the fall of 1963, following that point Russian missile deployments in "hardened" sites would rapidly remove the "aggressive" option

6. *The National Security Policy from Truman to Eisenhower*, Richard Challener, pp. 39-49

7. *The National Security: Its Theory and Practice 1945-1960*, Oxford University Press, Norman A. Graebner editor, 1968

8. *The Assassinations*, Scott, Peter Dale; Hoch, Paul; Stetler, Russell. 1976. New York: Vintage Books, p. 137; with the author's thanks to Phil Dragoo.

9. *TIME* Magazine, "The Nation: Helms Makes a Deal", November 14, 1977. Full article online at: http://www.time.com/time/magazine/article/0,9171,912005,00.html With the author's appreciation to Albert Doyle

10. *James Jesus Angleton: The CIA and the Craft of Intelligence*, Michael Holzman pp. 174 and 181, also consider Angleton's statement to the Church Committee in which he stated that "it is inconceivable that a secret intelligence arm of the government has to comply with all the overt orders of the government;" IBID, p. 202

11. Memorandum for Director Central Intelligence from General Counsel Houston, Report of Criminal Violations to the Department of Justice, February 23, 1954 and Memorandum for Deputy Attorney General, Department of Justice from CIA General Counsel Houston, Washington D.C., March 1, 1954

12. The text of the Houston testimony is provided in *A Terrible Mistake: The Murder of Frank Olson and the CIA's Secret Cold War Experiments*, H.P. Albarelli Jr. Trine Day Publishing, 2009, pp. 535-540

13. Information about the PBFORTUNE and PBSUCCESS projects is sourced from a CIA History Staff analysis prepared by Gerald K. Haines in June, 1995. The study is titled *CIA and Guatemala Assassination Proposals: 1952-1953* and is available online. Key sources for the CIA Historical study are referenced as noted in the text. http://en.wikisource.org/wiki/CIA_and_Guatemala_Assassination_Proposals:_CIA_History_Staff_Analysis

14. Given the high level meetings attended by "SEEKFORD" it seems most probably that the crypt applies to Tracy Barnes, the PBSUCCESS operations leader

15. *End note: sources include: Bureau of Inter-American Affairs, "Alternative Policy Lines, 1953." and NSC, "Guatemala," 19 August 1953, FRUS 4:1074–1086.Cable to Dulles, "Conference with ...," 4 August 1952, Box 69 (S).Memorandum to Dulles, "Guatemalan Situation," 9 July 1952, Box 67 (S) and memorandum to Dulles, "Conference with...," 4 August 1952, Box 69 (S). "Chronology of Meeting's Leading to Approval of Project A," 8 October 1952, Box 69 (S); to [ ] "Guatemala," 8 October 1952, Box 69 (S); and to Dulles, "Guatemala Situation," 9 July 1952, Box 69*

16. Sources include memorandum *to [ ] "Guatemala Communist Personnel to be Disposed of During Military Operations of CALLIGERIS," (Castillo Armas), 18 September 1952, Box 134 (S)*

17. Sources include *report #3 to [ ] "Liaison between CALLEGERIS and General Trujillo of Santo Domingo," 18 September 1952, Box 134 (S). The CIA study noted that "assignation a nasty but frequent tool of Guatemalan politics. Arbenz himself benefited from the killing of his arch rival for the presidency Francisco Arans in 1949.")*

18. Sources include Memo *"Conferences," 1 December 1952, Box 134 (S). Memo "Current Planning of Calligeris Organization," 12 December 1952, Box 134 (S). See also, Acting Chief, [ ] Branch, Western Hemisphere Division that reported in November 1952 that Castillo Armas was studying PW use of liquidation lists. Memorandum for the record, "PW Conferences" 5 November 1952, Box 151 (S). The case officer also reported that the Arbenz government had targeted Castillo Armas for assassination. 10 March 1953, Box 15D (S)*

19. *The Old Boys: The American Elite and the Origin of the CIA*, Burton Hersh, Tree Farm Books, 2001, pp. 344-346

20. *The Night Watch*, David Phillips, p. 36

21. The term "cadre" was used by James Angleton to describe the tightly knit and bonded first generation of senior CIA officers, individuals extremely loyal to the Agency and trusted by each other.

22. *The Night Watch*, David Phillips, 1977, p. 37

23. Phillips resigned in 1974, at the age of 52, some eight years before the standard retirement age. At the time he was a Division Chief, in charge of the Western Hemisphere. *The Night Watch*, David Phillips, 1977, p. vii

24. Sources include *"Chief's CALLIGERIS Briefing Notes," J [ ] "Cost of Support for PBSUCCESS," 17 September 1954, Box 43 (S). He listed the 20 silencers resent. See also [ ] to Headquarters, 6 January 1954, Box 75 (S) and [ ] 2 to Headquarters, 21 January 1954, Box 1 (S). Also report #5. [ ]." 18 September 1952, Box 73 (S) and [ ] Chief, memo for the record, "Pbt conference Held at*

[ ] " 13 February 1954, Box 74 (S). See also [ ] to Headquarters, 4 January 1954, Box 1 (S). The Headquarters Registry cop of the pouch manifest for 8 January 1954, Box 97 (S) list the manual "A Study of Assassinations." A handwritten note of the original manifest says the pouch was carried to [ ] by [ ]. The serial assassination study is in Box 145 (S)

25. "A Study of Assassinations" provided Appendix 2 of A Terrible Mistake by H.P. Albarelli Jr., pp. 720-729

26. Dispatch to [ ], "Training," 6 June 1954, Box 75 (Secret, PBSUCCESS, Rybat). [ ] and Memorandum to LINCOLN Station, 16 May 1954, "Tactical Instructions (part II)" (S) and To LINCOLN "Instructions" Nerve War Against Individuals," 9 June 1954, Box 50 (S)

27. Sources include COS Guatemala City, to Western Hemisphere Division, undated, Box #6, (C) and Guatemala City 553 to LINCOLN, 14 May 1954. Also the COS dispatch Guatemala City to LINCOLN, 14 May 1954, Box 145 (S). [ ] and Memo for the record, "Weekly PBSUCCESS Meeting with [ ]" 9 March 1954, Box 154 (TS). Even before this meeting [ ] suggested that the top Guatemalan leadership needed to be assassinated during the first hours of the revolution. They had to be "pulled out by the roots." If we waited [ ] argued, "If too many of these birds get out they will be back in about three years." See [ ] Tape 17, Box 209 (S). [ ] Sec [ ] "Administrative Details." 15 April 1954, Box 70 (S); [ ] memo for the record, "Meeting" 2 March 1954, Box 70 (S)

28. Sources include: Chief, Economic Warfare, [ ] memo to All Staff Officers, "Selection of individuals for Disposal by Junta Group." 31 March 1954, Box 145 (S). We know [ ] visited [ ] on this date from the [ ] visitors log book. He signed into [ ] on 31 March and [ ] Log Book for 31 March 1954, Box 138 (S) also Memo, Box 145 (S)

29. Sources include: "Disposal List Home Addresses," copied from an attachment to dispatch, [ ] to [ ] 1 June 1954. Box 145, (S). It contained 15 name, also [ ] routing slip for the attachment, (Dispatch dated 25 May 1954), Box 145 (Secret, Rybat, [ ] draft memo, "Present Status and Possible Future Course of PBSUCCESS," 1 June 1954, Box 145 (S and See "Contact Report," 2 June 1954, Box 146 (Secret, PBSUCCESS, Rybat). See also [ ] memo for the record, "Points Covered in H/W Discussion of June 1 and 2," 3 June 1954 and [ ] note for the file, "Disposal List Prepared by C/ EW," 1 June 1954, Box 145 (S).)

30. The Night Watch, David Phillips, Athenaeum Press, 1977. pp. 42-48 also Consortiumnews. com, Guatemala – 1954: Behind the CIA's Coup, Kate Doyle, available on line at: http://www. consortiumnews.com/archive/story38.html

31. The committee referred to was officially the "United States Senate Select Committee to Study Governmental Operations with Respect to Intelligence Activities," a Senate committee chaired by Senator Frank Church of Idaho; it began work in 1975 and was the precursor to the US Senate Select Committee on Intelligence, which investigated illegalities in intelligence work by both the CIA and FBI. The Congressional investigations were driven by activities revealed during the Watergate affair.

32. Congressional Record, House, 29 June 1954, pp. 9176-917; the quotes are from Johnson and Republican leader William Knowland are from the Congressional Record , 25 June 1954, pp. 8922-8926; also see also Congress, the CIA and Guatemala, 1954 – Stabilizing a Red Infection by David M. Barrett.

33. Wiley, *quoted in Immerman, pp. 103, 115, 156; Smathers, (CR), 28 May 1954, pp. 7336-8. For reference see Immerman, The CIA in Guatemala: The Foreign Policy of Intervention, Austin: University of Texas Press, 1982*

34. Congress, the CIA and Guatemala, 1954 – Stabilizing a Red Infection, David M. Barrett. Barrett's study, prepared for the CIA is available online at: https://www.cia.gov/library/center-for-the-study-of-intelligence/kent-csi/vol44no5/html/v44i5a03p.htm

35. *"Weekly PBSUCCESS meeting with [word(s) deleted]," 9 March 1954, CIA-Guatemala Records, 1952-1943, Box 1, National Archives; Smith quotation and Eisenhower-Knowland interaction, both in Immerman, pp. 151-153.*

36. Church Committee Report, p. 181

37. Church Committee Report, p. 200 and *Widows: Four American Spies, the Wives They Left Behind and the KGB's Crippling of American Intelligence*, Joseph and Susan Trento, 1989, p. 211

38. Volume X, State Department Memo, May 14, 1962

39. This view of Barnes is conveyed in *Death in Washington* by Donald Freed; Freed presents Barnes as being ultra- conservative and fiercely anti-Communist. Of special interest is that Freed states that in 1963, as head of Domestic Operations, Barnes organized a number of "fronts" inside the United States related to project QK/ENCHANT. Howard Hunt, working for Barnes in Domestic Operations, was cleared for QK/ENCHANT and the Bannister Detective Agency in New Orleans was cleared in the same program. Freed also relates that Barnes was involved with certain Fair Play for Cuba Committee activities in the same time frame. *Death in Washington: The Murder of Orlando Letelier*, Donald Freed, 1989, p. 46

40. For reference, Maheu was a former FBI agent, with a private investigations office in Washington and had no agency employee connection to the CIA. As with many cleared Lawyers, Doctors, professionals and business contacts, Maheu provided a totally deniable mechanism for contacts totally outside the Agency. Reference Foreign Relations of the United States, 1961-1963, Volume X, Department of State, 337. Memo: May 14, 1962. Memo prepared for briefing the Attorney General of the United States.

41. The initial agreement was later formalized in a 1952 Memorandum of Understanding between the CIA and the Army Chemical Corps Officer. *A Terrible Mistake*, Hank Albarelli Jr., 2009, p.65; see also p. 781 on 1975 memo and pp. 531-533 in reference to the DOD internal inquiry.

42. Various sources and references to the Berlin poisoning are found in *A Terrible Mistake*, Hank Albarelli Jr., 2009, pp781-782

43. *Did Ike Authorize a Murder?* George Lardner Jr., *Washington Post* Staff Writer, Tuesday, August 8, 2000; A23, article available at: http://www.washingtonpost.com/wp-dyn/articles/A52595-2000Aug7.html

44. *Flawed Patriot*, Bayard Stockton, pp. 160-161

45. *The Very Best Men*, Evan Thomas, p. 227

46. *Flawed Patriot*, p. 171

47. *A Terrible Mistake*, H. P. Albarelli Jr., pp. 659-653

48. *The Castro Obsession*, Don Bohning, 2006, pp. 25-26

49. IBID, pp. 24-26

50. *Someone Would Have Talked*, Larry Hancock, 2010 edition, pp. 389-391.

51. IBID, more details on Jenkins, including a report that certain of his trainees had later
    participated in the Kennedy assassination is found in Appendix I of *Someone Would Have
    Talked*

    For denial of off the record operatives see: http://www.maryferrell.org/mffweb/archive/viewer/
    showDoc.do?docId=51417&relPageId=80
    For off the record documents seen only by interal CIA see: http://www.maryferrell.
    org/mffweb/archive/viewer/showDoc.do?docId=51417&relPageId=78

52. IBID, p. 111-112

53. *JMARC Intelligence Plan; Counter Intelligence Plan for an FRD Security Service*, attachments
    to a CIA memo for the record prepared by R.D. Shea, June 2, 1962 – a debriefing interview
    with David Morales, GS-14, Chief of Counter Intelligence Section, Miami Base. It should
    be noted that Shea gave Morales high marks for initiative and efficiency and that Morales
    AMOT organization, first headed by Sanjenis and later by Tony Sforza, became the core of
    the JMWAVE connected Cuban Intelligence Service which also provided the majority of
    intelligence during the JMATE program which followed JMARC. The majority of key Cuban
    exile and Cuban domestic intelligence reports now available can be found to have come from
    AMOT sources.

54. *Decision for Disaster: Betrayal at the Bay of Pigs*, Grayston Lynch, 1998, p. 34

55. IBID, pp. 164-165 also *The Castro Obsession*, pp. 144-145

56. *Flawed Patriot: The Rise and Fall of CIA Legend Bill Harvey*, Bayard Stockton, 2006, pp.293- 296

57. *James Jesus Angleton, the CI and the Craft of Counter Intelligence*. Michael Holzman, pp. 141-142

58. *Flawed Patriot*, Bayard Stockton, pp. 146-147

59. Church Committee report, *Alleged Assassination Plots*, pp. 6-7

60. The Cuba project carried on in different forms for almost a decade, changing considerably in
    form, activities and leadership. Strictly for purposes of this study, we will discuss four different
    phases of the Cuba project: Phase 1/Pre-Bay of Pigs with Bissell and Barnes in charge, Phase
    2/Post Bay of Pigs regrouping with Bissell still officially in charge, Phase 3/ Mongoose era with
    Lansdale in charge and William Harvey leading the CIA portion of the effort designated Task
    Force W, and Phase 4 with the Special Group/RFK assuming management and Desmond
    Fitzgerald in charge of the CIA portion of the effort designated as Special Actions (SAS).

Several field officers would be a constant through all four phases including David Morales, David Phillips, Henry Hecksher, Rip Robertson and Carl Jenkins. In addition, the Castro assassination efforts went through two separate rounds, both involving John Roselli and Tony Varona with other undocumented attempts apparently being directed and organized field operations officers.

61. Both the IG report and the rebuttal, written by Tracy Barnes in support of the senior officer Richard Bissell, are reviewed in *The CIA's Probe of the Bay of Pigs Affair: Lessons Unlearned* by Michael Warner. His article is available online at: https://www.cia.gov/library/center-for-the-study-of-intelligence/csi-publications/csi-studies/studies/winter98_99/art08.html

62. *The Castro Obsession*, Don Bohning, p. 195 and *Someone Would Have Talked*, Larry Hancock, p. 54 and pp. 339-340

63. *The Night Watch*, David Phillips, p. 86

64. Phillips' book was published in 1977; the Taylor Report which evaluated the Bay of Pigs disaster was over a decade old at that point and it had clearly established that the Trinidad Plan morphed from a guerilla project to something much different many months in advance; the only element that had changed following that was the choice of a landing site. In his book Phillips blamed Dean Rusk for forcing the selection of an alternative landing site at the relatively last minute. *The Night Watch*, David Phillips, p. 102

65. *Harper's Magazine*, "The Kennedy Vendetta," Taylor Branch and George Cliff III, 1975

66. *The Castro Obsession*, Don Bohning, p. 20

67. IBID, p. 21

68. Accordingly, UNIDAD — composed of some 27 different groups - was not informed of the Bay of Pigs landing and Castro militia, alerted by rumors of an impending military invasion, conducted extensive searches and operations and managed to take the majority of the UNIDAD leadership into custody, breaking the back of the movement within Cuba. After the Bay of Pigs, the remaining UNIDAD leader, Alberto Fernandez complained bitterly to the CIA about not being briefed and having their warnings disregarded in favor of the Agencies' trust in Manuel Artime, one of the actual leaders of the invasion brigade. *Someone Would Have Talked*, Larry Hancock, Appendix D, "The Way of Wave"

69. *The Castro Obsession*, Don Bohning, pp. 23-24

70. IBID, pp. 29 and 44

71. IBID, pp. 29 and 63

72. IBID, pp. 31-34 and 48

73. IBID, p. 48

74. *Betrayal at the Bay of Pigs*, Grayston Lynch, pp. 29-30

75. IBID, p. 159 and *The Castro Obsession*, Don Bohning, p.46. Bohning presented the issue of disbanding the Brigade Hawkins and Esterline, who did not picture it as a serious problem. He

also discussed it with selected exile leaders who made it clear to him that indeed it would have been – they might simply have decided to take over Guatemala and they had the manpower, weapons and air power to do so. In fact one of the exile commanders told Bohning that it would indeed have been a "very big problem" and Kennedy had made the right decision

76. Leon was believed to have been a Colonel in Batista's Secret police; since Morales had worked with the secret police while in Cuba it is possible the two men might have known each other previously. *The Castro Obsession*, Don Bohning, p. 144

77. *Someone Would Have Talked*, Larry Hancock, pp. 113-115

78. For reference, the National Intelligence Estimates (NIE's) are prepared by the National Intelligence Council and draw on views and data from the entire intelligence community. Foreign Relations of the United States/State Department, VI Document 617 pp. 1149-1163; Document 620 pp. 1168-1174; FRUS X Document 271 pp. 668-672; Document 315 pp. 772-776 and FRUS XI Document 347 pp. 834-836.

79. Memorandum for Chief WH/4 (Bissell), Subject CI Program for the JMATE Project, April 20, 1961

80. Online document reference at Mary Ferrell website: http://www.maryferrell.org/mffweb/ archive/viewer/showDoc.do?mode=searchResult&absPageId=486828

81. *CIA Mexico City Station History*, Anne Goodpasture. Also, CIA office Barney Hidalgo talked to author Dick Russell about being stationed at JMWAVE, serving as a counter intelligence officer and as a case officer for former Brigade members and checking out exiles coming into the Keys. He described being in line of command under Desmond Fitzgerald [after Fitzgerald had taken over the Cuba project in 1963] but receiving little direction from him and providing little information in turn. Hidalgo made several trips to Mexico City for various purposes was well acquainted with David Phillips. "I didn't know Phillips agents and he didn't know mine." Hidalgo was involved in lots of dirty tricks against Castro supporters in MC and apparently also against the Communist Party in Mexico. *The Man Who Knew Too Much*, Dick Russell, p. 262.

82. For references to Sforza, see *Someone Would Have Talked*, Larry Hancock, pp. 114, 270 and 342 also RIF 104-10103-10024

83. Bissell's removal seems to have been a combination of his earlier failure and the general lack of any results from JMMATE through the rest of 1961. Bohning relates his being chewed out for lack of performance by both the President and RFK. *The Castro Obsession*, Don Bohning, pp. 82-83 also *James Jesus Angleton, The CIA and the Craft of Intelligence*, Michael Holzman, p. 190

84. David Morales assignment per *Sons and Brothers: The Days of Jack and Bobby Kennedy*, Richard Mahoney, 199, p. 396

85. *The Castro Obsession*, Don Bohning, pp. 72-75

86. Someone Would Have Talked, Larry Hancock p. 18, also RIF 104-10111-10049; RIF 104-10111-10114; RIF 1993.08.02.10:19:58:180060. Morales support of the Christ

team – as crypt Zamka – is in RIF 104-10260-10407: document available at: http://www.maryferrell.org/mffweb/archive/viewer/showDoc.do?docId=37632&relPageId=2

Very little is known about how the Christ team managed to infiltrate Cuba or how they obtained the electronics equipment for "bugging" the Chinese office. Although speculative, it should be noted that John Martino owned a small Miami electronics firm and worked on electronics projects in the Havana casinos. When arrested in Havana, he spoke of being there in an effort to expand his electronics business in Cuba.

87. *Flawed Patriot*, Bayard Stockton, pp. 146-147

88. IBID pp. 114-115 also 160-161

89. IBID pp. 116-117 and pp. 191-192

90. IBID, documents presented on pages 152-158 As will be discussed later, burglary attempts to recover certain of these documents from Harvey's private residence and safe may be of considerable relevance to our discussion of the Kennedy assassination

91. The Roselli surveillance study information is provided by researcher John Sanders, readers are also referred to Sanders detailed study and writing on Roselli, available as an appendix in the 2010 version of *Someone Would Have Talked*

92. *Flawed Patriot*, Bayard Stockton, pp. 138-139

93. Church Committee report, *Alleged Assassination Plots*, pp. 6-7

94. *The Secret War against Hanoi*, Richard Shultz, Jr., pp. 1-37.

95. Hurwitch, unpublished memoirs, p. 130 cited by Bohning in *The Castro Obsession*, p. and Schlesinger in response to a question by Bohning, pp. 79-80

96. *CIA Mexico City Station History*, Anne Buttermer, available online at the Mary Ferrell website

97. *Eyeball to Eyeball*, Dino Brugioni, 1990, p. 99. Summary of force deployment, *Defcon 2*, Norman Polmar and John Gresham, 2006, pp. 64-68.

98. *Flawed Patriot*, Bayard Stockton, pp. 132-133

99. IBID, 137-141

100. *The Last Investigation*, Gaeton Fonzi, pp. 128-129. It should be noted that Phillips had personally responded very emotionally to the Bay of Pigs disaster. He himself referred to it as the worst day of his life, describing going home and spending several hours alternating between drinking and throwing up. While Phillips seems to have gone to great lengths in his biography to disguise his true thoughts about JFK, his brother has claimed that David Phillips was extremely critical of JFK and his policies. *Someone Would Have Talked*, Larry Hancock, p. 146

101. IBID, Appendix H, The Way of JMWAVE

102. *The Last Investigation*, Gaeton Fonzi, pp. 132-133

103. *The Castro Obsession*, Don Bohning, pp. 120-121

104. NARA Record Number: 104-10074-10379, Station Asset Report. Available online line through the Mary Ferrell Foundation: http://www.maryferrell.org/mffweb/archive/textsearch/advancedResults.do
also NARA Record Number 104-10263-10055; Subject: VICTOR DOMINADOR ESPINOSA HERNANDEZ; CARLOS EDUARDO HERNANDEZ SANCHEZ; JOHN KOCH GENE; ACELO PEDROSO

105. *Someone Would Have Talked*, Larry Hancock, p. 357-358

106. *The Last Investigation*, Gaeton Fonzi, p. 50

107. IBID, p. 50

108. *Defcon 2*, Norman Polmar and John Gresham, pp. 218-221 also *One Minute to Midnight*, Michael Dobbs, p. 17

109. *Eyeball to Eyeball*, Dino Brugioni, pp. 86-89

110. IBID, pp. 107-108

111. IBID, p. 110-114

112. *One Minute to Midnight*, Michael Dobbs, p. 178-181. Readers are referred to Dobbs' book for the most comprehensive description of Soviet atomic weapons and their deployment inside Cuba

113. *The Last Investigation*, Gaeton Fonzi, pp. 48-49

114. *The Castro Obsession*, Don Bohning, Interview with Sam Halpern, pp. 153-154

115. RIF 198-10005-10015, Draft memorandum "Utilization of Operators," Army March, 1963, Califano papers, Box 3, folder 2

116. From January to November 1963, JMWAVE had planned some 88 Cuban missions of all types including supply, intelligence, cache placement; 15 were cancelled, and of the remainder only four had involved actual sabotage attempts. *Blonde Ghost*, David Corn, p. 112

117. Details and sources on the background and evolution of the TILT operation are from *Someone Would Have Talked*, Larry Hancock, pp. 19-22

118. Documents are available on the Mary Ferrell web site: http://www.maryferrell.org/mffweb/archive/viewer/showDoc.do?docId=28964&relPageId=2

119. Later in 1963 the LEDA's sister ship, the REX, would be compromised in a Cuba mission, both boats would be exposed and it would turn into a considerable public relations problem for all concerned

120. In 1975 an extensive description of the mission was written by Miguel Acoca and a Robert K. Brown. It included numerous photographs and was published in Solider of Fortune Magazine. The subtitle of the article was "A Plot to Destroy JFK and Invade Cuba." The article is available online at: http://www.maryferrell.org/mffweb/archive/viewer/showDoc.

do?docId=28888&relPageId=2

121. RIF 1993.08.04.16:25:36:340007; copy available at: http://www.maryferrell.org/mffweb/archive/viewer/showDoc.do?docId=105573&relPageId=208

122. *Rearview Mirror*, William Turner, p. 194

123. NARA RIF: 1993.08.04.16:25:36:340007; available online at: http://www.maryferrell.org/mffweb/archive/viewer/showDoc.do?docId=105573&relPageId=228

124. RIF 1993.08.04.16:25:36:340007; the 250 page file may be found at: http://www.maryferrell.org/mffweb/archive/viewer/showDoc.do?absPageId=1174849

125. reference Chief JMWAVE dispatch to Chief SAS; NARA RIF 1993.08.04.16:25:36:340007; copy available online at: http://www.maryferrell.org/mffweb/archive/viewer/showDoc.do?docId=105573&relPageId=223

126. *Someone Would Have Talked,*, pp. 196-198 also 205

127. Material for this section on Kennedy back channel contacts with Fidel Castro is largely based in the article *JFK and Castro: The Secret Quest for Accommodation*, written by National Security Archive Senior Analyst Peter Kornbluth and published in the October 1, 1999 issue of *Cigar Aficionado* magazine. Additional information, discussion, notes and documents is contained in a separate study on the National Security Archives web site titled *Kennedy Sought Dialogue with Cuba*, posted November 24, 2003. This study is available online at: http://www.gwu.edu/~nsarchiv/NSAEBB/NSAEBB103/index.htm

The *Cigar Aficionado* article may be found at: http://www.cigaraficionado.com/webfeatures/show/id/JFK-and-Castro_7300

128. Further information can be found at: http://www.gwu.edu/~nsarchiv/NSAEBB/NSAEBB269/doc03.pdf

129. Recollections of CIA officer Sam Halpern as described by Jefferson Morley, *Our Man in Mexico City*, p.165

130. Halpern and Sanchez's remarks are described by Jefferson Morley, *Our Man in Mexico*, pp. 165-167

131. *Someone Would Have Talked*, Larry Hancock, p. 170-175 on the Terrell armory theft and Chapter 11 on Ruby's Cuban interests, "Cuba, the Guns, New Orleans and Everything."

132. *The Castro Obsession*, Don Bohning, p. 192-193

133. IBID, p. 195. Readers are referred to Bohning's chapter on the "autonomous groups," Chapter 11

134. RIF 104-10308-10091, Memoranda for the Record, Relationships between AMBIDDY -1 (Artime) and Ray, Henry Hecksher, July, 10 1963. At this time Hecksher was chief of Special Operations (Cuba Project) under Fitzgerald, stationed in Washington and responsible for AMWORLD

135. RIF 104-10308-10093. Memoranda from Henry Hecksher; subject: Kidnapping of Cuban Dignitaries Abroad

136. *The Castro Obsession*, Don Bohning, p. 171

137. IBID, p. 171

138. It seems apparent that the telephone calls were quite positive and suggestive of imminent negotiations, unfortunately we have no transcripts. Attwood did prepare a chronology of his activities with Howard and the Cubans and it is available at the National Security Archives and may be viewed at: http://www.gwu.edu/~nsarchiv/NSAEBB/NSAEBB103/631108.pdf

139. Oval Office audio tape, November 5, 1962; playable version available at: http://www.gwu.edu/~nsarchiv/NSAEBB/NSAEBB103/index.htm

140. *Inside Echelon*, Duncan Campbell; article originally published in Telopolis, Hannover, Germany; July, 25, 2000. Available online at: http://www.100megsfree4.com/farshores/s_ech03.htm

141. Letter to the Editors: "I Chose Freedom - Why Victor Norris Hamilton Left U.S.A. and Decided to Live in U.S.S.R;" *The Current Digest of the Soviet Press*, Vol. XV, NO. 29

142. RIF's 104-10098-10055 Memorandum from Mexico City to Director and 104-10529-10298 Memorandum from Director to Mexico City with information from JMWAVE

143. RIF's 104-10098-10055 Memorandum from Mexico City to Director and 104-10529-10298 Memorandum from Director to Mexico City with information from JMWAVE

144. The CIA provided "Watch Lists" to the NSA as did other federal agencies; to date all efforts to obtain lists for the period in question have been fruitless, including requests during Government investigations and Congressional inquiries.

145. *Cold Warrior*, Tom Mangold, p. 43

146. IBID, p. 51

147. IBID, pp. 231 and 313

148. IBID, pp. 328 and 339. Privately Kalaris is rumored to have mentioned that at least one of the unmentionables was a series of grisly morgue photos of Robert Kennedy

149. *James Jesus Angleton, The CIA and the Craft of Intelligence*, Michael Holzman, pp. 139-142 and Chapter 9

150. IBID, p. 160, p. 219 and p. 220

151. *A Very Private Woman*, Nina Burleigh, 1998, pp 246-248

152. *Cold Warrior*, Tom Mangold, pp. 302-306

153. IBID, p. 308

154. *Survivors Guilt*, Vincent Palamara, 2005, p. 19, 52 and 53

155. *The Last Investigation*, Gaeton Fonzi, 1993, pp. 232-236

156. *The Man Who Knew Too Much*, Dick Russell, 2003, p. 348

157. RIF 104-10221-10154; available at http://www.maryferrell.org

158. NARA Record Number: 124-10369-10057. The author has confirmed visits to the Martino home in Miami by an individual identified by Martino's son as Felipe Vidal; Martino's wife also remarked on frequent and ongoing visits to their home by an American named "Rip," almost certainly CIA operations officer Rip Robertson

159. *Someone Would Have Talked*, Larry Hancock, 2010, Chapter 1, "They're Going to Kill Kennedy."

160. For more details on David Morales and his career see *Someone Would Have Talked*, Chapter 8 "We took care of that SOB didn't we?" and Appendix B, "Crossing Paths in the CIA."

161. *The Last Investigation*, Gaeton Fonzi, 1993, Chapter 42, "On the Trail of the Shadow Warrior" also *The War That Never Was*, Bradley Ayers, 1976, p. 27

162. The Morales/Roselli connection was corroborated in interviews with Morales' long time friend and business partner Reuben Carbajal; sources include interviews with Carbajal by Robert Dorff and personal communication between the author and Dorff.

163. *Someone Would Have Talked*, Larry Hancock, 2010, pp. 17-18

164. *Harper's Magazine*, "The Kennedy Vendetta," Tyler Branch and George Crile III, August, 1975

165. RIF 104-10057-10102, Memorandum to JMWAVE, Chief Special Affairs Staff, Feb. 2, 1964, specific page referring to Cadick (Robertson) and Martino available at: http://www.maryferrell.org/mffweb/archive/viewer/showDoc.do?docId=50552&relPageId=6

166. *Someone Would Have Talked*, Larry Hancock, 2010, pp. 107-108

167. *The Last Investigation*, Gaeton Fonzi, p. 232-242

168. Escalante's disclosure came during a 1995 Nassau meeting organized by Wayne Smith, chief of the Center for International Policy in Washington. Attendees included Gaeton Fonzi, Dick Russell, Noel Twyman, Anthony Summers, Peter Dale Scott, Jeremy Gunn, John Judge, Andy Kolis, Peter Kornbluh, Mary and Ray LaFontaine, Jim Lesar, John Newman, Alan Rogers, Russ Swickard, Ed Sherry, and Gordon Winslow as well as Escalante and other high-level Cuban officials including Carlos Lechuga Arturo Rodriguez, a State Security official. Escalante himself revealed details of Cuesta's remarks.

169. RIF's 124-10220-10320 and 104-10221-10154; documents available on the Mary Ferrell web site. Many years later, Hargraves would relate details of his own travel to Dallas and his presence there on November 22, 1963 to researcher and author Noel Twyman. That information is available in the eBook edition of Twyman's *Bloody Treason* and will be discussed later in this study.

170. *Someone Would Have Talked*, Larry Hancock, pp. 126-132 and 276-277

171. IBID, pp. 270-271

172. *Someone Would Have Talked*, Larry Hancock, 2010, pp. 88-89 and pp. 55-56. Potential "patsies" were individuals with a history of public support for Castro and some personal time in Cuba itself. The first individual reportedly considered was a Los Angeles based ex-Marine, FPCC advocate who had traveled to Cuba and was known to be a good man with a rifle [Vaughn Marlowe a.k.a. Snipes]; the other individual had actually fought with Fidel's guerrillas in Cuba, only to be captured by Batista forces and deported back to the U.S. [Garrett Trapnell]. For a detailed discussion on the Marlowe incident, readers are referred to Dick Russell's book on Richard Case Nagell, *The Man Who Knew Too Much* and, *Someone Would Have Talked*, Hancock's Chapters 2 and 4. The author has personally confirmed details of the Marlowe incident in personal exchanges with him.

173. *Our Man in Mexico*, Jeff Morley, pp 164-165. Given the extreme level of FBI surveillance on Roselli from 1961-1963, it remains extremely suspicious that no records at all have ever been released relating to Roselli's known trips to Florida.

174. IBID, pp. 172-173

175. *Someone Would Have Talked*, Larry Hancock, 2010, pp. 140-143; For discussion of Quiroga and Bringuier, IBID, pp. 38-40 also *Our Man In Mexico*, Jefferson Morley pp. 171-177

176. *Our Man In Mexico*, Jefferson Morley pp. 174-175 and 154-155

177. IBID, p. 156

178. IBID, pp. 175-177

179. For background and credibility assessment of both Martino and Nagell refer to *Someone Would Have Talked* by Hancock, the CD "Keys to the Conspiracy" by Hancock and *The Man Who Knew Too Much* by Russell. For background on Oswald's mysterious contacts in New Orleans refer to *Oswald in New Orleans: Case of Conspiracy with the CIA* by Harold Weisberg and *Oswald and the CIA*, John Newman, 2008, Chapter seventeen.

180. *Someone Would Have Talked*, Larry Hancock, 2010, pp. 47 -47 also *Oswald and the CIA*, John Newman, pp. 346-347

181. IBID, pp 45-46

182. *Oswald and the CIA*, John Newman, 2008, p. 328

183. A detailed account of the FBI's activities as well as an analysis of Carlos Bringuier's affiliations and activities can be found in the 2008 edition of *Oswald and the CIA* by John Newman, pp. 218-345; further details on exile New Orleans activities and camps can be found in *Someone Would Have Talked*, Larry Hancock, 2010, pp. 59-62 and 96

184. IBID, pp. 34-37, Chapter 11 and Chapter 13

185. It may be difficult for younger readers to accept the fact that in 1963 anyone would think that the public would have accepted something as apparently insane as Castro sponsoring the assassination of an American president, essentially committing suicide in doing so. However,

we know that at the height of the Cuban missile crisis, Castro sent Moscow a telegram which Khrushchev interpreted as encouraging the Russians towards an atomic exchange – accepting the total destruction of Cuba – in he face of an American invasion of Cuba. The telegram remains unpublished and authorities disagree on that interpretation, however Khrushchev's interpretation reflects the view of a "fanatical" Fidel Castro, common at the time. *On the Brink; Americans and Soviets Reexamine the Cuban Missile Crisis*, James Blight and David Welch, 1989, pp. 342-344

186. Readers without access to Newman's book are referred to his JFK Lancer November in Dallas presentation available at JFK Lancer. Materials from Professor Newman's presentation were prepared for posting by Joseph Backes: http://www.jfklancer.com/backes/newman/newman_1a.html

187. Background information on the Mexico City station is taken from *Our Man In Mexico City; Winston Scott and the Hidden History of the CIA*, Jefferson Morley, 2008 and the official CIA station history prepared by Anne Goodpasture, available at: http://www.maryferrell.com

188. Since Oswald had written the Russian US embassy early in 1963, and received a reply at that time, with no related FBI contacts in response it appears that his remarks to the Russians (like many of his other statements) were extremely inconsistent. His actual lack of fear of the FBI can be seen in his request to talk to an FBI agent after his arrest during a street protest in New Orleans that summer.

189. Unless of course certain CIA officers such as David Phillips were already quite aware of Oswald's visit and the fact that he would be visiting both the Cuban and Soviet embassies in a attempt to travel to Cuba. Given that knowledge, Oswald would most likely have also been under physical surveillance from the CIA station team. Excluding that Americans entering the Cuban embassy were certainly intelligence targets, even under the U.S. laws prohibiting travel to and from Cuba and there are numerous reports of American Cuban travelers being identified and monitored. Phillip's remark that Oswald, as an American simply visiting the Cuban and Soviet embassies would not even have been "on the radar" was disingenuous at best given what we now know of Mexico City station activities and resources. The only difference is that without prior knowledge, the station would be tracking an individual whose name and identity were not known to them (or whose identity had been compartmentalized in a SAS (Cuba project) operation involving Phillips but not the rest of the Mexico City station.

190. *Someone Would Have Talked*, pp. 146-148.

191. The exact source of the tap is unknown, we do not know if it was a tap on a Russian embassy phone in which case the callers could have been located anywhere in the city or a tap on the Cuban embassy phone, which would indicate the callers had to actually be either at the Cuban embassy (unlikely since it was closed and the call was adamantly denied by Duran) or calling from the actual location of the Cuban embassy phone tap – indicating that the callers performing the impersonation were CIA employees. Of course the CIA itself would have immediately known the answer to that question.

192. *Our Man In Mexico*, Jefferson Morley, pp. 236-237

193. After the CIA had consistently denied that the Oswald tapes were still in existence at the time

of the President's murder, both in internal communications and on a variety of other occasions, it appears that approximately a week later, in his presentation of an initial inquiry into events in Mexico City, Director McCone told President Johnson that "our expert monitor says the voice is identical with the voice of 1 October known to be Oswald's." There are a great many issues with that statement including that the fact that we now know the CIA's own translator characterized the October 1 speaker as being a very poor Russian speaker. And the speaker's identify was identifiable simply because the man referred to himself by name, as "Oswald". No details of who listened to the tape or how they certified the caller as Oswald are recorded and given the fact that the Agency was still stating that all tapes had been erased, McCone's statement not only remains questionable but so does his grasp of the overall subject. *Our Man in Mexico*, Jefferson Morley, p. 216

194. *Cold Warrior*, Tom Mangold, pp. 230-231

195. The full story of Bradford's research and his efforts to clarify the issue - along with an official confirmation from the Johnson library that that a section of the tape related to the Hoover call had been intentionally erased - are available on the Mary Ferrell web site at: http://www. maryferrell.org/mffweb/archive/viewer/showDoc.do?mode=searchResult&docId=361

196. *Deep Politics II*, Peter Dale Scott, p. 12 and Anthony Summers, *Not in Your Lifetime*, p. 277

197. Goodpasture ARRB testimony, 12-15-1999, p. 147 available on the Mary Ferrell web site: http://www.maryferrell.com

198. *Our Man in Mexico*, Jefferson Morley, pp. 155-156. This incident involved Eldon Henson and details can be found in a 7/20/73 CIA memo on Eldon Henson and the Cuban Embassy, RIF: 104-10132-10243. The document is available online at the Marry Ferrell site: http://www. maryferrell.org/mffweb/archive/viewer/showDoc.do?docId=49131&relPageId=2c

199. *Man in Mexico City*, Jefferson Morley, pp. Chapter 15; pp. 196-197 on Jane Roman

200. IR 73214 of 4 Oct 63: "Mr. David Phillips, newly appointed Chief PBRUMEN [Cuba] Ops in MEXI will arrive 7 October EAL FL 655 for two days consultations WAVE" (NARA #104-10046-10003). For reference WAVE was the SAS field station in Miami.

MEXI 6344 011831Z, PS 61-1. The full text of the cable is as follows: "*Bulk materials under TN 251905, Pouch number 4083, pouched one October to be held in registry until picked up by Michael C. Choaden presently TDY HQS.*"

201. Professor Newman posits that the Kostikov link reveals the hand of James Angleton in a conspiracy against President Kennedy.

202. *Someone Would Have Talked*, Larry Hancock, 2010, pp. 302-305

203. RIF's 104-10098-10055 Memorandum from Mexico City to Director and 104-10529-10298 Memorandum from Director to Mexico City with information from JMWAVE

204. Biographical summary of Russell D. Matthews, excerpted from Vol. 5, Issue 12 of Penn Jones *Continuing Inquiry* newsletter; available as exhibit 19-4, *Someone Would Have Talked*

205. The report concerning Roselli/Ruby meetings in Florida comes from Washington DC investigative reporter Scott Malone. Malone received a call from an individual claiming to be an FBI agent who had investigated Roselli's murder. In doing so the agent had come across Miami office surveillance files on Roselli detailing the meetings. Malone taped his conversation, described it in his article "The Secret Life of Jack Ruby" and later played the tape for authors writing a biography of Roselli. As noted above, it is impossible to verify this story since all the Miami office Roselli files seem to have gone missing.

206. A great deal has been written about John Roselli, implying that his part in a conspiracy would have reflected Mafia control of the Kennedy assassination. Much has also been written presenting Roselli and John Martino, as agents of Sam Giancana, Santos Trafficante or Carlos Marcello. Newer studies of Roselli and Martino bring such assumptions into serious question, presenting a much different picture of Roselli's real, long term business and his personal alliance to Meyer Lansky and CIA officer William Harvey. Interested readers will find a good bit of that new research in the work of researcher John Sanders, presented in the 2010 edition of *Someone Would Have Talked*.

207. Letter of March 2, 1977 from the Chief of the IRS Intelligence Division Robert Potrykus of Dallas Texas, hand delivered to Ted Gunderson, Special Agent in Charge of the Dallas FBI office. There is no record of an FBI response to the IRS letter.

208. Ruby's mood swings, his assertive and confident behavior (trying to enter the room where Oswald was being held and later even impersonating a newsman at the Oswald press appearance in front of numerous officers who knew his true identity) during the afternoon and evening of the assassination were quite dramatic and Kantor describes them in considerable detail. It is quite possible that the huge swings in emotion were further stimulated by the fact that Ruby had been reportedly been taking amphetamines for a couple of weeks preceding the assassination. At the time Doctors wrote proscriptions for the drug, "preludin," as a diet pill but the drug also increased alertness, energy, confidence, concentration, talkativeness and even euphoria in the short term.

209. *Someone Would Have Talked*, Larry Hancock, 2010, pp. 118-119

210. IBID, Chapter 11, "Cuba, The Guns, New Orleans and Everything!" and pp. 171-175

211. IBID, pp. 201-202

212. IBID, pp. 159 and 207

213. Authors' private communications with John Sanders and Sanders' 2009 conversations with Peter Noyes. More detail on Roselli's background and business connection is contained in the 2010 edition of *Someone Would Have Talked*, courtesy of John Sanders

214. *Someone Would Have Talked*, Larry Hancock, 2010, pp. 278-282, also The Ruby Cover-Up, 1977 pp. 85-101

215. *The Ruby Cover-Up*, Seth Kantor, pp. 112 – 115; *Forgive My Grief Vol. 1*, Penn Jones Jr., pp. 78-91

216. *Someone Would Have Talked*, Larry Hancock, 2010, p. 305

217. IBID, pp. 204-205

218. *The Ruby Cover-Up* Seth Kantor, 1978, Chapter 8 "The Weekend" and *Someone Would Have Talked*, Larry Hancock, 2010, pp. 278-282

219. *The War That Never Was*, Bradley Earl Ayers, 1976, pp. 36-38

220. It remains a matter of controversy to what extent President Kennedy was personally aware of the Castro assassination efforts. Certainly he knew that such things had been proposed by members of his administration (Defense Secretary McNamara had broached it in at least one meeting) and there is considerable evidence that Robert Kennedy was well aware that efforts had been made to kill Castro; certainly all the 1963 coup projects then in progress and endorsed by the Special Group Augmented, assumed that Castro would have to somehow be eliminated before any coup could proceed. Still, it seems very likely that although Kennedy might well have heard such talk, those involved would have been proceeding at their own initiative, as they had with the efforts to kill Castro during the Eisenhower administration. Deniability remained the watchword. It is almost impossible to conceive that Kennedy would be encouraging a direct dialog with Fidel Castro if he had known of active plans not just to oust him but actually to kill him.

221. *Someone Would Have Talked*, Larry Hancock, 2010, pp. 126-130

222. Although much attention has been paid to Dallas FBI Special Agent Hosty due to his contacts with Lee and Marina Oswald, an area that has not received nearly enough attention is the pre-assassination activities of Dallas FBI agents assigned to the Cuban community. For example, we now know that S.A. Walter Heitman was very much involved in investigations within the local Dallas/Fort Worth exile community and that he played a major role in JFK related investigations following the assassination. However, we have absolutely no documents of any exile investigations that he might have done prior to November 22; that could be very revealing in regard to this study. *Someone Would Have Talked*, p. 170

223. IBID, pp. 72-74

224. IBID,, pp. 65-70

225. IBID, pp. 182-183

226. IBID, pp. 143-145, 210-212 and 228-230

227. *The Media and the Social Construction of the Kennedy Assassination*, Ross Franklin Ralston, A PHD Dissertation in the Department of Sociology, Iowa State University, 1999, pp. 45-50

228. Author's interviews with James Richards, March, 2011. It is of further interest that Robertson continued to command highly effective Cuban exile combat teams beyond missions into Cuba. In 1964-1965 he and a team of 18 exiles ("Low Beam") participated in the hostage rescues in the Congo, Operation Dragon. Other Cuban exiles piloted B-26 aircraft in air support of the operation. During that mission Robertson introduced himself with the alias "Carlos," an interesting coincidence given David Phillips' fictional book, *The Carlos Contract*, featuring "El Indio" and other characters. Robertson and the Cuban exiles activities in the Congo are described in *Dragon Operations: Hostage Rescues in the Congo*, Major Thomas P. Odom,

Leavenworth Papers, No. 14, pp. 78, 116-117

229. "Cadre" is a term used by James Angleton to describe the original core of officers who joined the CIA, especially within its covert divisions; the "cadre" was felt to be exceptionally loyal to the Agency and its mission.

230. *Our Man In Mexico*, Jefferson Morley, pp 232-234

231. *The Nasty Career of CIA Director Richard Helms*, Jefferson Morley, Slate Magazine, Friday, Nov. 1, 2002

232. Church Committee report, *Alleged Assassination Plots*, pp. 6-7

233. For the purpose of reference, readers are referred to a chronology of events which the author presents as supporting the evolution of the Dallas conspiracy during 1963 – that chronology is provided as Appendix A to this work.

234. James Angleton quote, "A mansion has many rooms and there were many things going on during the period of the (antiwar) bombings and *I'm not privy to who struck John*," New York Times, Dec. 25, 1974

235. Phillips had become quite friendly with Walsh who was working in DC as a private investigator. He had become close enough to have lunch with Phillips on a fairly regular basis and Phillips remark was made in the casual context of one of those lunches. In a separate but perhaps relevant incident, an interview by author Jim Hougan with Frank Terpil, one of Phillips former subordinates at JMWAVE, Terpil, stated that Phillips early retirement from the CIA was an assignment and the retirement itself totally phony. *Someone Would Have Talked*, p. 152; IBID for the Phillips quotation.

236. Angel Murgado, a Brigade 2506 member captured and imprisoned in Cuba went on to become acquainted with both Manuel Artime and Robert Kennedy circa 1963. He said that he went to Washington on at least one trip with Artime, who met personally with RFK. Murgado has reported that there was a fear, which RFK was aware of, that some anti-Castro Cubans might attempt to assassinate JFK and that he was asked to watch for any indications of such activity.

237. The identity of the pilot who was in Dallas is unknown. The only known exile pilot acquainted with Artime was a long time associate of Artime and Quintero, named Hector Varone. Varone is shown in photographs with the two men and in one photo taken in 1960, where he and Artime are shown with a DC-3 in the background. Beyond this circumstantial association, there is nothing further which places Varone in Dallas with January. The Artime/Varone photo may be viewed on the *LIFE* web site at: http://www.life.com/image/50555291

238. *Someone Would Have Talked*, 2010, Larry Hancock, pp. 206-297

239. Department of Justice Memorandum, Miami Florida, September 16, 1970

240. RIF 104-10117-10341 Security support to Project Venom

241. RIF 180-10109-10154, Ellis interview notes, 08/05/78. With thanks to researcher Larry Haapanen who brought the interview notes to the author's attention.

242. Fonzi notes that Phillips appeared to be under intense stress during the interview, lighting and smoking three different cigarettes at the same time. Given Phillips known expertise as a professional actor and legendary "cool", putting him under that amount of tension seems quite significant.

243. Talking with an *Arizona Times* reporter in 1973, Morales described his current job as Consultant to the Deputy Director for Operations Counter Insurgency and Special Activities. He did not point out that this position reported to the Joint Chiefs of Staff but did say that he at been American Counsel in Cuba at the time of the Castro revolution.

244. *The Last Investigation,* Gaeton Fonzi, pp. 388-389

245. Actually, there appears to be some disagreement on his date of death, officially it is cited as 1978 while at least one family member maintains it was 1984. Personal conversation between the author and researcher Zach Robertson, 2011.

246. *Failed Patriot,* Bayard Stockton, pp. 243-247

247. IBID, pp. 255-257

248. IBID, pp. 302-305

CPSIA information can be obtained at www.ICGtesting.com
Printed in the USA
BVOW081210211112

306137BV00003B/92/P